THE CASE AGAINST

Q

THE CASE AGAINST

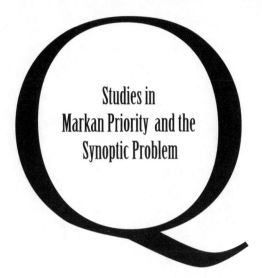

Studies in
Markan Priority and the
Synoptic Problem

M A R K   G O O D A C R E

TRINITY PRESS INTERNATIONAL
Harrisburg, Pennsylvania

Trinity Press International, P.O. Box 1321, Harrisburg, PA 17105
Trinity Press International is a division of The Morehouse Group.

Cover design: Trude Brummer

Library of Congress Cataloging-in-Publication Data
Goodacre, Mark S.
    The case against Q: studies in Markan priority and the synoptic problem /
Mark Goodacre.
      p. cm.
    Includes bibliographical references and index.
    ISBN 1-56338-334-9 (alk. paper)
    1. Q hypothesis (Synoptics criticism)   I. Title.
  BS2555.52 G66 2001
  226′.066 – dc21

                                   2001048084

Printed in the United States of America

02   03   04   05   06   07   08   10 9 8 7 6 5 4 3 2 1

CONTENTS

PREFACE

The Case Against Q comprises a series of studies on the Synoptic Problem in which the theory of Markan Priority is affirmed while the existence of Q, the hypothetical second source behind Matthew and Luke, is challenged. I have tried but have found myself unable to be persuaded that there ever was such a document, and this book represents my endeavors to explain why I find Luke's use of Matthew, as well as Mark, to be more plausible. It is with an inevitable degree of apprehension that a scholar towards the beginning of his career embarks on a project as controversial as the attempt to argue against the existence of Q. I am therefore grateful to all those who have helped me to develop my ideas, both by offers of encouragement and by robust criticism, whether on internet discussion groups like *Crosstalk* and *Synoptic-L*, among whom I would particularly want to mention Stevan Davies, William Arnal, Stephen Carlson and Jeff Peterson, or on occasions when I have read parts of this book in earlier versions: Chapter 5 at the University of Oxford Post-Graduate New Testament Seminar (June 1998) and the Society of Biblical Literature Annual Meeting, Synoptics Section, Orlando (November 1998); Chapter 6 at the British New Testament Conference, Glasgow (September 1998); Chapter 7 at the British New Testament Conference, Bristol, Synoptic Evangelists Section (September 1999); and Chapter 9 at the Society of Biblical Literature Annual Meeting, Q Section, Boston (November 1999). Chapter 6 is a revised version of an article originally published in *JSNT* 80 (2000): 31–44, gratefully used with permission. Parts of Chapters 1, 3, and 8 incorporate revisions of a paper read at the Synoptics Section of the Society of Biblical Literature Annual Meeting, Nashville (November 2000), published as "A Monopoly on Marcan Priority? Fallacies at the Heart of Q," *Society of Biblical Literature Seminar Papers 2000* (Atlanta: Society of Biblical Literature, 2000), 538–622. I am grateful to John S. Kloppenborg Verbin and Elizabeth Struthers Malbon for some helpful feedback on that paper.

Stephen Carlson read a large part of the manuscript and made innumerable valuable comments. Barbara Shellard read several chapters and made many helpful remarks. I am also most grateful to Jeff Peterson, with whom I have had many useful discussions about the ideas contained here; and I would like to thank Mark Matson for similarly useful feedback. John S. Kloppenborg Verbin and John Ma. Asgeirsson provided helpful comments on an earlier version of Chapter 9. My thinking on the Synoptic Problem owes a massive debt to my teachers, especially E. P. Sanders, Eric Franklin, and John Muddiman. But I am also indebted to my colleagues in Birmingham, especially David Parker, who has often been happy to engage in discussion of the topics covered here. Michael Goulder, who was the subject of my doctoral dissertation, subsequently my first book, has become a valued friend since I came to Birmingham; and in spite of my criticism of his work in *Goulder and the Gospels,* his ideas have nevertheless inspired much of the discussion in this book.

It would be utterly inadequate for me to try to express here my gratitude to my wife, Viola, here for her patience and support. Nor does thanking my parents, Janet and Selwyn, for their encouragement adequately express my gratitude, and I would like to dedicate this book to them.

MARK GOODACRE
University of Birmingham

The Case Against Q web site:
http://ntgateway.com/Q

ABBREVIATIONS

While I have tried to avoid the use of abbreviations as far as possible, the following standard abbreviations are found:

ABD Anchor Bible Dictionary

ABRL Anchor Bible Reference Library

AnBib Analecta biblica

ANRW Aufstieg und Niedergang der römischen Welt

Ant. Josephus, *Antiquities of the Jews*

BETL Bibliotheca ephemeridum theologicarum lovaniensium

BZNW Beiheft zur *ZNW*

CBQ *Catholic Biblical Quarterly*

DBI *Dictionary of Biblical Interpretation*

EKKNT Evangelisch-katholischer Kommentar zum Neuen Testament

ET English Translation

ETL *Ephemerides theologicae lovanienses*

ExpT *Expository Times*

Hist. Eccl. Eusebius, *Historia ecclesiastica*

HTKNT Herders theologischer Kommentar zum Neuen Testament

HTR *Harvard Theological Review*

ICC International Critical Commentary

IDB *Interpreter's Dictionary of the Bible*

IDBSupp *Interpreter's Dictionary of the Bible, Supplementary Volume*

IQP	International Q Project
JBL	*Journal of Biblical Literature*
JSNT	*Journal for the Study of the New Testament*
JSNTSup	Journal for the Study of the New Testament Supplement Series
JSOTSup	Journal for the Study of the Old Testament Supplement Series
JTS	*Journal of Theological Studies*
LXX	Septuagint
NA^{26}	Nestle-Aland, *Novum Testamentum Graece,* 26th edition, 1979
NA^{27}	Nestle-Aland, *Novum Testamentum Graece,* 27th edition, 1993
NHS	Nag Hammadi Studies
NovT	*Novum Testamentum*
NovTSup	Supplements to Novum Testamentum
NTS	*New Testament Studies*
SBL	Society of Biblical Literature
SBLDS	SBL Dissertation Series
SNTS	Studiorum Novi Testamenti Societas
SNTSMS	Studiorum Novi Testamenti Societas Monograph Series
TPI	Trinity Press International
UBS	United Bible Societies
WMANT	Wissenschaftliche Monographien zum Alten und Neuen Testament
WUNT	Wissenschaftliche Untersuchungen zum Neuen Testament
ZNW	*Zeitschrift für neutestamentliche Wissenschaft*

Chapter One

FIRST IMPRESSIONS

It is at an early point in their university education that students of religious studies are introduced to Q. It is one of the basics, a tool of
the trade that needs to be grasped from the beginning. This lost document has become an elementary resource for knowledge about the New
Testament, a staple of introductory courses on Christian Origins and indispensable for research into the historical Jesus. In the unlikely event
that a lecturer should fail to mention Q, students will find reference to
it in the first books on the Gospels that they read.

That is, of course, if they have not heard of it already, for Q is no
longer confining itself to classrooms, libraries and scholars' studies but
is emerging to develop a new celebrity status. Books based on Q are
big business, journalistic articles tell its story, television programs take
it for granted, and one can even listen to Q on the car stereo or the
Walkman.[1] It is easy to see why it is becoming so popular. In an age that
has seen some wonderful archaeological discoveries, people are excited
to think that there might be a lost document lying behind our Gospels,
just waiting to be rediscovered, an excitement intensified by the thought
that this document might be our earliest source of information on what
Jesus actually said. One popular edition of Q entices the reader with the

---

1. E.g. Charlotte Allen's "The Search for a No-Frills Jesus," *Atlantic Monthly* 278, 6 (Dec.
1996): 51–68, and *From Jesus to Christ,* the major American television series from PBS (1998).
However, Q has achieved much greater notoriety in the U.S.A. than it has in Europe. None of
the three recent British television series on Jesus, *Lives of Jesus* (BBC, 1996), *The Jesus Files*
(CTVC, 1999) and *Son of God* (BBC, 2001; it aired in the U.S.A. as *Jesus: The Complete
Story,* Discovery Channel, 2001) even mentioned Q. We will see more evidence in due course
for the higher profile that Q has in America in comparison (especially with Britain). Marcus
Borg (Editor), Jacob Needleman (Narrator), Thomas Moore (Introduction), *The Lost Gospel
Q: The Original Sayings of Jesus* (Ten Speed Press, Audio, 1998), an audio version of the book
listed in n. 2. The blurb for the tape is startling even by the standards of sensationalist literature
on Q: "The Lost Gospel Q brings the reader closer to the historical figure of Jesus than ever
before. The sayings within this book represent the very first gospel. Lost for two thousand years,
it's a window into the world of ancient Christianity. Here are the actual words of Jesus — the
original Sermon on the Mount, Lord's Prayer, and Beatitudes, as well as parables, aphorisms,
and guidance on living a simple and compassionate life."

promise that "these are the original words of Jesus, preserved and written by his contemporaries"[2] while another unashamedly announces itself as "the first full account of the lost gospel of Jesus' original followers."[3]

Q plays this kind of key role not only in the popular literature, but also in scholarly works on Jesus. Our generation has seen Q placed at the heart of historical Jesus research,[4] elementary in reconstructing Jesus' sayings, across a broad spectrum of scholarship.[5] The much-respected German exegete Gerd Theissen, while noting that many different pictures of Jesus are produced by scholars dependent on Q nevertheless claims that "Q is certainly the most important source for reconstructing the teaching of Jesus."[6] Likewise the Jesus Seminar raises Q to a special prominence in its own weighing of Jesus' sayings, embedding its importance for Jesus research in its very premises.[7]

Further, anyone with even a passing acquaintance with recent New Testament scholarship will realize that the importance of Q is not limited to its role in Jesus research. Recent years have seen a proliferation of interest in Q as a document worth studying in isolation from the Gospels of Matthew and Luke in which its content is embedded. Its genre, its strata, its theology, the communities behind it — all this has become the subject of intense speculation and careful research. Entire doctoral dissertations are devoted to the analysis of Q[8] and the Society of Biblical

---

2. Thomas Moore, *The Lost Gospel Q: The Original Sayings of Jesus* (ed. Marcus J. Borg and Mark Powelson; trans. Ray Riegert; Berkeley, Calif.: Ulysses Press, 1996).

3. Burton L. Mack, *The Lost Gospel: The Book of Q and Christian Origins* (San Francisco: HarperSanFrancisco, 1993).

4. For an excellent commentary on the role Q has played and is now playing in Jesus Research see John S. Kloppenborg, "The Sayings Gospel Q and the Quest of the Historical Jesus," *HTR* 89:4 (1996): 307–44, with responses by Helmut Koester (345–49) and Ron Cameron (351–54).

5. This continues in spite of E. P. Sanders's seminal *Jesus and Judaism* (London: SCM, 1985), which steers clear of Q; cf. further his *The Historical Figure of Jesus* (London: Allen Lane, 1993) and E. P. Sanders and M. Davies, *Studying the Synoptic Gospels* (Philadelphia: Trinity Press International; London: SCM, 1989). Sanders is followed in this by N. T. Wright, *Jesus and the Victory of God: Christian Origins and the Question of God,* vol. 2; London: SPCK, 1996).

6. Gerd Theissen and Annette Merz, *The Historical Jesus: A Comprehensive Guide* (ET, London: SCM, 1998), 29.

7. Acceptance of the existence of the "Sayings Gospel Q" is one of the seven "pillars of scholarly wisdom." See Robert W. Funk, Roy W. Hoover and the Jesus Seminar, *The Five Gospels: The Search for the Authentic Words of Jesus* (Sonoma, Calif.: Polebridge, 1993), 3 and 9–19.

8. Recent examples include Alan Kirk's University of Toronto Ph.D. thesis, now published as *The Composition of the Sayings Source: Genre, Synchrony, and Wisdom Redaction in Q* (NovTSup, 91; Leiden: Brill, 1998) and William E. Arnal's Ph.D. thesis, now published as William E. Arnal, *Jesus and the Village Scribes: Galilean Conflicts and the Setting of Q* (Minneapolis: Fortress, 2001).

Literature has its own Q Section.[9] Where Q once functioned largely as a "sayings source," it is now taken seriously as an important historical and religious artifact in its own right.

The increase of interest in Q proceeds from and interacts with its transformation from "source" to "Gospel."[10] For just as Q is now found in both the classroom and the public arena, so too it has emerged from the texts of Matthew and Luke, in which it used to be embedded, and onto a stage of its own, no longer simply an aspect of the solution to the Synoptic Problem, but now with a distinctive profile and place in early Christianity. Where it was once simply a source, the sayings source, the Synoptic Sayings Source or *Logienquelle*, it has now become something much more major — a Gospel in its own right, *The First Gospel* in fact (Jacobson), now known variously as the Sayings Gospel Q, the Gospel of Q or *The Gospel Behind the Gospels*.[11]

In this widespread new fascination with Q, there is a feature of its history and profile that is increasingly being played down, for not only has Q changed from a "source" into a "Gospel," but also it is forgetting its origin as a hypothesis, indeed a derivative hypothesis, the function of which was to account for the origin of the double tradition material on the assumption that Matthew and Luke were redacting Mark independently of one another. Many books and articles on Q now fail to mention this key element in Q's identity, dispensing with the word "hypothesis" and treating Q simply as part of the established literature of early Christianity.

There are genuine grounds for anxiety here. It is not simply that our teachers taught us to be suspicious of claims so dogmatically asserted or

---

9. The Q Section has been meeting since 1990. Before that SBL had a Q Seminar (1985–89). Publications emerging from the Q Seminar and Q Sections of SBL include John Kloppenborg, ed., *Conflict and Invention: Literary, Rhetorical, and Social Studies on the Sayings Gospel Q* (Philadelphia: Trinity Press International, 1995).

10. Arland Jacobson, *The First Gospel: An Introduction to Q* (Foundations & Facets; Sonoma, Calif.: Polebridge, 1992), Chapter 2 charts Q's rise "From Source to Gospel"; cf. James M. Robinson, "The Sayings Gospel Q" in *The Four Gospels 1992: Festschrift Frans Neirynck* (ed. F. Van Segbroeck et al.; BETL 100.1; Leuven: Leuven University Press, 1992), 361–88. This is well documented, with some critical remarks, by Frans Neirynck, "From Source to Gospel," *ETL* 71 (1995): 421–30. Neirynck prefers to keep to the term "source" but this is rapidly becoming a minority position.

11. Ronald A. Piper, ed., *The Gospels behind the Gospels: Current Studies on Q* (NovTSup, 75; Leiden: Brill, 1994). This book is one of the most important published on Q in recent years for it gives an international perspective, featuring articles by almost all of the key figures in Q research, including Frans Neirynck, Christopher Tuckett, John Kloppenborg, Arland Jacobson, James Robinson, and Paul Hoffmann. Further, Ronald Piper's fine introduction is probably the best available essay on the current state of Q studies.

assumed, but those of us who are teachers ourselves might be worried about the impression that the new student receives, for it is rare in the recent literature to find a careful account of the origin of the Q hypothesis, at the very least locating the postulation of Q as an element in the discussion of the Synoptic Problem. In one widely used textbook, for example, James Dunn's *Unity and Diversity in the New Testament,* Q makes its first appearance early on,[12] but without any explanation of the term. There is no list of abbreviations or a glossary or an introduction that clarifies the meaning of this symbol. The cause for concern is that books like this have "undergraduates primarily in mind."[13] It is likely that many of the undergraduates who read books like this will assimilate the views without having time to check elsewhere for details about what "Q" might be. Q is simply added to the student's armory without encouraging any thinking about the matter.

It is not that Q is only taken for granted in books where it is a tangential concern. John Dominic Crossan's scholarly yet popular *The Historical Jesus*[14] uses a stratified Q as bedrock in its reconstruction of the life of the historical Jesus. Like the Gospel of Thomas it is regarded as vital in the attempt to recover the primary stratum of Jesus material. There are many references to Q but it is not described as a hypothesis and never is it suggested that its existence might be open to question. Indeed, Crossan talks about the *Sayings Gospel Q* in italics throughout, the format he reserves for concrete extra-canonical texts like *Gospel of Thomas* and *Gospel of Peter,* with which Q is indexed at the end of the book.[15]

While the careful reader of *The Historical Jesus* will be able to infer that the text of the *Sayings Gospel Q* has to be reconstructed[16] and that this was a text used by Matthew and Luke,[17] nowhere is the origin of the Q hypothesis explained for the reader new to the discipline. The

12. James D. G. Dunn, *Unity and Diversity in the New Testament: An Enquiry into the Character of Earliest Christianity* (London: SCM, 1977), 35.

13. Ibid., xiii.

14. John Dominic Crossan, *The Historical Jesus: The Life of a Mediterranean Jewish Peasant* (Edinburgh: T & T Clark, 1991).

15. J. D. Crossan, *The Historical Jesus,* 503–4. Notice, however, that Crossan provides a little more information in his more recent *The Birth of Christianity: Discovering What Happened in the Years Immediately After the Execution of Jesus* (Edinburgh: T & T Clark, 1999), 110, "The *Q Gospel,* therefore, is a hypothetical document whose existence is persuasively postulated to explain the amount of non-Markan material found with similar order and content in Matthew and Luke."

16. *The Historical Jesus,* 310.

17. Ibid., 328, 429.

question of Q is closed, its existence apparently more certain than that of the *Gospel of Thomas,* the *Gospel of Peter* and the *Egerton Gospel,* all of which are at least introduced and explained with references given for further research.[18] In the case of the *Sayings Gospel Q,* Crossan only refers us to bibliography for the issue of Q's stratification.[19] The many readers whose first experience of New Testament criticism is this international bestseller are simply and subtly encouraged to assimilate the Q hypothesis into their thinking.

But these examples are not isolated ones. The phenomenon is common, and is found across a broad spectrum of books. Whether they deal with the New Testament, or Christian Origins, or the Gospels or Jesus or just Q, the existence of this "Sayings Gospel" is often taken for granted. It is true of textbooks designed for undergraduates, popular books designed for mass readership and scholarly works designed for the specialist. The existence of Q seems more certain than ever; its hypothetical character is apparently becoming a thing of the past, a matter seldom mentioned, let alone discussed.

The Tangibility of Q

So why is Q apparently becoming so much more tangible? For while it has been widely assumed now for over a century, it is only relatively recently that its status has been elevated in this dramatic way, respected and relied upon by scholars who have not published anything on the Synoptic Problem. It is partly, no doubt, that scholars have been numbed to old-fashioned source-critical questions and it is hardly surprising that they eschew the tedious task of rehearsing issues that they regard as having been long solved. But it is also clear that the apparent elevation in Q's status has itself generated a fresh rhetoric, a rhetoric that then reinforces the situation that it is attempting to describe. For as soon as Q began to leave the arena of the Synoptic Problem and source criticism, the language of theory and hypothesis was quickly replaced with the language of "discovery." Once an artifact of this importance has been "found," scholars are naturally loath to lose it again.

The archaeological metaphors have no doubt been suggested, largely consciously, by the relatively recent discovery of the Gospel of Thomas,

---

18. Ibid., 427–29.
19. Ibid., 429, where Crossan refers to Kloppenborg.

with which Q is alleged to have much in common.[20] The link is often explicit, as when Q and Thomas are treated together in the *Q Thomas Reader*,[21] which opens with the lines:

> "Q and the Gospel of Thomas are two examples of sayings gospels that have survived. And even they were lost until modern times."[22]

Similarly, Burton L. Mack's introductory chapter on "the discovery of a lost gospel" concludes with the triumphant claim that "the shards of a lost text have finally been pieced together."[23] The metaphor is becoming a major one, now appearing in the title of one of the most important, recent studies on Q, John S. Kloppenborg Verbin's *Excavating Q*.[24]

The choice of archaeological metaphors to describe the Q hypothesis has probably played an important role in reinforcing the consensus view on its existence. One can hardly "undiscover" a document, and the subtle impression is conveyed that those who doubt its existence have somehow not caught up with the present. It is as if Q skeptics are always at home discussing maps and routes while the rest of the party has long since left home and begun to explore. Consonant with this impression, and at the same time intensifying it, is what one might call the myth of inevitable scholarly progress. There is a widespread view that it is futile to go back and dig up old foundations, to go back over matters that were established long ago.[25] Why not accept the sound results of a century's worth of good scholarship and get on instead with building on those pillars of scholarly wisdom?

The most significant scholarly development in this area has been "The International Q Project," which has been engaging in the attempt to construct a database of reconstructions of Q, providing evaluations and

---

20. See Chapter 9 below.

21. John S. Kloppenborg, Marvin W. Meyer, Stephen J. Patterson, and Michael G. Steinhauser, *Q Thomas Reader* (Sonoma, Calif.: Polebridge, 1990).

22. Quoted from James M. Robinson's Foreword, ibid., vii. It needs to be noted, however, that in Michael Steinhauser's introduction to "The Sayings Gospel Q," there is some limited discussion of the Synoptic Problem and the two-source theory (8–13), and the term "discovery" is here placed in inverted commas (6).

23. Burton L. Mack, *The Lost Gospel*; Part One is entitled "The Discovery of a Lost Gospel" and Chapter One is entitled "Finding the Shards."

24. John S. Kloppenborg Verbin, *Excavating Q: The History and Setting of the Sayings Gospel* (Minneapolis: Fortress; Edinburgh: T & T Clark, 2000); cf. Arland Jacobson's use of the metaphor, distinguishing between a "raid" and a "serious expedition," the latter the claimed keynote of his investigation of Q, *The First Gospel*, 1–2.

25. Cf. James M. Robinson and Helmut Koester, *Trajectories in Early Christianity* (Philadelphia: Fortress, 1971). Robinson clearly regards the era of source criticism as belonging to a past, referring to "the triumph of the two-document hypothesis," established by the 1920s (5).

thus, ultimately, reconstructing the wording of Q.[26] The most important fruit of this endeavor is the publication *The Critical Edition of Q*.[27] Although the argument is seldom made explicitly, one cannot help thinking that the apparent success in reconstructing Q itself functions as an implicit argument for its existence, for it reinforces the feeling that this "gospel" must have had a tangible existence. How easy would it be to reconstruct a phantom?[28]

Q's Textual Trappings

Thus Q now has all the characteristics of an established text, not only a *Critical Edition* but also a synopsis, a concordance, a "reader"[29] and its own versification system. The latter is one of the more extraordinary developments in the study of Q in recent years and it has become the

26. This work is currently being published incrementally under the general editorship of James M. Robinson, Paul Hoffmann, and John S. Kloppenborg, entitled *Documenta Q. Reconstructions of Q Through Two Centuries of Gospel Research Excerpted, Sorted, and Evaluated*. The first volume (sent free to every member of SNTS) was Shawn Carruth and Albrecht Garsky; volume editor: Stanley D. Anderson, *Q 11:2b–4* (Leuven: Peeters, 1996); so far the following volumes have also appeared: Shawn Carruth and James M. Robinson; volume editor: Christoph Heil, *Q 4:1–13, 16. The Temptations of Jesus — Nazara* (Leuven: Peeters, 1996); Albrecht Garsky, Christoph Heil, Thomas Hieke, and Josef E. Amon; volume editor Shawn Carruth, *Q 12:49–59. Children against Parents — Judging the Time — Settling out of Court* (Leuven: Peeters, 1997); Paul Hoffmann, Josef E. Amon, Ulrike Brauner, Thomas Hieke, M. Eugene Boring, Jon Ma. Asgeirsson; volume editor Christoph Heil, *Q 12:8–12. Confessing or Denying — Speaking against the Holy Spirit — Hearings before Synagogues* (Leuven: Peeters, 1997); Paul Hoffmann, Stefan H. Brandenburger, Ulrike Brauner, and Thomas Hieke; volume editor Christoph Heil, *Q 22:28–30. You Will Judge the Twelve Tribes of Israel* (Leuven: Peeters, 1998).

27. James M. Robinson, Paul Hoffmann, and John S. Kloppenborg Verbin; managing editor Milton Moreland, *Critical Edition of Q in a Synopsis, Including the Gospels of Matthew and Luke, Mark and Thomas, with English, German and French Translations of Q and Thomas* (Hermeneia; Minneapolis: Fortress, 2000). The text was given in reports over several years in *JBL*: *JBL* 109 (1990): 499–501; 110 (1991): 494–98, 111 (1992): 500–508; 112 (1993): 500–506; 113 (1994): 495–500; 114 (1995): 501–11 and 116 (1997): 521–25.

28. Austin Farrer is partly to blame for this perception. He wrote that "it is notorious that Q cannot be convincingly reconstructed. No one reconstruction, to say the least of it, is overwhelmingly evident, and no proposed reconstruction is very firmly patterned" ("On Dispensing with Q," *Studies in the Gospels: Essays in Memory of R. H. Lightfoot* [ed. D. E. Nineham; Oxford: Blackwell, 1955], 55–88, reproduced online at *The Case Against Q* web site, *http://ntgateway.com/Q*, 57). Another important reconstruction of Q was produced before the International Q Project began their work, Athanasius Polag's *Fragmenta Q: Textheft zur Logienquelle* (Neukirchen-Vluyn: Neukirchner Verlag, 1979).

29. Frans Neirynck, *Q-Synopsis: The Double Tradition Passages in Greek* (Leuven: Leuven University Press, 1988); W. Schenck, *Synopse zur Redenquelle der Evangelien* (Düsseldorf: Patmos Verlag, 1978). See too notes above and 30 below. John S. Kloppenborg, *Q Parallels: Synopsis, Critical Notes and Concordance* (Foundations and Facets: New Testament; Sonoma, Calif.: Polebridge, 1988). This work is already a classic, a research tool in some ways useful to Q skeptics as well as Q theorists. John S. Kloppenborg et al., eds., *Q Thomas Reader*, see n. 21 above.

standard remarkably quickly.[30] It is now common to see references of
the nature "Q 6:47–49" and so on, following Luke's versification. "Q
6:47–49" means the Q text allegedly underlying Matt 7:24–27 // Luke
6:47–49, or the Q text that can be reconstructed on the basis of Matt
7:24–27 // Luke 6:47–49.[31] Scholars point out that this is "a convenience
and a mere convention"[32] and this is largely true; it is much less tedious
to write "Q 6:47–49" than it is to write "the Q passage that can be
reconstructed on the basis of Matt 7:24–27 // Luke 6:47–49" every
time that one wants to refer to it; and it is also easier to read.

Yet this feature of current Q research comes across to the newcomer as
bizarre. Like many other features in the study of Q the system inevitably
tends to obscure the hypothetical nature of the document to which it
refers. It has the clear potential to mislead students by giving them the
impression of an established document, concrete enough to have its own
verse numbers, the existence of which it would be foolish to question.

This feeling of security that current Q studies generate is accentuated
still further by the fact that scholars continue to argue about its precise
wording. Members of the International Q Project, while having come
to a consensus on the key points of the Critical Text of Q, nevertheless
naturally disagree over details, and some of the individual opinions are
felt to be weighty enough to be worth special notice.[33] Likewise, those
outside of the project will accept its broad findings and debate just a
point here or a point there.[34] The impression given is that the argument
concerns merely the finer details of a text, the existence and overall character of which is unshakeable. In this important respect Q scholarship is
aligning itself with the discipline of textual criticism; the broad consensus
is established in the near unanimous use by scholars of the latest version
of Nestle-Aland's critical text, but individual scholars will debate about

---

30. The system originated in the Q Seminar of SBL. The earliest published reference to it
that I can find is James M. Robinson, "The Sermon on the Mount/Plain: Work Sheets for the
Reconstruction of Q" in *Society of Biblical Literature. 1983. Seminar Papers* (ed. Kent Harold
Richards; Society of Biblical Literature Seminar Paper Series, 22; Chico, Calif.: Scholars Press,
1983), 451–54 (451–52).

31. Descriptions of the convention are often somewhat lax. Michael Steinhauser, for examples, says: "In citing Q scholars usually make use of the Lukan versification of Q texts.... For
example, Q 4:1–13 refers to the Q text Luke 4:1–13 (parallel to Matt 4:1–11)" (ibid., 5).
More accurately Q 4:1–13 surely refers to the Q text *allegedly underlying* Matt 4:1–11 // Luke
4:1–13.

32. Shawn Carruth et al., eds., *Q 11:2b–4*, vii.

33. Minority views among the General Editors are also recorded in the critical apparatus.

34. For example Dale Allison, *The Jesus Tradition in Q* (Harrisburg, Pa.: Trinity Press International, 1997), 24, n. 102, "Although the International Q Project prints the Matthean form
of Q 12:23 (see Matt 6:25), this is probably secondary."

one reading or another. Indeed the attempted alignment of Q studies with biblical textual criticism is explicit in the work of the International Q Project who use sigla and language borrowed from biblical textual criticism.[35] The incautious reader might easily and mistakenly assume that the reconstruction of a "Critical Text of Q" is more than superficially akin to the reconstruction of a critical text of a document like the Gospel of Matthew. For while the reconstruction of the latter is a matter of weighing witnesses to a document with recognizable parameters, well attested in antiquity, the reconstruction of Q essentially remains a piece of source criticism, comparing texts in order to reconstruct one of their supposed sources.

There is little doubt, then, that for most newcomers to the discipline, the interested outsider as well as the new student, Q will give the impression of being a concrete entity with recognizable parameters, a Gospel that has been "discovered," a once-lost text that has been found. The problematic element in this is that the newcomer is often refused access to the all-important fact that Q remains a hypothesis. This is not to say that the Q theory is problematic simply because it is a hypothesis, for we all use hypotheses all the time, some of which are very good hypotheses. The point is, rather, that the progress of the Q theory, its acceptance by so many, takes place in the context of rhetoric that discourages one from thinking about the question of its existence. In other words, it is not that ever-increasing numbers of students are trying and testing the Q hypothesis and finding it to be plausible. Instead, with its hypothetical nature hidden from view, students are not given the opportunity to ask the vital question of whether or not Q is a necessary hypothesis, to examine whether or not the theory might be correct.

Of course many students will, however, be curious about this enigmatic "text" and they might well, out of intellectual curiosity, seek an alternative. What might such students find? The answer to this question would depend on where they were living and where they looked. In the United States the dominant alternative to the Q theory combines opposition to Q with a rejection of Markan Priority. There have been, over the last generation or so, many publications from a group that has followed

---

35. For the sigla and language, see the works cited in nn. 26 and 27 above. For an example of the explicit use of such language in relation to the reconstruction of Q, see Alan Kirk, *The Composition of the Sayings Source,* 227, "The IQP's decision to exclude 12.35–38 (unattested in Matthew) from Q is based upon the consideration that standard arguments advanced for its inclusion, while not without weight, are insufficient to warrant a far-reaching text-critical decision."

William Farmer in reviving the Griesbach hypothesis, the theory that
Matthew's is the first Gospel, that Luke used Matthew and that Mark
used them both. It is a mark of their success in organizing and marketing
themselves[36] that their views have gained a hearing in America, and that
they are now regarded as presenting there the chief rival or indeed the
only alternative[37] to the two-source theory. This provincial impression[38]
tends to obscure the challenge from British Q skeptics by aligning them
with it or, worse, regarding them as in some way more peculiar than the
Griesbachian alternative.[39]

Markan Priority Without Q

But Austin Farrer's live alternative to the Q theory,[40] which has been advocated with vigor by a number of scholars, most notable among whom
is Michael Goulder,[41] is less well known outside of the United Kingdom

---

36. This is not meant pejoratively. In a world in which the two-source theory is consensus, careful thinking about how to organize and advertise the alternatives is required. Most
importantly, a core of neo-Griesbachians have organized themselves into an "Institute for the
Renewal of Gospel Studies," the research team of which recently produced Allan J. McNicol
with David L. Dungan and David B. Peabody, eds., *Beyond the Q Impasse: Luke's Use of
Matthew: A Demonstration by the Research Team of the International Institute for Gospel
Studies* (Valley Forge, Pa.: Trinity Press International, 1996). For an article review of this, see
Mark Goodacre, "Beyond the Q Impasse or Down a Blind Alley?" *JSNT* 76 (1999): 33–52.
For further reflections on the Griesbach hypothesis, see below, Chapter 2.

37. See, for example, J. Tyson, "The Synoptic Problem" in his *The New Testament and
Early Christianity* (New York; London: Macmillan; Collier Macmillan, 1984), 148–58. Arland
Jacobson claims, "The Griesbach Hypothesis has succeeded in establishing itself as the only
real alternative to the Two Document Hypothesis" (*The First Gospel*, 5–6). Jacobson seems
simply to be ignorant of the Farrer theory, cf. p. 17, "Of these six [viz. possible direct-copying
relationships among the Synoptics], only one has any considerable scholarly support today,
namely the Griesbach hypothesis."

38. It is worth noting that while the Griesbach Hypothesis has never taken off the United
Kingdom, there are several advocates of the Farrer theory in the U.S.A., Edward Hobbs, "A
Quarter Century Without Q," *Perkins School of Theology Journal* 33/4 (1980): 10–19 (reproduced online at *The Case Against Q* web site, *http://ntgateway.com/Q*); E. P. Sanders and
M. Davies, *Studying the Synoptic Gospels*. Indeed the theory originated in the U.S.A. with two
former SBL Presidents, James Hardy Ropes, *The Synoptic Gospels* (Cambridge, Mass.: Harvard University Press, 1934; Second Impression with New Preface, London: Oxford University
Press, 1960) and his student Morton Scott Enslin, *Christian Beginnings* (New York: Harper
and Brothers, 1938; reprinted, Harper Torchbooks; New York: Harper and Brothers, 1956).

39. Stephen Patterson, for example, regards Goulder's views as "more obscure" than Griesbach (Review of C. M. Tuckett, *Q and the History of Early Christianity*, *JBL* 117 (1998):
744–46 (esp. 744); also at *SBL Review of Biblical Literature*, *http://www.bookreviews.org*).

40. Austin Farrer, "On Dispensing with Q," see n. 28 above.

41. The two key publications by Michael Goulder on this theory are *Midrash and Lection
in Matthew* (London: SPCK, 1974) and *Luke: A New Paradigm* (JSNTSup, 20; Sheffield:
Sheffield Academic Press, 1989). There are also several important articles, all of which will
be mentioned in due course. For those unfamiliar with Goulder's work, a useful recent piece
is "Is Q a Juggernaut?" *JBL* 115 (1996): 667–81 (reproduced online at *The Case Against Q*

where it originated.[42] Since this theory combines Markan Priority with Luke's knowledge of Matthew, ignorance of it tends to lead to the false impression that dispensing with Q entails dispensing also with Markan Priority, an impression intensified by the way in which Markan Priority and the Q theory have become so closely intertwined in the scholarship of the last century or so. It is as if, for many, shots fired against Q naturally count as shots fired against Markan Priority and scholars are not surprisingly on their guard. Markan Priority and Q are regarded as sisters, sisters who are, it seems, fond of one another for they are seldom seen apart. Ignorance of the Farrer theory in North America only adds to this feeling of family fondness.[43]

The situation in Germany is still starker, though less consideration is given for the neo-Griesbachian alternative.[44] Willi Marxsen famously stated that the two-source theory was so strongly assured that it had gone beyond the status of hypothesis to a finding[45] and the passage of years, in which the challenge of Goulder and others has been mounted, does not seem to have made any impact at all on this kind of perception. As Michael Goulder recently pointed out,[46] Dieter Lührmann seems to think that the alternatives to the Q theory are either Matthean Priority or Proto-Luke.[47] And one can hardly help noticing that Gerd Theissen

---

web site, *http://ntgateway.com/Q*). For a survey entitled "Goulder and His Critics," see Mark Goodacre, *Goulder and the Gospels: An Examination of a New Paradigm* (JSNTSup, 133; Sheffield: Sheffield Academic Press, 1996), Chapter 1.

42. Though see n. 38 above for those like Ropes and Enslin who advocated the same theory less systematically earlier on. The theory is also anticipated in E. W. Lummis, *How Luke Was Written* (Cambridge: Cambridge University Press, 1915). See also A. W. Argyle, "Evidence for the View that St Luke Used St Matthew's Gospel," *JBL* 53 (1964): 390–96 and R. T. Simpson, "The Major Agreements of Matthew and Luke Against Mark," *NTS* 12 (1965–66): 273–84, reprinted in *The Two Source Hypothesis: A Critical Appraisal* (ed. A. J. Bellinzoni, J. B. Tyson, and W. O. Walker; Macon, Ga.: Mercer University Press, 1985), 381–95; for more recent defenses of the Farrer theory, see n. 55 below.

43. There are, of course, honorable exceptions, especially recently, e.g., John Kloppenborg, ed., *The Shape of Q: Signal Essays on the Sayings Gospel* (Minneapolis: Fortress, 1994), 2–3; John S. Kloppenborg Verbin, *Excavating Q*, 38–43; Zeba Antonin Crook, "The Synoptic Parables of the Mustard Seed and the Leaven: A Test-Case for the Two-Document, Two-Gospel, and Farrer-Goulder hypotheses," *JSNT* 78 (2000): 23–48.

44. This is in spite of the publication of H.-H. Stoldt, *Geschichte und Kritik der Markushypothese* (Göttingen: Vandenhoeck & Ruprecht, 1977; 2d ed. 1986), which is a defense of the Griesbach Hypothesis. Cf. my *Goulder and the Gospels* (JSNTSup, 133; Sheffield: Sheffield Academic Press, 1996), 31–32 on the reception of Farrer and Goulder in Germany. The Synoptic Problem is hardly discussed in recent German literature, but for a rare exception, see W. Schmithals, *Einleitung in die drei ersten Evangelien* (De Gruyter Lehrbuch; Berlin and New York: Walter de Gruyter, 1985), 44–233.

45. W. Marxsen, *Introduction to the New Testament* (ET, Philadelphia: Fortress, 1968), 118.

46. Michael Goulder, "Is Q a Juggernaut?" 668, n. 11.

47. "I consider the assumption that Matthew and Luke used a second source in addition

and Annette Merz are more willing to discuss doubts about the existence of Jesus than they are doubts about the existence of Q.[48]

Thus the standard reaction, especially to those outside the United Kingdom,[49] seems to be the equation of Q skepticism with doubts about Markan Priority. Helmut Koester asserts with misplaced confidence that "All attempts to disprove the two-source hypothesis favor the priority of Matthew or some earlier form of Matthew which was possibly written in Aramaic."[50] Likewise, Raymond Brown spends twelve pages discussing the Synoptic Problem without even mentioning the Farrer theory or any proponent of it. Neither Farrer, nor Goulder nor even Sanders are mentioned in Brown's bibliography to the Synoptic Problem.[51] Worse still are occasions when the Farrer theory is misunderstood or misrepresented, as when Craig Blomberg describes Michael Goulder's *Luke: A New Paradigm* as a "defense of the Augustinian model," suggesting that one has "but to read" it to find out how implausible its theories are.[52]

It is hardly surprising, in these circumstances, that Q skeptics who believe strongly in Markan Priority seldom get a hearing outside the U.K. Widespread ignorance of, as well as confusion about, the Farrer theory has played an important part in supervising the dominance of the Q hypothesis. The newcomer to the discipline, whose time is limited, rarely gets the chance to engage with Markan Priority alongside Q skepticism. The danger in this for the Q theory is twofold. First, it means that the

---

to Mark to be assured, despite all criticism. Neither the priority of Matthew nor proto-Luke hypotheses can resolve the Synoptic Problem to any comparable extent" ("Q: Sayings of Jesus or Logia?" in R. Piper, ed., *Gospel Behind the Gospels*, 97–116 [esp. 97].)

48. Gerd Theissen and Annette Merz, *The Historical Jesus*. "The Logia Source" is introduced on pp. 27–29 without any indication of alternatives to it. The question of the existence of Jesus is dealt with on pp. 122–23.

49. Though sometimes even within British scholarship. Morna Hooker, *A Commentary on the Gospel According to St. Mark* (London: A & C Black, 1991), surprisingly lists several possible alternatives to the two-source theory, not one of which is Farrer's.

50. Helmut Koester, *Ancient Christian Gospels: Their History and Development* (London: SCM; Philadelphia: Trinity Press International, 1990), 130. Cf. Burton Mack, *Lost Gospel*, "Even today there are scholars who continue to resist the two-source theory and to favor Matthew as the earliest gospel" (20).

51. Raymond E. Brown, *Introduction to the New Testament* (ABRL; Garden City, N.Y.: Doubleday, 1997), 111–24.

52. Craig L. Blomberg, *Jesus and the Gospels: An Introduction and Survey* (Leicester: Apollos, 1997), 90, n. 27. It seems that Blomberg has "but to read" the book to find out what its theory is. The same unfortunate mistake is made even more blatantly and inexplicably by one of the key scholars writing from the Griesbachian perspective, David L. Dungan, *A History of the Synoptic Problem: The Canon, the Text, the Composition and the Interpretation of the Gospels* (Anchor Bible Reference Library; New York: Doubleday, 1999), "the modified Augustinian hypothesis proposed by B. C. Butler and Austin Farrer" (369); again on 376, 378 and 384–85.

dominance of Q is maintained partly by means of ignorance of a key alternative but second, and more seriously, the dominance of Q is maintained by means of the false impression that the alternatives have been discussed and dispensed with, alternatives that are on the whole implausible not because of their rejection of Q but because of their rejection of Markan Priority. As long as Markan Priority is thought necessarily to entail belief in Q, the two-source theory will remain dominant. Markan Priority is not going to collapse and the vulnerability of Q will not be perceived while it continues to takes refuge under the wing of the more plausible, primary tenet of the two-source theory.

But what of those who do take seriously the idea of Markan Priority without Q? Some have found the key elements in Goulder's theory persuasive, most prominently E. P. Sanders and Margaret Davies in their textbook *Studying the Synoptic Gospels*,[53] support for Goulder that is all the more striking in that it appeared before the latter's magnum opus *Luke: A New Paradigm* and, further, which represents some movement, at least for Sanders, from his earlier position. Given Sanders's importance on the international scene, it is surprising that his study has not yet made more impact on synoptic scholarship, though this may be simply a matter of time.[54]

While several others have developed the thesis of Markan Priority without Q,[55] all are less well known than Goulder who has practically

---

53. "We think that Matthew used Mark and undefined other sources, while creating some of the sayings material. Luke used Mark and Matthew, as well as other sources, and the author also created sayings material. . . . Goulder has not persuaded us that one can give up sources for the sayings material. With this rather substantial modification, however, we accept Goulder's theory: Matthew used Mark and Luke used them both" (*Studying*, 117). This modified version of Goulder's thesis is essentially the one that will be argued in this book.

54. For Sanders's earlier views, see E. P. Sanders, "The Argument from Order and the Relationship between Matthew and Luke," *NTS* 15 (1968–69): 249–61 and "The Overlaps of Mark and Q and the Synoptic Problem," *NTS* 19 (1972–73): 453–65. For a recent endorsement of Sanders and Davies's position, see Jonathan Knight, *Luke's Gospel* (New Testament Readings; London and New York: Routledge, 1998), 11–16.

55. John Drury, *Tradition and Design in Luke's Gospel* (London: Darton, Longman and Todd, 1976), though see also other publications listed below, p. 118, n. 31. Eric Franklin, *Luke: Interpreter of Paul, Critic of Matthew* (JSNTSup, 92; Sheffield: Sheffield Academic Press, 1994); H. Benedict Green, "The Credibility of Luke's Transformation of Matthew," *Synoptic Studies: The Ampleforth Conferences of 1982 and 1983* (ed. C. M. Tuckett; JSNTSup, 7; Sheffield: JSOT Press, 1984), 131–56 and now *Matthew: Poet of the Beatitudes* (JSNTSup, 203; Sheffield; Sheffield Academic Press, 2001). See also n. 38 above for the contributions by Edward Hobbs, James Hardy Ropes and Morton Scott Enslin and n. 53 above for E. P. Sanders and Margaret Davies. Recent publications defending the Farrer theory include Mark Goodacre, *The Synoptic Problem: A Way Through the Maze* (The Biblical Seminar, 80; Sheffield: Sheffield Academic Press, 2001); "Fatigue in the Synoptics," *NTS* 44 (1998): 45–58 (reproduced on *The Case Against Q* web site, *http://ntgateway.com/Q*); Mark Goodacre, "A Monopoly on Marcan Priority? Fallacies at the Heart of Q," *Society of Biblical Literature Seminar Papers 2000* (At-

become the lineally accredited spokesman for the Farrer theory, to the extent that it is sometimes even called "the Goulder theory" or "the Farrer-Goulder theory."[56] In some ways this has been a great thing, for a theory could not want for a more gifted advocate than Goulder. In other ways it has been a liability, for Goulder has combined Q skepticism with what are often seen to be the less palatable theses of the lectionary origin of Scripture and the notion that the evangelists were highly creative authors who used minimal source material. For this reason, the term "Farrer theory" is preferable and the recent term "Farrer-Goulder theory" should be abandoned. Not only does the latter marginalize the contributions of other key figures, but it also tacitly suggests that the theory of Markan Priority alongside Luke's use of Matthew necessarily involves Goulder's take on it.[57] On the matter of creativity, David Catchpole consistently plays off the Q hypothesis against Goulder's view that Matthew has created non-Markan material without any other sources. "Matthean creativity" and "the Q hypothesis" are held to be opposites.[58] On the lectionary question Graham Stanton simply remarks that "with a wave of the lectionary wand, Q was consigned to oblivion."[59]

---

lanta: Society of Biblical Literature, 2000), 538–622 (reproduced on *The Case Against Q* web site, *http://ntgateway.com/Q*); Mark Matson, "Luke's Rewriting of the Sermon on the Mount," *Society of Biblical Literature Seminar Papers 2000* (Society of Biblical Literature Seminar Paper Series, 39; Atlanta: Society of Biblical Literature, 2000), 623–50; Jeffrey Peterson, "A Pioneer Narrative Critic and His Synoptic Hypothesis," *Society of Biblical Literature Seminar Papers 2000* (Society of Biblical Literature Seminar Paper Series, 39; Atlanta: Society of Biblical Literature, 2000), 651–72; and Barbara Shellard, *New Light on Luke: Its Purpose, Sources and Literary Context* (JSNTSup, 215; Sheffield: Sheffield Academic Press, 2002).

56. Christopher Tuckett, *Q and the History of Early Christianity* (Edinburgh: T & T Clark, 1996), 6. Frans Neirynck, "The Synoptic Problem," in Raymond E. Brown, Joseph A. Fitzmyer, Roland E. Murphy, eds., *The New Jerome Biblical Commentary* (Englewood Cliffs, N.J.: Prentice Hall, 1990), 587–95 (esp. 595); John S. Kloppenborg Verbin, *Excavating Q*, 38–43. Tuckett also talks about "Goulder-Farrer" (*Q*, 11, 32). Cf. my *Goulder and the Gospels*, 21–22.

57. John Drury and Eric Franklin, for example, each contribute something of key importance unrepresented by Goulder: Drury's stress on Luke as a literary artist picks up on Farrer's stress on the same and is a useful antidote to Goulder's fundamentally source- and redaction-critical approach (see further pp. 117–19 below). Franklin stresses Luke's critical attitude to Matthew alongside a rejection of Goulder's no-additional-sources view (see further pp. 64–66 below).

58. David Catchpole, *The Quest for Q* (Edinburgh: T & T Clark, 1993), for example, p. 16. This is of course an entirely natural and proper procedure — Catchpole is attempting to demonstrate the plausibility of the Q theory over its main rival, Michael Goulder's theory. What I am here attempting to point out is that one can have Goulder's insights about Luke's use of Matthew without necessarily having Matthean creativity on the scale that Goulder demands. See further p. 70 n. 49 below.

59. Graham N. Stanton, "Matthew, Gospel of," *DBI*, ad loc. It needs to be noticed, however, that Goulder does not in any way associate the lectionary theory with his argument against Q in his major work *Luke: A New Paradigm*. See *Goulder and the Gospels*, Part 3, especially 301–2.

A Fragile Consensus

Once more, then, the Q theory retains its dominance without trouble. For while Goulder is rightly perceived as the Farrer theory's chief spokesperson, his more problematic theories become stumbling blocks in the way of acceptance of the key thesis of Luke's use of Matthew and Mark. It is rarely asked whether we might accept some and not all of his ideas, as of course we do with many a Q theorist. Thus one might be troubled by aspects of Tuckett's views on Q, or Kloppenborg's or Jacobson's or Catchpole's or Neirynck's, without one's faith in Q being shaken. When it comes to Goulder, on the other hand, any element of difficulty is not allowed the luxury of standing to one side to let the major thesis make its way through to the front. Indeed, this is one of the strengths of Sanders and Davies's *Studying the Synoptic Gospels,* that they are able to see the wood for the trees, discerning where the strength lies (Luke's use of Matthew and Mark) and where the weaknesses lie (high creativity with minimal sources).

This is not to say, of course, that there are not proper, well-considered attempts to answer Goulder for there are indeed several, including careful studies by, among others, David Catchpole, Frans Neirynck, and Christopher Tuckett, all of which need to be taken seriously. But it has been necessary to establish the extent to which the vast majority of scholarship, especially outside the United Kingdom, is ignoring, confusing or misrepresenting the case against Q. Q maintains its dominance because, among other things, the alternative is unknown, or it is confused with theories involving Matthean Priority, or it is rejected because elements of one expression of it (Goulder's) are thought to be unpalatable.

Yet more important than any of these considerations, the language of Q theorists and the widespread failure to consider alternatives to it, is the simple fact that Q has been consensus for a long time. Its dominance is largely a function of the fact that it has been assumed for a century. Most scholars therefore begin with Q and write books assuming Q without investigating the matter carefully for themselves. There is nothing wrong with this; we all take a great deal on trust and do not have the time or energy carefully to reexamine every matter taken for granted in New Testament scholarship. But this means, of course, that the fact of majority acceptance of Q cannot itself function as an argument for the existence of Q. The fragile nature of some of the consensus positions of the past should be enough to remind us that numbers do not necessarily carry weight, and that establishing the truth is not a matter of counting heads. One of the most exciting features of New Testament scholarship, or indeed of any academic discipline, is the potential for current paradigms to be overturned, for basic positions to be rethought. Those who remain optimistic about New Testament scholarship will not regard the reexamining of basic suppositions as a waste of time.[60] The questioning of Q might well turn out to be a healthy procedure for Q theorists and Q skeptics alike.

But let us not be under any illusions. Even if the Q-accepting majority is largely made up of "lazy" believers in Q,[61] who inherit and pass on the consensus without investigating the Synoptic Problem carefully for themselves, Q is not going to vanish overnight. As Michael Goulder once pointed out, there is a lot at stake in this theory.[62] Every time that Q is assumed, it appears to gain ground, for a working hypothesis soon appears to be a plausible hypothesis. The repeated presupposition of a theory does not function as a reliable means of testing it.

If we were to dispense with Q, it would not be without tears. For Q has been all over the world, loved by everyone, feminists and liberation theologians,[63] the sober and the sensational, the scholar and the layperson, a document with universal appeal. Indeed one of the keys to its success has been its ability to woo both conservatives and radicals alike. While conservatives, for example, are drawn by its early witness to sayings of Jesus, others have seen its lack of a Passion Narrative as witnessing to an alternative stream of early Christianity, one not based on the proclamation of a crucified Christ. For those at one end of the theological spectrum, Q can give us a document of Jesus material from before 70, written within a generation of the death of Jesus. For those at

60. For a recent example of the healthy questioning of a consensus issue, see Richard Bauckham, ed., *The Gospel for All Christians: Rethinking the Gospel Audiences* (Grand Rapids: Eerdmans; Edinburgh: T & T Clark, 1998).

61. Again, I do not use this term disparagingly but take it over from two New Testament scholars who described themselves to me this way. I suspect that there are many like them.

62. Michael Goulder, "Farrer on Q," *Theology* 83 (1980): 190–95 (esp. 194).

63. For feminist perspectives on Q, see Luise Schottroff, "Itinerant Prophetesses: A Feminist Analysis of the Sayings Source Q" in R. Piper, ed., *The Gospel Behind the Gospels,* 348–60 and "The Sayings Source Q" in Elisabeth Schüssler Fiorenza, ed., *Searching the Scriptures,* vol. 2, *A Feminist Commentary* (New York: Crossroad, 1994; London: SCM, 1995), 510–34; Amy-Jill Levine, "Who's Catering the Q Affair? Feminist Observations on Q Paraenesis" in Leo G. Perdue and John G. Gammie, eds., *Paraenesis: Act and Form, Semeia* 50 (1990): 145–61; Elisabeth Schüssler Fiorenza, *Jesus: Miriam's Child, Sophia's Prophet: Critical Issues in Feminist Christology* (London: SCM, 1995), 139–44. On the ramifications of Q for liberation theology, see James M. Robinson, "The Jesus of Q as Liberation Theologian" in R. Piper, ed., *The Gospel Behind the Gospels,* 259–74.

the other end of the spectrum, Q aligns itself with the Gospel of Thomas to form a "trajectory" in early Christianity that contrasted radically with emerging orthodoxy, and which only "canonical bias" can now obscure from our view.[64]

With so much apparently against a scholar who remains skeptical about Q — the sentimental attachment to the familiar, the meta-morphosis of Q into a gospel with ever more concrete features, the archaeological metaphors, alternatives that are unpalatable, unpersua-sive or unknown — such matters suggest that there might be little hope for success for someone attempting to mount a case against Q, let alone in achieving the vision of a world without Q. But the situation is not as hopeless as it might at first sound; reports of Q's discovery might yet turn out to have been greatly exaggerated. For Q's departure from the arena of source-critical debate, its elevation to a new canonical status, is nursing an ignorance among students about the Synoptic Problem that is likely, in time, to generate a reaction. One picks up hints in the scholarly community that perhaps Q studies have gone far enough, that perhaps it is time for a change.

It is a thought that is encouraged by the fact that New Testament scholarship remains in the process of a massive transformation, utilizing new methods that Synoptic Problem scholars rarely allow to impinge on their work, giving rise to the feeling that current trends in New Testament studies have actually overtaken Synoptic Problem scholarship, leaving the latter a sadly washed up relic of the old way of doing things, wedded as it is to historical-critical methods at their most narrowly conceived. It is seldom, if ever, asked, for example, how far the study of the Synoptic Problem might be transformed by interaction from the new methods like narrative criticism or the study of the New Testament in fiction and film and this in spite of the clear potential for profitable interaction between the methods new and old. The difficulty with the current scene is, as I will attempt to show, not only that the standard arguments for the Q theory are flawed, but also that contemporary synoptic scholars are

---

64. One of the starkest examples of Q entering the discussion of canonical bias comes in John Dominic Crossan's comments on Mack's *Lost Gospel*, "Even if every apocryphal gos-pel, discovered or discoverable, be judged late, derivative, and dependent, here magnificently presented is a lost gospel already inside the biblical canon, already inside the walls that ecclesi-astical scholarship consistently raises against the contamination of the New Testament gospels by their earlier or contemporary alternatives." (Excerpt is from the publisher's publicity for the book.) Note too, in addition to the comments on Crossan's *Historical Jesus* earlier, that *Sayings Gospel Q* is indexed under "Extracanonical Writings" (503–4).

ignoring the potential for stimulating interaction between the traditional methods and some of the newer perspectives.

There are reasons, then, for optimism about the future of synoptic scholarship. Students who were introduced to Q at an early stage in their university education might enjoy hearing news of a different view. The brighter students, those with inquiring minds, will no doubt enjoy examining the evidence to see whether the Q hypothesis is indeed the best option, or whether this might be an occasion for using Occam's Razor. And scholars also might enjoy a challenge to the consensus view. Such challenges at least keep us honest and help us to clarify our thinking. There is surely nothing to lose, except perhaps a document that no one has ever found.

Chapter Two

SETTING IN PLACE THE CORNERSTONE
The Priority of Mark

The case against Q has been impeded for some time by confusion over the role played in it by the theory of Markan Priority. With the exception of Sanders and Davies, Q skeptics have tended to take Markan Priority for granted in their attempts to dispense with Q.[1] John Drury, Eric Franklin, H. Benedict Green, Michael Goulder and Austin Farrer himself have all begun with the consensus position of Markan Priority and have built their case against Q from there. In his article, "On Dispensing with Q," Farrer does not so much as mention any argument for the theory of Markan Priority on which he is building[2] and on one occasion Michael Goulder spoke, in passing, of Markan Priority as a fact.[3]

---

1. I use the term "Q skeptic" to signify those whose difficulty with the two-source theory is Q and not Markan Priority. Of course adherents of the Griesbach theory are also skeptical of the existence of Q and so in that sense they are also Q skeptics, but their difficulties over Q operate within a framework the fundamental point of which is the rejection of Markan Priority.

2. Austin Farrer, "On Dispensing with Q." The theory of Markan Priority is implicit throughout the article and often provides the model for seeing how Luke might have proceeded in his use of Matthew. But it is assumed rather than argued. Cf. Austin Farrer, *A Study in St Mark* (Westminster: Dacre, 1951), which begins by noting the nineteenth-century shift of scholarly opinion to "the well-grounded conviction that St Mark's is the earliest written of the Gospels, and that the other three (two of them more particularly) knew and used his work" (1). See further below, pp. 38–39.

3. Michael Goulder, "Is Q a Juggernaut?" 670, "But Luke's use of Mark is a fact (or generally accepted as one), while Q is a mere postulate." One should not make too much of this, however, for Goulder is in context contesting a point about conclusions that might be drawn from the minor agreements *among those who share the assumption of Markan Priority* (here referring to himself, Frans Neirynck and Christopher Tuckett). Perhaps the more careful statement would have been to say, "But Luke's use of Mark is generally accepted as a given; the focus of our disagreement is over the postulate Q." Robert Derrenbacker's comment that "Michael Goulder has recently stated that Markan priority is no longer theory but 'fact'" ("The Relationship of the Gospels Reconsidered," *Toronto Journal of Theology* 14 [1998]: 83–88, 83) is an overstatement. Two further qualifications might be added: first, Michael Goulder attempts a statistical argument for Markan Priority in *Midrash and Lection in Matthew* (London: SPCK, 1974), 122–23, with a view to attempting to demonstrate the accuracy of his "midrashic" view later (474–75). However, the argument is fallacious — see my *Goulder and the Gospels*, 86–87. Second, see his "Some Observations on Professor Farmer's 'Certain Results....'" in C. M. Tuckett, ed., *Synoptic Studies: The Ampleforth Conferences of 1982 and 1983* (JSNTSup,

19

It is not difficult to see why most Q skeptics have taken this course of action. When one is arguing for a minority position, it is natural to devote energy to arguing for what is controversial or unorthodox in one's view and to leave agreements with the status quo largely taken for granted. Unfortunately, however, this strategy has had mixed results. One of the most troubling elements has been the confusion that has ensued from those who have apparently not managed to distinguish between the kind of Q skepticism that builds on Markan Priority and the very different variety for which the rejection of Markan Priority is at the top of the agenda.[4] And, further, the lack of stress on Markan Priority among adherents of the Farrer theory has tended to focus opponents' attention solely on what is different from the two-source theory without encouraging due consideration of its essential similarity in building on the same foundation, working first and foremost with Matthew's and Luke's use of Mark.[5]

With a view, then, to joining hands with Q theorists on the one side, and creating some distance from the Griesbach hypothesis on the other side, the aim of this chapter is to provide an account of why the Priority of Mark remains a plausible theory and a sound building block for the study of Synoptic relationships.[6] The Griesbach Hypothesis is currently advocated by a research team made up of Lamar Cope, David Dungan, Thomas Longstaff, Allan McNicol, David Peabody, and Philip Shuler. Under the inspiration of the late William Farmer,[7] they have been press-

---

7; Sheffield: JSOT Press, 1984), 99–104, in which Goulder argues against William Farmer's contribution to the same volume.

4. See above, pp. 10–13.

5. See, for example, John Kloppenborg Verbin's treatment of the Farrer theory together with the Griesbach and the "Augustine" theories, *Excavating Q*, 38–43 (under the title "Other Solutions"). Of course Kloppenborg points out that the Farrer theory involves the shared postulate of Markan Priority (38), but the discussion focuses on its difference from the two-source theory and its alleged similarity to Griesbach and Augustine.

6. I will not discuss the (so-called) Augustine hypothesis (Matthew → Mark → Luke) since it is does not currently have any significant support. However, some of the observations made in this chapter will be relevant also to this solution. See H. G. Jameson, *The Origin of the Synoptic Gospels: A Revision of the Synoptic Problem* (Oxford: Basil Blackwell, 1922); John Chapman, *Matthew, Mark and Luke: A Study in the Order and Interrelation of the Synoptic Gospels* (London: Longmans, Green, 1937); B. C. Butler, *The Originality of St Matthew: A Critique of the Two-Document Hypothesis* (Cambridge: Cambridge University Press, 1951) and most recently, in a modified form, the late J. W. Wenham, *Redating Matthew, Mark and Luke: A Fresh Assault on the Synoptic Problem* (London: Hodder & Stoughton, 1991).

7. I was sorry to hear of the death of Professor Farmer on December 30, 2000, while I was preparing this manuscript. I have had the privilege of meeting Professor Farmer on several occasions over the last five years or so, and he has always gone out of his way to be encouraging, gracious, and enthusiastic about my work. In spite of my own disagreement with him, I am grateful for what he has done to "renew gospel studies" by challenging us to think in fresh

ing their case with clarity and vigor now for some years, and as well as considerable individual academic contributions,[8] they have collaborated to produce the first detailed verse-by-verse exposition of Luke on the assumption that he read Matthew alone, and further works are in the pipeline.[9] Although few scholars appear to have changed their minds about Markan Priority as a result of their research, one important and quantifiable result has been achieved by adherents of the Griesbach hypothesis — they have pointed to weaknesses in some of the standard arguments for Markan Priority and have thus caused proponents of it to think carefully about the theory and to attempt to articulate the arguments for its existence more carefully.[10]

The clearest example is the argument from order.[11] Once given as the key reason for belief in Markan Priority,[12] this argument holds that

---

ways, for refusing to accept the consensus simply because it is the consensus, but most of all for encouraging scholars to work together in the kind of collegial spirit that is all too often lacking in the discipline.

8. Important recent publications include William R. Farmer, *The Gospel of Jesus: The Pastoral Relevance of the Synoptic Problem* (Louisville: Westminster/John Knox, 1994); Allan McNicol. *Jesus' Directions for the Future: A Source and Redaction-History Study of the Use of the Eschatological Traditions in Paul and in the Synoptic Accounts of Jesus' Last Eschatological Discourse* (New Gospel Studies, 9; Macon, Ga.: Mercer University Press, 1996); David B. Peabody, "Luke's Sequential Use of the Sayings of Jesus from Matthew's Great Discourses. A Chapter in the Source-Critical Analysis of Luke on the Two Gospel (Neo-Griesbach) Hypothesis" in *Literary Studies in Luke-Acts. Essays in Honor of Joseph B. Tyson* (ed. Richard P. Thompson and Thomas E. Phillips; Macon, Ga.: Mercer University Press, June 1998), 37–58; David L. Dungan, *A History of the Synoptic Problem: The Canon, Text, the Composition and the Interpretation of the Gospels* (Anchor Bible Reference Library; New York: Doubleday, 1999).

9. Allan J. McNicol et al., *Beyond the Q Impasse.* For a detailed analysis see my "Beyond the Q Impasse or Down a Blind Alley?" See also Robert J. Derrenbacker, Jr., "The Relationship of the Gospels Reconsidered"; and the reviews by John Kloppenborg Verbin, *CBQ* 61 (1999): 370–72, and Christopher Tuckett, *JBL* 117 (1998): 363–65. I am grateful also to Timothy A. Friedrichsen for lending me a copy of his (as yet unpublished) excellent, detailed review article. The forthcoming work is David B. Peabody, ed., with Lamar Cope and Allan J. McNicol, *One Gospel from Two: Mark's Use of Matthew and Luke* (Harrisburg, Pa.: Trinity Press International, 2002).

10. Cf. Arland Jacobson, *The First Gospel,* 6, "Even if such challenges are finally judged to be of little merit, consideration of them may lead to greater methodological clarity."

11. The authoritative work here is David Neville, *Arguments from Order in Synoptic Source Criticism: A History and Critique* (New Gospel Studies 7; Leuven: Peeters, 1994; Macon, Ga.: Mercer University Press, 1994). For a careful and nuanced recent discussion of the argument from order, see John S. Kloppenborg Verbin, *Excavating Q,* especially 18–28.

12. Notice, however, that the simple form of the argument from order is still sometimes given as a major argument in favor of Markan Priority, for example Stephen J. Patterson, *The Gospel of Thomas and Jesus* (Sonoma, Calif.: Polebridge, 1993), 13, "In the case of Markan priority, the strength of the thesis has traditionally been that Mark seems to dictate the order followed by Matthew and Luke.... Thus, the strongest argument for Markan Priority concerns a common synoptic order." Compare also Robert W. Funk, Roy Hoover and the Jesus Seminar, *The Five Gospels: The Search for the Authentic Words of Jesus* (Sonoma, Calif.: Polebridge, 1993), 10–12.

Mark apparently "dictates" the parallel sequences found in Matthew and Luke.[13] However, in its simplest form at least, the argument from order points to nothing more striking than that Mark is the "middle term" among the Synoptics.[14] Those who now defend some kind of argument from order tend to reconfigure it in terms of the plausibility of the redactional procedure that the differences in order imply. So where Matthew departs from Mark's order, it is straightforward to imagine why, in the light of his literary preferences, he might have made those changes, and so too Luke.[15] But while in the judgment of most, these kinds of argument remain plausible as explanations of Matthew's and Luke's redactional procedures on the assumption of Markan Priority, it is difficult for them to function as strong arguments in favor of Markan Priority unless they are accompanied by arguments against the plausibility of the reverse procedure, Mark's use of Matthew and Luke. On the whole, this has not happened in recent arguments from order. While useful arguments are put forward for the theory that Matthew's and Luke's procedure is "readily explicable,"[16] the case is not often accompanied by an exposition of the implausibility of Mark's procedure on the Griesbach hypothesis, and it is this latter that is also required. Markan Priorists' arguments from order have, in other words, become essentially defensive, reacting against the Griesbachians' formal argument from order without attempting to go on the counteroffensive. At present, therefore, the argument from order used by Markan Priorists can indeed play a supportive role, illustrating the plausibility of Matthean and Lukan dependence on Mark, as part of a general redaction-critical argument in favor of Markan Priority,[17] but it will be unconvincing to

---

13. See B. H. Streeter, *The Four Gospels: A Study of Origins, Treating of the Manuscript Tradition, Sources, Authorship and Dates* (London: Macmillan, 1924), 151: "[t]he relative order of incidents and sections in Mark is in general supported by both Matthew and Luke; where either of them deserts Mark, the other is usually found supporting him."

14. The decisive moment is B. C. Butler's exposure of the (so-called) "Lachmann Fallacy," *The Originality of St Matthew*, 62–71. For helpful discussion of Mark as the middle term, see E. P. Sanders and M. Davies, *Studying the Synoptic Gospels*, Chapter 3. See also John S. Kloppenborg Verbin, *Excavating Q*, 18–28; Mark Goodacre, *The Synoptic Problem*, Chapter 2.

15. See especially Christopher M. Tuckett, *The Revival of the Griesbach Hypothesis: An Analysis and Appraisal* (SNTSMS 44; Cambridge: Cambridge University Press, 1983).

16. See, for example, J. A. Fitzmyer, *Luke I–IX*, 71.

17. This argument from redaction criticism is now made ever more frequently by adherents of Markan Priority, e.g., Graham Stanton, Joseph Fitzmyer, and Ulrich Luz — see further below, pp. 75–77. On one level it is convincing; no synoptic theory can hope to be persuasive unless it has the potential to explain the evangelists' redactional procedures plausibly. However, it is the most clearly subjective kind of argument in favor of Markan Priority and will only be convincing to those working with the same sets of assumptions, within the same framework as

those who are not already inclined to accept Markan Priority on other grounds.

What, then, of other arguments for the priority of Mark? Is the situation within New Testament scholarship as problematic as William Farmer has consistently maintained?[18] The best way ahead will be to attempt to lay out why the theory of Markan Priority might still emerge as more plausible than its chief rival, Markan Posteriority, asking repeatedly whether the evidence makes better sense on the assumption that Matthew and Luke both knew Mark, or whether it makes better sense on the assumption that Mark knew Matthew and Luke.

The Dates of the Gospels

The natural place to begin any study of relative priority among related documents might be the attempt to see whether the documents under consideration show any signs of their respective dates. Have historical events, outside of those directly connected with the life of Jesus, impinged in any way on the Synoptics in such a way as to provide clues about the dates of their composition? On the whole, scholars have tended to fight shy of asking this question in the context of discussions about the Synoptic Problem, perhaps because of the general uncertainty about the dates of the Gospels. But this may have been a mistake. For while it is difficult to pinpoint the dates for any of the Gospels precisely, what evidence we do have points generally in the direction of a date no later than 70 for Mark, but clearly post-70 for both Matthew and Luke. Indeed one might almost say that this view approaches consensus, a consensus that emerges not simply because scholars have already made up their mind about Markan Priority but also because of certain clues in the texts. The evidence is not, of course, conclusive but it is, at the very least, suggestive.

One of the clearest hints that Matthew and Luke know of the events of 70 comes in the following piece of double tradition material:

Markan Priorists. Useful arguments in favor of Markan Priority require more than some kind of plausible account of Matthew's and Luke's alleged procedure on the assumption of their use of Mark.

18. See, for example, William R. Farmer, "The Current State of the Synoptic Problem," *Literary Studies in Luke-Acts: Essays in Honor of Joseph B. Tyson* (Macon, Ga.: Mercer University Press, 1998), 11–36. Having analyzed some recent literature, with a special focus on W. D. Davies and D. C. Allison's arguments for Markan Priority in *Matthew,* 1:97–127, Farmer claims that "Unless defenders of the Two Source Theory can produce new arguments to defend that theory, and renew critical confidence in it, source criticism in Gospel studies appears destined to remain at an impasse" (36).

Matt 23:37–39	Luke 13:34–35
Ἰερουσαλὴμ Ἰερουσαλήμ, ἡ ἀποκτείνουσα τοὺς προφήτας καὶ λιθοβολοῦσα τοὺς ἀπεσταλμένους πρὸς αὐτήν, ποσάκις ἠθέλησα ἐπισυναγαγεῖν τὰ τέκνα σου, ὃν τρόπον ὄρνις ἐπισυνάγει τὰ νοσσία αὐτῆς ὑπὸ τὰς πτέρυγας, καὶ οὐκ ἠθελήσατε. ἰδοὺ ἀφίεται ὑμῖν ὁ οἶκος ὑμῶν ἔρημος. λέγω γὰρ ὑμῖν, οὐ μή με ἴδητε ἀπ᾽ ἄρτι ἕως ἂν εἴπητε· εὐλογημένος ὁ ἐρχόμενος ἐν ὀνόματι κυρίου.	Ἰερουσαλὴμ Ἰερουσαλήμ, ἡ ἀποκτείνουσα τοὺς προφήτας καὶ λιθοβολοῦσα τοὺς ἀπεσταλμένους πρὸς αὐτήν, ποσάκις ἠθέλησα ἐπισυνάξαι τὰ τέκνα σου ὃν τρόπον ὄρνις τὴν ἑαυτῆς νοσσιὰν ὑπὸ τὰς πτέρυγας, καὶ οὐκ ἠθελήσατε. ἰδοὺ ἀφίεται ὑμῖν ὁ οἶκος ὑμῶν. λέγω [δὲ] ὑμῖν, οὐ μὴ ἴδητέ με ἕως [ἥξει ὅτε] εἴπητε· εὐλογημένος ὁ ἐρχόμενος ἐν ὀνόματι κυρίου.
"Jerusalem, Jerusalem, killing the prophets and stoning those who are sent to you! How often would I have gathered your children together as a hen gathers her brood under her wings, and you would not! *Behold, your house is forsaken and desolate.* For I tell you, you will not see me again, until you say, 'Blessed is the one who comes in the name of the Lord!'	"Jerusalem, Jerusalem, killing the prophets and stoning those who are sent to you! How often would I have gathered your children together as a hen gathers her brood under her wings, and you would not! *Behold, your house is forsaken.* And I tell you, you will not see me until [when he comes] you say, 'Blessed is the one who comes in the name of the Lord!'

For any post-70 reader, the words "your house is forsaken" would naturally evoke thoughts about the destruction of the Temple, and under such circumstances it seems likely that this may have been the reason for its inclusion by Matthew and Luke. Josephus provides an analogy for the way this oracle functions here:

There was one Jesus, the son of Ananus, a plebeian and a husbandman, who, four years before the war began, and at a time when the city was in very great peace and prosperity, came to that feast whereon it is our custom for every one to make tabernacles to God in the temple, began on a sudden to cry aloud, "A voice from the east, a voice from the west, a voice from the four winds, a voice against Jerusalem and the holy house, a voice against the bridegrooms and the brides, and a voice against this whole people!" This was his cry, as he went about by day and by night, in all the lanes of the city. (*Jewish War* 6.300–301)

Although the oracle is familiar to New Testament scholars, especially those writing on the historical Jesus, many do not notice that there is a parallel here between the way that Jesus ben Ananus's doom oracle functions in Josephus and the way Jesus' oracle functions in both Matthew and Luke. Josephus is writing from the perspective of the post-70 situation, drawing attention to Jesus ben Ananus's oracle, along with other, similar portents, in order to evoke the feeling that Jerusalem's inevitable doom, known to his readers, had been clear if only the people had cared to look for it. Both oracles, Matthew 23:37–39 // Luke 13:34–35 and *Jewish War* 6.300–301, have the same threefold focus on the people, the city, the temple. Just as Jesus ben Ananus cries "a voice against Jerusalem...," so too Jesus laments "Jerusalem, Jerusalem...." Just as ben Ananus singles out "the holy house," so too Jesus says "behold your house is forsaken." Just as ben Ananus raises "a voice against this whole people," so too Jesus exclaims "how often would I have gathered your children...."

In both cases, we may be dealing with pre-70 traditions,[19] but in both cases the oracles could not fail to evoke thoughts about 70 to post-70 readers. Perhaps, like Josephus, Matthew and Luke intended the oracle to function in precisely that way. In the same context, Josephus gives the extraordinary report of voices heard in the temple, "we are departing from hence" (μεταβαίνομεν ἐντεῦθεν, *Jewish War* 6.299), just as here in Matthew and Luke the implication is that God has left the temple. So, while not conclusive, the evidence is at least suggestive — Matthew and Luke both stress a passage in which the temple's desolation is central.[20]

---

19. I leave open the question of whether or not this is a *vaticinium ex eventu* in either Josephus or the Gospels. The importance here is to notice the way in which a prophecy set in the pre-70 period may function in a post-70 literary context.

20. Luke, for example, stresses this material by placing it in the center of his narrative, a narrative flanked by Jerusalem at the beginning (Luke 1) and the end (Luke 24). For a reading of Luke sympathetic to the view that the Temple is central, see Jonathan Knight, *Luke*. There has been some resistance to the notion that this passage postdates 70, perhaps partly because of the later dating it might imply for Q, on other grounds usually felt to be a document that predates 70. While within Q scholarship the force of "your house is forsaken" is felt to be an overwhelming sign of post-70 redaction by Paul Hoffmann, "The Redaction of Q and the Son of Man: A Preliminary Sketch" in Ronald Piper, ed., *The Gospel Behind the Gospels*, 159–98 (especially 191) and Matti Myllykoski, "The Social History of Q and the Jewish War" in *Symbols and Strata: Essays on the Sayings Gospel Q* (ed. Risto Uro; Suomen Eksegeettisen Seuran Julkaisuja. Publications of the Finnish Exegetical Society 65; Helsinki: Finnish Exegetical Society; Göttingen: Vandenhoeck & Ruprecht, 1996), 143–99, it is not essential to the point I am making here. Even if Hoffmann and Myllykoski are wrong and Q did not know of the events of 70, the fact that both Matthew and Luke stress a passage in which this is such a major theme could point to a post-70 date. For the question of dating, see also Michael Goulder, *Luke*, 61–62.

This piece of double tradition is not the only place where the Synoptics hint at their knowledge of the destruction of Jerusalem. Another famous example comes in Matthew's parable of the Great Banquet.

πάλιν ἀπέστειλεν ἄλλους δούλους λέγων· εἴπατε τοῖς κεκλημένοις· ἰδοὺ τὸ ἄριστόν μου ἡτοίμακα, οἱ ταῦροί μου καὶ τὰ σιτιστὰ τεθυμένα καὶ πάντα ἕτοιμα· δεῦτε εἰς τοὺς γάμους. οἱ δὲ ἀμελή-σαντες ἀπῆλθον, ὃς μὲν εἰς τὸν ἴδιον ἀγρόν, ὃς δὲ ἐπὶ τὴν ἐμπορίαν αὐτοῦ· οἱ δὲ λοιποὶ κρατήσαντες τοὺς δούλους αὐτοῦ ὕβρισαν καὶ ἀπέκτειναν. ὁ δὲ βασιλεὺς ὠργίσθη καὶ πέμψας τὰ στρατεύματα αὐτοῦ ἀπώλεσεν τοὺς φονεῖς ἐκείνους καὶ τὴν πόλιν αὐτῶν ἐνέ-πρησεν. τότε λέγει τοῖς δούλοις αὐτοῦ· ὁ μὲν γάμος ἕτοιμός ἐστιν, οἱ δὲ κεκλημένοι οὐκ ἦσαν ἄξιοι. (Matt 22:4–8)

Again he sent other servants, saying, "Tell those who are invited, 'Behold, I have made ready my dinner, my oxen and my fat calves are killed, and everything is ready; come to the marriage feast.'" But they made light of it and went off, one to his farm, another to his business, while the rest seized his servants, treated them shame-fully, and killed them. *The king was angry, and he sent his troops and destroyed those murderers and burned their city.* Then he said to his servants, "The wedding is ready, but those invited were not worthy." (Matt 22:4–8)

This element intrudes into a story that can be told quite adequately without it (as in the parallel versions in Luke 14:15–24 and Thomas 64). It seems likely that Matthew is thinking here of the fall of Jerusalem, and he hopes that his readers see the allusion, all the more stark for the way in which it intrudes into the parable. The burning of the city, the climax of the sequence of events in Matthew 22:7, is a major element in Josephus's account of the war.[21]

When we turn to Mark such elements appear to be lacking. This would, of course, be little more than an argument from silence if it were not for the clear contrast between Matthew and Luke, on the one hand, and Mark, on the other, something troubling for the view that Mark wrote his Gospel in dependence on Matthew and Luke with their clear hints of the events of 70. Indeed, in triple tradition passages, in which

---

21. See, for example, Titus's command, "So he gave orders to the soldiers both to burn and to plunder the city" (τοῖς δὲ στρατιώταις ἐμπιμπράναι καὶ διαρπάζειν ἐπέτρεψεν τὴν πόλιν, *Jewish War* 6.353).

Mark is, according to the Griesbach hypothesis, redacting Matthew and Luke, it appears that he must have been careful to play down Matthew's and Luke's clearest allusions to the events of 70, substituting material that made the connection much less obvious:

Matt 24:15, 21–22	*Mark 13:14, 19–20*	*Luke 21:20–21, 23–24*
"So when you see the desolating sacrilege spoken of by the prophet Daniel, standing in the holy place (let the reader understand), then let those who are in Judea flee to the mountains.... For then there will be great tribulation, such as has not been from the beginning of the world until now, no, and never will be. And if those days had not been shortened, no human being would be saved; but for the sake of the elect those days will be shortened.	"But when you see the desolating sacrilege set up where it ought not to be (let the reader understand), then let those who are in Judea flee to the mountains.... For in those days there will be such tribulation as has not been from the beginning of the creation which God created until now, and never will be. And if the Lord had not shortened the days, no human being would be saved; but for the sake of the elect, whom he chose, he shortened the days.	"But when you see <u>Jerusalem surrounded by armies,</u> then know that its desolation has come near. Then let those who are in Judea flee to the mountains ... For great distress shall be upon the earth and wrath upon this people; they will fall by the edge of the sword, and be led captive among all nations; <u>and Jerusalem will be trodden down by the Gentiles,</u> until the times of the Gentiles are fulfilled.

On the Griesbach hypothesis, Mark here sides primarily with Matthew over against Luke, though it is the latter who has the clearest allusions to the events of 70. Instead of a Jerusalem surrounded by armies and downtrodden by "the Gentiles," Jesus in Mark speaks obliquely about the "desolating sacrilege set up where it ought not to be." It is possible, of course, that Mark had reasons to avoid being too explicit about what had happened in 70, but it is even more likely that he simply did not know about it.

But are there any other indications that Mark's Gospel is closer in time to the events it is narrating than are Matthew and Luke? There is one other hint. It is a small hint; it is only suggestive, and it is easy to miss, but it is nevertheless worth noting. Mark mentions that Simon of Cyrene, who carried Jesus' cross, was "the father of Alexander and Rufus" (Mark 15:21), a detail absent from the parallels in Matthew and Luke (Matt 27:32 // Luke 23:26). This passing reference to "Alexander and Rufus" is one of the few places in the whole gospel tradition where someone is identified by means of their children's names. To say the least, it is not standard practice. The obvious reason that Mark mentions this character's children is that they are expected to be known by at least some of the readers.[22] Here, then, we have a hint that Mark's Gospel does not perceive itself to be a long way, in time, from the events it is relating, for the sons of one of the characters in the story are apparently known to Mark's readers. Insofar as there are any indicators at all, then, they all point in the direction of Markan Priority. Together, these different elements add up to the kind of evidence that is troubling for the Griesbach hypothesis.

Finally, Luke perceives itself to be a second generation document. Not only does its preface mention the πολλοί ("many") who have attempted to compose narratives (1:1), but also it mentions the tradents through whom Luke has additional knowledge (1:2). Unlike Mark, Luke is self-conscious about its secondary and derivative nature. While this does not require the theory that Luke postdates Mark, the evidence is clearly more conducive to that theory than it is to the Griesbach hypothesis.

Mark's Omissions

Mark's Gospel is considerably shorter than both Matthew and Luke. One of the most pressing issues, therefore, for adherents of the Griesbach hypothesis is to provide an account of why Mark omitted the material their theory dictates that he omitted.[23] Furthermore, this needs to be studied alongside the additions Mark allegedly makes and some account of the relationship between the omissions and the additions will be nec-

---

22. Some commentators have even speculated that this is the same Rufus mentioned in Romans 16:13, though this is rejected by Ernest Best, "Mark's Readers: A Profile," in *The Four Gospels 1992. Festschrift Frans Neirynck,* vol. 2 (ed. F. Van Segbroeck et al.; BETL, 100; Leuven: Leuven University Press, 1992), 839–58 (esp. 857).

23. Cf. E. P. Sanders's and Margaret Davies's useful comment on "a major presupposition behind the two-source hypothesis: Everything is from a source, and no one would leave out anything important," *Studying the Synoptic Gospels,* 79. While it will not do simply to point to the fact that, on the Griesbach hypothesis, Mark omits a lot from Matthew and Luke, much may nevertheless be gained by looking at precisely what the theory dictates that he left out. In particular, is any pattern discernible in Griesbach's Mark's alleged omissions?

essary. What kind of profile of Mark the evangelist emerges, and how plausible a picture is it?

The issue of omissions is focused by the fact that on the Griesbach hypothesis, Mark's rationale is sometimes held to have involved a quest for unity, drawing together in one shorter Gospel some of the divergent elements in his sources. Farmer, for example, summarizes Mark's purpose by saying, "The evangelist Mark, under the auspices of the Pauline gospel, unified within the collective consciousness of the church the diverse and sometimes diverging accounts of Matthew and Luke."[24] Given this alleged aim, the scholar's attention is naturally drawn to material Mark omitted from his alleged sources, and especially the material that is shared by both Matthew and Luke that is not in Mark, the double tradition. What is it about this material, which represents concurrent testimony of the two other Synoptic Evangelists, that caused Mark to omit it? Can we see in it a distinctly un-Markan profile? In Mark's alleged quest for unity, what is it about this particular subset of material that Mark found unhelpful?[25]

It has to be said that the double tradition does not have a particularly un-Markan profile. Indeed, there are places in Mark where the insertion of double tradition might have been highly conducive to his purposes, both literary and theological. One of the clearest and most famous examples is the omission of the Lord's Prayer. Both theologically and in

---

24. William Farmer, *Gospel of Jesus*, 24. Cf. William R. Farmer, "Reply to Michael Goulder" in C. M. Tuckett, ed., *Synoptic Studies*, 105–9, in which this is presented as the consensus position among adherents of the Griesbach hypothesis, "One hundred years of work with Mark, assuming his Gospel to be the earliest, has produced no consensus among the Markan priorists which can begin to compare to the consensus shared by all critics who regard Mark as third: Mark is a unifying figure, a reconciling churchman, a mediating, but self-consistent, theologian — dynamic in his irenicism" (109).

25. William Farmer describes "the Q material" as "simply writings that Luke copied from Matthew but that Mark did not incorporate into his work," which, on the Griesbach hypothesis, is correct. But he goes on to say, "This partly explains why it is so difficult to identify the extent or purpose of Q. That Q could have produced an intelligible theology is explained by the fact that Luke selected from Matthew only material that was useful for his Gentile readers. This explains the appeal of Q to some modern theologians. It is generally free of Jewish *Tendenz*" (*Gospel of Jesus*, 21). Regardless of the somewhat questionable characterization of the Q material, this reading of what constitutes Q does not take seriously the key element in the previous statement, "that Mark did not incorporate into his work." With Griesbach, the double tradition is constituted primarily by that which Mark omitted from the combined witness in Matthew and Luke. For, on the Griesbach hypothesis, there is no distinction as far as Luke is concerned between triple tradition and double tradition — Luke takes both kinds of material from Matthew. In relation to this, I am a little puzzled by the tendency among adherents of the Griesbach hypothesis to refer to Luke's use of Matthew as taking us "beyond the Q impasse," for on their theory Luke takes over far more of (what we would call) triple tradition from Matthew than he takes over of (what we call) double tradition. See further on this methodological point my "Beyond the Q Impasse or Down a Blind Alley?" 40–42 and 51.

terms of structure and literary preference, it seems that the Lord's Prayer would find a place in Mark. Almost every element in it finds a parallel in Mark, and some of his favorite themes are stressed. They might be enumerated as follows:

1. Οὕτως οὖν προσεύχεσθε ὑμεῖς..., In this way therefore should you pray (Matt 6:9) // ὅταν προσεύχησθε, λέγετε..., When you pray, say...(Luke 11:2)

The presumption of corporate prayer is a feature also of Mark, including two contexts using similar themes to those found in the prayer. Mark 11:24–25, which follows on from the Cursing of the Fig Tree, has Jesus exhort his disciples, διὰ τοῦτο λέγω ὑμῖν, πάντα ὅσα προσεύχεσθε καὶ αἰτεῖσθε... καὶ ὅταν στήκετε προσευχόμενοι.... "Therefore I say to you (pl.), Whatever you (pl.) pray and ask.... And when you (pl.) stand praying...." Likewise in Gethsemane, Jesus exhorts Peter with the plural imperative, γρηγορεῖτε καὶ προσεύχεσθε, "Watch (pl.) and pray (pl.)" (Mark 14:38).

2. πάτερ ἡμῶν ὁ ἐν τοῖς οὐρανοῖς..., *Our Father in heaven* (Matt 6:9) // πάτερ, *Father* (Luke 11:2)

The address of God as "Father" is apparently congenial to Mark. In Jesus' prayer in Gethsemane, he famously addresses God with the words ἀββᾶ ὁ πατήρ, "Abba, Father" (Mark 14:36).

3. ἐλθέτω ἡ βασιλεία σου, *May your kingdom come* (Matt 6:10 // Luke 11:2)

The coming of God's kingdom is at the heart of Jesus' proclamation in Mark's Gospel, from his opening words, ἤγγικεν ἡ βασιλεῖα τοῦ θεοῦ ("the kingdom of God is at hand," Mark 1:14) and throughout the Gospel, and most famously in his parables of the kingdom. Indeed of all the evangelists, Mark is the one who has the most explicitly future kingdom, in which prayer for its coming might have been quite at home.

4. γενηθήτω τὸ θέλημά σου, *May your will be done* (Matt 6:10)

Doing God's will is so important for Mark that he makes it the means of defining fictive kinship, ὃς [γὰρ] ἂν ποιήσῃ τὸ θέλημα τοῦ θεοῦ, οὗτος ἀδελφός μου καὶ ἀδελφὴ καὶ μήτηρ ἐστίν, "for whoever does the will of God, this is my brother and sister and mother" (Mark 3:35). And it is a key element in Jesus' prayer in Gethsemane, ἀλλ᾽ οὐ τί ἐγὼ θέλω ἀλλὰ τί σύ, "but not what I wish, but what you wish" (Mark 14:36 // Matt 26:39 // Luke 22:42).

5. καὶ ἄφες ἡμῖν τὰ ὀφειλήματα (Luke ἁμαρτίας) ἡμῶν, ὡς καὶ ἡμεῖς ἀφήκαμεν τοῖς ὀφειλέταις ἡμῶν, And forgive us our debts, as we forgive our debtors (Matt 6:12; cf. Luke 11:4)

This theme of reciprocal forgiveness is very close to Mark 11:25, in material parallel to that which is adjacent to the Lord's Prayer in Matthew (6:14):

Matt 6:14	*Mark 11:25*
Ἐὰν γὰρ ἀφῆτε τοῖς ἀνθρώποις τὰ παραπτώματα αὐτῶν, ἀφήσει καὶ ὑμῖν ὁ πατὴρ ὑμῶν ὁ οὐράνιος.	ἀφίετε εἴ τι ἔχετε κατά τινος, ἵνα καὶ ὁ πατὴρ ὑμῶν ὁ ἐν τοῖς οὐρανοῖς ἀφῇ ὑμῖν τὰ παραπτώματα ὑμῶν.

The clause in the Lord's Prayer might thus, once again, be described as congenial to Mark.

6. καὶ μὴ εἰσενέγκῃς ἡμας εἰς πειρασμόν, *And lead us not into temptation* (Matt 6:13 // Luke 11:4)

This theme is another that appears directly in Mark, and in the context of exhortation to pray. In Gethsemane, Jesus says to Peter, γρηγορεῖτε καὶ προσεύχεσθε, ἵνα μὴ ἔλθητε εἰς πειρασμόν, "Watch and pray, lest you come into temptation" (Mark 14:38, cf. Matt 26:41 // Luke 22:46).[26]

In short, it is surprising, on the assumption of Markan Posteriority, that Mark omitted the Lord's Prayer. There is an ideal literary context available for it in Mark 11:24–25, and almost every element within it appears to be highly conducive to Mark's theological interests. It could hardly be that Mark dislikes the repetition of liturgical set-pieces since the Eucharistic Words (Mark 14:22–25) have a key function in his Passion Narrative. All in all, from what we can gather of Mark's interests and editorial practice, combined with the Griesbachian theory that Mark was in some sense the Church's document, aiming at unifying two diverging literary predecessors, there are problems with the notion that he has omitted double tradition like this.[27]

---

26. For a useful exposition of the links between the Lord's Prayer and Mark's Gospel, see further Michael Goulder, "The Composition of the Lord's Prayer," *JTS* 14 (1964): 32–45. Goulder thinks that the links are so close that it is likely that Matthew has composed the prayer himself on the basis of Jesus' teaching and practice in Mark. For the place of the Lord's Prayer in the Q hypothesis, and its relevance to the question of Luke's use of Matthew, see below, pp. 64–65.

27. The question has not, on the whole, been tackled by adherents of the Griesbach hypoth-

Mark's Additions

On its own, however, this kind of example would only be suggestive. One of the key questions for the notion that Mark succeeded Matthew and Luke is what Mark, on this assumption, has added to his primary literary sources. The question is an interesting one, and is capable of even more focusing than is possible over his alleged omissions, because there is so little material that appears in Mark alone. The three primary examples[28] are

> Mark 7:33–36: Healing of a Deaf Mute
> Mark 8:22–26: Blind Man of Bethsaida
> Mark 14:51–52: Man Running Away Naked

The question that these rather limited examples of special Mark raise see above,is whether they are best regarded, in line with Markan Priority, as mutual omissions by Matthew and Luke or whether, in line with the Griesbach hypothesis, they are best regarded as Markan additions to his literary source material. There are several reasons for thinking that Markan Priority, and the theory of mutual omission by Matthew and Luke, is the more plausible. There are common elements in the first two examples, the Healing of the Deaf Mute and the Blind Man of Bethsaida,

---

esis. William Farmer, *Gospel of Jesus*, Chapter 4, gives an entire chapter on the Lord's Prayer in the Griesbach hypothesis but focuses solely on alleged pastoral difficulties with Q theorists' claim that the Lukan form of the prayer might have predated Matthew's. He does not comment at all on the omission of the prayer by Mark. I am grateful to David Peabody for showing me a section relating to Mark 11:24–25 from the forthcoming volume of the Research Team of the International Institute for the Renewal of Gospel Studies, *One Gospel from Two: Mark's Use of Matthew and Luke*. The Research Team point to "the fragmentary presentation of the Lord's Prayer" here and observe that Matthew and Luke stand in their own right as reliable attestations of the prayer. On the general issue of omissions from Matthew and Luke under the Griesbach hypothesis, see also Thomas R. W. Longstaff, "Crisis and Christology: The Theology of Mark" in *New Synoptic Studies: The Cambridge Gospel Conference and Beyond* (ed. William R. Farmer; Macon, Ga.: Mercer University Press, 1983), 373–92.

28. Sometimes the Seed Growing Secretly (Mark 4:26–29) is also listed as special Mark; see classically C. H. Dodd, *Parables of the Kingdom* (Rev. ed.; London: Nesbet & Co., 1961), 137. However, the Wheat and the Tares (Matthew 13:24–30) appears in the identical context in Matthew, featuring much of the same wording. Although the Gospel of Thomas features both parables (Seed Growing Secretly in Thomas 21 and Wheat and Tares in Thomas 57), it seems likely that, on the assumption of Markan Priority and given the placement, Matthew thought of the Wheat and the Tares as a version of the Seed Growing Secretly, or on the assumption of Matthean Priority, vice versa. For a full statement of the material Mark adds on the assumption of the Griesbach hypothesis, see W. D. Davies and Dale C. Allison, *A Critical and Exegetical Commentary on the Gospel According to Saint Matthew* (The International Critical Commentary on the Holy Scriptures of the Old and New Testaments; Edinburgh: T & T Clark, 1988), 1:108–9. They list eighteen passages covering forty verses.

that might straightforwardly explain the omission.[29] First, both healings involve the use of saliva (Mark 7:33 and 8:23). Since there are no examples of healings using physical agents like this anywhere in Matthew and Luke, this element may be important. Second, both healings involve the element of secrecy that is so often standard in Mark (7:33, 36; 8:23, 26). In both incidents, it is a twofold secrecy: first Jesus takes the man to one side and then after the healing, he issues the command not to tell anyone. The same twofold secrecy is absent from Matthew and occurs only once in Luke, in the healing of Jairus's daughter, in direct parallel with Mark (Mark 5:35–43 // Luke 8:49–56; contrast Matt 9:23–26).

Furthermore, the healing of the Blind Man of Bethsaida clearly places some kind of limit on Jesus' ability; the healing is not instantaneous but takes time. Matthew and Luke are here on a trajectory that stretches out across Christian history; Matthew's and Luke's Jesus, always able to heal instantaneously, is the one familiar to most. It is with Mark's Gospel that we are afforded a brief glimpse into a slightly more gritty, more realistic picture of Jesus, a Jesus who does not always heal everyone immediately. Indeed, this coheres with other elements in Mark's presentation of Jesus' healing which are also absent from Matthew and Luke. In spite of Peter Head's welcome corrective to an oversimplistic appeal to Christological arguments for Markan Priority,[30] there are certain features in Mark's approach that, on the assumption of Markan Priority, are consistently avoided by Matthew and Luke. Where Mark's Jesus "could not do" (οὐκ ἐδύνατο... ποιῆσαι, Mark 6:5) any "mighty work" (δύναμις) in his hometown, except that he laid hands on a few sick people and healed them,[31] Matthew's Jesus, by contrast, only "did not do" many mighty works there (οὐκ ἐποίησεν, Matt 13:58).[32] Likewise, where Jesus heals many (καὶ ἐθεράπευσεν πολλοὺς κακῶς ἔχοντας ποικίλαις νόσοις) in Mark 1:34, he heals "all those who were ill" (καὶ πάντας τοὺς κακῶς ἔχοντας ἐθεράπευσεν) in the Matthean parallel (Matt 8:16) and "each

---

29. In Luke's case here, it needs to be added that this pericope is part of his Great Omission, Mark 6:45–8:26.

30. Peter M. Head, *Christology and the Synoptic Problem: An Argument for Markan Priority* (SNTSMS, 94; Cambridge: Cambridge University Press, 1997).

31. Many commentators gloss over the latter clause in Mark's account, which clearly qualifies and possibly contradicts the previous οὐκ ἐδύνατο... comment. However, it seems likely that Mark is pointing specifically to Jesus' inability to do any δύναμις (cf. Mark 6:2 — they had heard the rumor that he could perform mighty works), even if he did lay hands on some sick people, i.e., performed minor healings.

32. See Peter Head, *Christology and the Synoptic Problem*, 66–83 for an excellent discussion of this pericope (and literature cited there), and pages pp. 71–73 for a critique of the standard views on Matthew's καὶ οὐκ ἐποίησεν... over against Mark's οὐκ ἐδύνατο... ποιῆσαι.

one" in Luke (ὁ δὲ ἑνὶ ἑκάστῳ αὐτῶν τὰς χεῖρας ἐπιτιθεὶς ἐθεράπευσεν αὐτούς, Luke 4:40).

Of course it is possible that one of Mark's aims was to correct the more reverential picture of Matthew and Luke, so "reprimitivizing" the tradition. The question, however, is whether this view, on which Mark adds only a small number of archaizing traditions and primitivizing redactions at the expense of much congenial material in Matthew and Luke, is more plausible than the alternative possibility, that these incidents are ones omitted by Matthew and Luke in accordance with their general redactional policies. The question to which we inevitably return concerns the profile of Mark the redactor. On the Griesbach hypothesis, Mark apparently takes care to include the majority of those incidents to which Matthew and Luke bear united witness.[33] The extent of Mark's care over his predecessors' concurrent testimony draws attention in a stark way to the few examples of special Markan material. The interpreter cannot help asking what it is about the Blind Man of Bethsaida and the Deaf Mute that is so important to Mark that they find their way, as special cases, into his Gospel. And the scarcity of such special Markan material only focuses the further question: why does so little else make it into the Gospel? Is it that Mark had little access to further traditions?

The Place of Oral Tradition

This problem is illustrated and so compounded further by questions over the place of oral tradition in Christian origins. On the assumption that Matthew is writing first, there appears to be a wealth of material available to him. So too Luke, on the Griesbachian assumption that he has used only Matthew, appears to have a large amount of additional tradition at his disposal. Then, however, when Griesbach's Mark writes, using Matthew and Luke, there seems to be a striking lack of additional material available to the author. All he adds is a small handful of stories, none of which is particularly striking. And he adds virtually no fresh sayings material at all.[34]

---

33. The miracles are particularly important to Griesbach's Mark — only the Centurion's Boy (Matt 8:5–13 // Luke 7:1–10) is omitted. On the Griesbach hypothesis, the double tradition is constituted by the material Mark has omitted from the concurrent witness of Matthew and Luke (see above, p. 29) and the Centurion's Boy is one of the only healing miracles actually recorded in the double tradition, though see also Matt 12:22 // Luke 11:14.

34. One of the few examples is Mark 9:49, πᾶς γὰρ πυρὶ ἁλισθήσεται, "for everyone will be salted with fire," reinforces the point. As usual, the redaction critic asks: is it more likely that

Those who believe that Mark came third therefore have to make sense of a situation in which Mark stands out from much of early Christianity. After all, Papias's comment that he prefers "the living voice" to the written word, written presumably after the composition of Mark (even on the assumption of the latter's posteriority),[35] does not suggest that oral traditions were in abeyance at this time. So too the Gospel of Thomas,[36] that most self-consciously oral text, features both Synoptic and non-Synoptic material that appears to have been gleaned from oral tradition. If one accepts a date for Thomas anywhere in the region from the late first to the mid-second century, it would seem to confirm further that oral tradition did not die a death somewhere in the late first century.[37]

Every piece of evidence we have available for this period suggests that oral traditions were healthy, widespread, and popular. So whether one dates Mark in the 60s or in the 90s of the first century, we will expect him to have been familiar with a good number of oral traditions of the Jesus story. In other words, while the theory of Markan Priority allows us to paint a plausible picture of the place of oral tradition in the composition of each of the Synoptic Gospels, the Griesbach Hypothesis implies some real isolation for Mark. It becomes an anomaly in early Christianity. We cannot help wondering why it is that Mark apparently relies on this oral tradition so little, why it is that the stories of the Blind Man of Bethsaida and the Deaf Mute are the best he could manage.

This troubling situation is intensified by a striking feature of Mark's style. For of all the canonical Gospels, Mark's is the most blatantly colloquial, the most "oral" in nature. Many of the most famous features of Mark's Gospel suggest a more intimate relationship with oral traditions than can be the case with Griesbach's rather literary Mark,

---

this obscure saying is one of the very few pieces that Mark adds to his literary sources Matthew and Luke or is it more likely that it is one of the few pieces that both Matthew and Luke omit from Mark? On balance, the latter seems more likely.

35. ... τὰ παρὰ ζώσης φωνῆς καὶ μενούσης, Eusebius, *Hist. Eccl.* III, 39, 1.

36. Increasing numbers of scholars are inclined to see at least some influence on Thomas from Synoptic-like oral traditions of the life of Jesus. See G. Theissen and A. Merz, *The Historical Jesus*, 37–41 for a good introduction to the issues. For a nuanced recent treatment of the question of Thomas's relation to the Synoptics and oral traditions, see Risto Uro, "*Thomas* and the Oral Gospel Tradition" in *Thomas at the Crossroads: Essays on the Gospel of Thomas* (ed. Risto Uro; Edinburgh: T & T Clark, 1998), Chapter 1.

37. Moreover, Helmut Koester's important 1957 study of patristic citations of the Gospels claims that the same thing is true of the second century more broadly: oral traditions did not cease the moment that the Synoptists had set pen to papyrus. See Helmut Koester, *Synoptische Überlieferung bei den apostolischen Vätern* (Berlin: Akademie-Verlag, 1957).

whose main task was the intricate, painstaking conflation of Matthew and Luke. Mark has a vigorous pace, with the use of καὶ εὐθύς (*and immediately...*) that borders on obsessive and a frequent use of the historic present, which even today is a feature only of the most colloquial writing. Further, Mark's love of visual detail ("the green grass," Mark 6:39; "he was in the stern, asleep on the cushion," 4:38) and its abrupt ending (16:8) are all features suggestive of a Gospel that is particularly oral in nature. Indeed it is perhaps for these reasons, as well as because of its length, that Mark has been the Gospel that has lent itself most readily in modern times to oral performance. In other words, it would be odd if the most "oral" of the Synoptic Gospels turned out also to be the third Gospel, dependent almost entirely, except for a handful of verses, on two much more literary predecessors, both of whom, like those who also came later, apparently had rich access to oral traditions of Jesus' actions and sayings.[38] As with much of the evidence, it is possible that this is the case, but it is not the most natural interpretation of the data.

Moreover, the anomaly is underlined and further illustrated by the fact that Griesbach's Mark is involved in a compositional procedure that does not do justice to the oral nature of this Gospel. In order to make sense of Markan posteriority, the Griesbach hypothesis supposes that Mark was generated by a careful process of conflation, which requires a high degree of literary attention on the author's part in order for it to become the middle term among the Synoptics.[39] Yet the colloquial Mark, with its color, its rough edges and its pace, does not look like the bookish, literary figure implied by the theory.[40]

---

38. See also the useful comment by Leander E. Keck, "The greater the role of oral tradition in early Christianity, the less viable the Griesbach hypothesis becomes, because this hypothesis forces the whole discussion into strictly literary terms. Streeter's hypothesis...can be adapted far more easily to take account of oral tradition than can any hypothesis insisting that the solution lies in a genealogical relation among three documents" ("Oral Traditional Literature and the Gospels," 103–22 in *The Relationships Among the Gospels: An Interdisciplinary Dialogue* (ed. William O. Walker; Trinity University Monographs in Religion 5; San Antonio: Trinity University Press, 1978), 120–21. The contrast between "Griesbach" and "Streeter," however, is artificial. It is not the "genealogical relation between three documents" that is problematic about Griesbach; it is the fact that for Griesbach, Mark comes third. On the Farrer theory there is a genealogical literary relationship between Mark, Matthew and Luke which need not preclude extensive interaction with oral tradition for each of the three Synoptists. See further below, pp. 64–66, for the place of oral tradition in the Farrer theory.

39. For a study of this issue from the perspective of the Griesbach hypothesis, see Thomas R. W. Longstaff, *Evidence of Conflation in Mark? A Study in the Synoptic Problem* (SBLDS, 28; Missoula, Mont.: Scholars Press, 1977).

40. I am grateful to Stephen Carlson for this point.

The Relationship Between Omissions and Additions

The question of Mark's alleged omissions and additions is most clearly focused, however, by asking about the relationship between them. In the introduction to their commentary on Matthew, W. D. Davies and Dale Allison ask this question:

> Can one seriously envision someone rewriting Matthew and Luke so as to omit the miraculous birth of Jesus, the sermon on the mount, and the resurrection appearances, while, on the other hand, adding the tale of the naked young man, a healing miracle in which Jesus has trouble healing, and the remark that Jesus' family thought him mad?[41]

Davies and Allison's rhetorical question causes us to reflect on the general profile of Mark the redactor as it is defined on the Griesbach hypothesis. The issue is not purely one of what Mark added and what he omitted. It is one of the consistency and coherence of the redactional procedure that the theory implies.[42]

On this hypothesis, Mark adds material that, as it happens, would have been uncongenial to Matthew and Luke (Blind Man of Bethsaida, etc.), material that seems an odd selection from what, one presumes, would have been available to him from his oral tradition. The handful of additions are balanced by the omission of material congenial to Mark like the Lord's Prayer, for which Mark has an obvious context into which it might have been inserted. But this negative judgment on the plausibility of Markan Posteriority is compounded still further by noticing that on the Griesbach hypothesis, Mark's tendencies pull in opposite directions.

One of the clearest ways of illustrating the difficulty is to look at the way in which, on the Griesbach Hypothesis, Mark, on the one hand, regularly adds material to help clarify material in his sources, but, on the other, goes to some lengths to make the material more enigmatic. First, the clarificatory material. After the call of Levi/Matthew, in all sources, there are said to have been many tax collectors and sinners seated with

---

41. Davies and Allison, *Matthew*, 1:109.

42. William Farmer ("Present State," 20) gives a brief and somewhat dismissive response to Davies and Allison, "At best this very misleading aggregative approach provides a nice rhetorical question, but it is difficult to see in it any 'compelling' reason for Markan priority." The difficulty with this response, however, is that "the consideration that needs to be explained" is not given, and the whole is treated under (Davies's and Allison's own) heading, "The Markan Additions," so that the issue of the relationship between additions and omissions is not touched on.

Jesus and his disciples (Matt 9:10 // Mark 2:15 // Luke 5:29). At this point Mark adds the somewhat redundant clarificatory clause, ἦσαν γὰρ πολλοὶ καὶ ἠκολούθουν αὐτῷ, "for they were many and they followed him." Likewise at 11:13, the narrator says, οὐδὲν εὗρεν εἰ μὴ φύλλα· <u>ὁ γὰρ καιρὸς οὐκ ἦν σύκων,</u> "When he came to it, he found nothing but leaves, *for it was not the season for figs*" (contrast Matt 21:18). Or at 16:4, he writes, καὶ ἀναβλέψασαι θεωροῦσιν ὅτι ἀποκεκύλισται ὁ λίθος· <u>ἦν γὰρ μέγας σφόδρα,</u> "And having looked up, they see that the stone was rolled back, *for it was very large*" (cf. Matt 28:2 and Luke 24:2).[43]

The addition of these somewhat redundant clarificatory clauses would appear to witness to a Gospel in which every effort is made to spell things out carefully for the reader. This looks like someone who, on the assumption of the Griesbach hypothesis, is editing Matthew and Luke to draw out what often appears to be transparently obvious. It is striking, therefore, that elsewhere Mark — again on the assumption of his use of Matthew and Luke — appears to be doing precisely the opposite thing, and making his sources more enigmatic, more gently suggestive, leaving the reader much more work to do. One of the best examples of this is the one to which Austin Farrer draws attention in Matt 17:9–13 // Mark 9:9–13.[44] Here, typically, Mark's text is allusive. Implying a knowledge both of the Hebrew Bible and of itself, Mark demands some work from his reader, who seems to be expected to have read the earlier part of the Gospel carefully, noticing that John the Baptist was aligned with Elijah because of his appearance (Mark 1:6; cf. 2 Kings 1:8) and that the story of John the Baptist, Herod, and Herodias is fashioned after and alludes to the stories of Elijah, Ahab, and Jezebel (Mark 6:14–29; 1 Kings 17–22). Now careful readers of Mark who know their Hebrew Bible will at this stage in Mark make a link, encouraged by the saying of Jesus here recorded. They will see that Elijah has indeed come, in John the Baptist, and that this confirms the Messianic identity of Jesus, which the disciples are now beginning to perceive (8:30). Further, and this is the key element, the sharp reader is expected to see that Jesus will meet an end that is similar to that of John — καὶ ἐποίησαν αὐτῷ ὅσα ἤθελον,

---

43. Since one of these redundant explanatory clauses does occur in a Matthean parallel to Mark, Matt 4:18 // Mark 1:16, ἦσαν γὰρ ἁλεεῖς, "for they were fishermen," we would have to assume that Griesbach's Mark saw this feature of Matthew and decided to replicate it on other occasions.

44. See Austin Farrer's much neglected *St Matthew and St Mark* (Westminster: Dacre, 1954), especially 4–7. I am grateful to Jeffrey Peterson for some useful discussion of this pericope.

καθὼς γέγραπται ἐπ' αὐτόν, "they did to him whatever they pleased, as it is written of him" (Mark 9:13) and so too the Son of Man will "suffer many things," also as "it is written" (πῶς γέγραπται ἐπὶ τὸν υἱὸν τοῦ ἀνθρώπου ἵνα πολλὰ πάθῃ καὶ ἐξουδενηθῇ, Mark 9:12). The reader of this passage in Mark, who reads in the context of both the Gospel and the Hebrew Bible, is left reflecting on the relationship between John the Baptist, the scriptures, Jesus' identity, suffering, messiahship, and the disciples' perception.

Here in Matthew, however, there is an additional concluding comment without parallel in Mark, τότε συνῆκαν οἱ μαθηταὶ ὅτι περὶ Ἰωάννου τοῦ βαπτιστοῦ εἶπεν αὐτοῖς, "Then the disciples understood that he was speaking to them about John the Baptist" (Matt 17:13). On the Griesbach Hypothesis, Mark has omitted this clarificatory remark of Matthew's, apparently preferring to make the account more gently suggestive, less explicit, less clear. This appears to run contrary to the impression we have of Mark from the clarificatory additions we see elsewhere. On the assumption of Markan Priority, on the other hand, Matthew's procedure is readily explicable. While most of Mark's rather banal clarificatory clauses get omitted by Matthew, here he is concerned to make the subtle, intra-textual and intertextual account of Mark as clear as possible. Matthew knows his Scriptures and he has been reading Mark and getting to know the book for some time. He sees what Mark is doing here but is concerned that his readers might miss it. So the allusive Mark, which prefers to keep things as subtle as possible, gets reworked when it is absorbed into Matthew, where matters are stated strongly and unambiguously.

The same feature of Mark, with the same kind of parallel in Matthew, occurs again in the incident concerning bread on the boat (Mark 8:14–21 // Matt 16:5–12). The Markan account is bizarre and somewhat difficult to fathom, even to contemporary readers, and it ends on an open question, addressed no doubt to the intended audience of the Gospel as well as to the disciples within the narrative, οὔπω συνίετε; ("Do you not yet understand?" Mark 8:21). Matthew, by contrast, adds here one of his clarificatory sentences, τότε συνῆκαν ὅτι οὐκ εἶπεν προσέχειν ἀπὸ τῆς ζύμης τῶν ἄρτων ἀλλὰ ἀπὸ τῆς διδαχῆς τῶν Φαρισαίων καὶ Σαδδουκαίων ("Then they understood that he did not tell them to beware of the leaven of bread, but of the teaching of the Pharisees and Sadducees," Matt16:12). Once again, on the Griesbach hypothesis, Mark is omitting clarificatory narration in order to make a scene more enigmatic, in contrast with his policy elsewhere of adding even the most trivial clarificatory explanations.

In summary, the Griesbach hypothesis has difficulties in dealing with Mark's alleged additions to and omissions from his sources. It is a hypothesis that succeeds only in placing several contrasting features of Mark into the kind of sharp relief that detracts from the plausibility of the thesis. Mark is, after all, a fascinating, rewarding piece of literature, and one of the greatest achievements of modern biblical scholarship, an enterprise these days all too keen to disparage itself, is its success in rehabilitating what was hitherto the most neglected Gospel. Scholars have come to delight in Mark's Gospel as a document that combines naïveté with profundity, the banal with the mysterious. The question source critics will inevitably ask is whether it is more likely that this is a work of brutish genius, the first attempt to write a "gospel of Jesus Christ" (1:1) by imposing a narrative on disparate traditional materials, or whether it is the complex product of contradictory elements in a redactional procedure that is rarely easy to fathom.

The point is one that adherents of the Griesbach hypothesis have not tended to appreciate. For if Mark is the first Gospel, then we will expect it to exhibit these fascinating and slightly self-contradictory traits. It seems likely that this evangelist is the first to attempt to compose a book in which differing materials from oral tradition are gathered together and subordinated to a narrative that reaches its climax in the death of Christ crucified. And if this is indeed the case, then scholarship has been right to stress Mark's creativity, his literary and theological genius even, for he is someone whose great achievement was the marriage of life of Jesus traditions with the kerygma of the suffering, dying Christ, in a genre in which the latter is the dominant element. All in all, adherents of the Griesbach hypothesis still have a long way to go to convince historical scholarship that this real jewel in its crown is nothing more than an embarrassing mistake.

The Phenomenon of Editorial Fatigue

While arguments about Mark's profile and the issue of additions, omissions, and the relationship between them, might prove to be helpful in the attempt to establish Markan Priority, one of the things that has remained frustrating for many Synoptic scholars is the lack of a category in which one can point clearly to activity that irreversibly establishes that Matthew and Luke both used Mark's Gospel. In an article published in *New Testament Studies* in 1998,[45] I argued that there may indeed be one such pointer, one that had generally been overlooked, for there is widespread evidence of "editorial fatigue" or "docile reproduction" in the way that Matthew and Luke were editing their Markan source, evidence that apparently confirms the hypothesis of Markan Priority.

Examples include Matthew's account of the Cleansing of the Leper (Matt 8:1–4 // Mark 1:40–45 // Luke 5:12–16), in which Matthew's location of the incident after the Sermon on the Mount leads to an introductory verse not paralleled in Mark, καταβάντος δὲ αὐτοῦ ἀπὸ τοῦ ὄρους ἠκολούθησαν αὐτῷ ὄχλοι πολλοί ("And when he had come down from the mountain, many crowds followed him," Matt 8:1), something that is simply not consonant with Matthew's virtual agreement with Mark[46] later in the same pericope, καὶ λέγει αὐτῷ ὁ Ἰησοῦς· ὅρα μηδενὶ εἴπῃς, ἀλλὰ ὕπαγε σεαυτὸν δεῖξον τῷ ἱερεῖ ("And Jesus says to him, 'See that you do not say anything but go, show yourself to the priest,'" Matt 8:4, cf. Mark 1:44). The private location taken for granted in Mark's account provides the setting for the command to silence. Matthew's different setting, characteristically introducing ὄχλοι πολλοί ("many crowds"),[47] makes the command to silence an absurdity.[48] Moreover, such commands to silence are much more rare in Matthew than they are in Mark. In other words, it seems that Matthew has rewritten the introduction to the pericope in accordance with its new

45. Mark Goodacre, "Fatigue in the Synoptics," *NTS* 44 (1998): 45–58, reproduced on *The Case Against Q* web site, *http://ntgateway.com/Q*. For a more limited appeal to a similar feature, see G. M. Styler, Excursus 4 in C. F. D. Moule, *The Birth of the New Testament* (3d ed.; London: Black, 1981), 285–316, and Davies and Allison, *Matthew,* 1:106–8. Against Styler, see Lamar Cope, "The Argument Revolves: The Pivotal Evidence for Markan Priority is Reversing Itself," in *New Synoptic Studies: The Cambridge Gospel Conference and Beyond* (ed. William R. Farmer; Macon, Ga.: Mercer University Press, 1983), 143–59 (esp. 150).

46. The only possible difference is that many reliable witnesses of Mark have ὅρα μηδενὶ μηδὲν εἴπῃς rather than ὅρα μηδενὶ εἴπῃς (Mark 1:44).

47. All five of Matthew's occurrences are — on the assumption of Markan Priority — redactional additions, here and at Matt 4:25, 13:2, 15:30 and 19:2.

48. The point is nicely illustrated if one looks at two recent attempts to transfer Matthew's Gospel to film. Pier Paolo Pasolini's *The Gospel According to St Matthew* (1964) retains the command to silence, but resets the scene so that it is now before and not after the Sermon, and a private encounter between Jesus and the leper. Regardt van den Bergh's *Matthew* (The Visual Bible, 1996), which features every single word of Matthew in the *New International Version* in order, is constrained to include both elements, the "many crowds" and the command to silence — and an otherwise powerful scene suffers by drawing attention to the contradiction in Matthew's account.

setting in the narrative, using characteristically Matthean language, but subsequently he has produced incoherence as a result of editorial fatigue, whereby he falls into docile reproduction of Mark.

Another example is provided by Matthew's account of the death of John the Baptist (Mark 6:14–29 // Matt 14:1–12). Whereas Mark calls Herod Antipas βασιλεύς ("king") four times in the passage (Mark 6:22, 25, 26 and 27), Matthew more correctly has τετραάρχης ("tetrarch," Matt 14:1),[49] precision that is typical of Matthew.[50] It is surprising, then, when Matthew (14:9) agrees with Mark (6:26) in calling him ὁ βασιλεύς ("the king"). That editorial fatigue has drawn him into this contradiction is confirmed by the strange plot in Matthew. Mark's version of the story, the one that has captured the imagination of countless later writers of fiction, is coherent: Herodias wanted to kill John because she had a grudge against him, but she could not "because Herod feared John, knowing that he was a righteous and holy man, and he protected him" (Mark 6:19–20). However in Matthew's version of the story, this element is not present. Herod and not Herodias wants him killed but does not because he fears the crowd (Matt 14:5).[51] Consequently, Mark's mention of Herod's "grief" (περίλυπος γενόμενος ὁ βασιλεύς, Mark 6:26) at the request for John's head is coherent: Herodias demanded something that Herod did not want. But Matthew's parallel mention of the king's grief (λυπηθεὶς ὁ βασιλεύς, Matt 14:9) makes no sense in an account in which "Herod wanted to put him to death" (14:5). Matthew is working from his Markan source, making characteristic changes in the early stages which he fails to sustain throughout.

Examples of the same feature in Luke include his version of the Healing of the Paralytic (Matt 9:1–8 // Mark 2:1–12 // Luke 5:17–26), in which Luke characteristically introduces the account with καὶ ἐγένετο ἐν μιᾷ τῶν ἡμερῶν καὶ αὐτὸς ἦν διδάσκων... ("And it came to pass on one of those days, and he was teaching," Luke 5:17), but the fresh introduction causes Luke to omit to mention entry into a house, unlike Mark in 2:1–2, where it is a major element in setting up the story. In agreement

---

49. He is called "tetrarch" by both Luke (3:19, 9:7; Acts 13:1; cf. Luke 3:1) and Josephus (*Ant.* 17. 188; 18. 102, 109, 122).

50. Matthew specifies that Pilate (Mark 15:1, 4, 9, 12, 14, 15, 43, 44) is ὁ ἡγεμών ("the governor," Matt 27:2, 11, 14, 15, 21, 27, 28:14), that "the high priest" (Mark 14:53) is "Caiaphas the high priest" (Matt 26:57) and that Herod the Great is indeed a "king" (ὁ βασιλεὺς Ἡρῴδης, 2:1, 3) and that Archelaus is not (2:22).

51. Matthew is here aligning his depiction of Antipas as weak but evil with his depiction of Herod the Great as frightened (2:3) but a murderer (2:16).

with Mark, however, Luke has plot developments that require Jesus to be in a crowded house of exactly the kind Mark mentions when in Luke 5:19 // Mark 2:4, the four men ascend onto a roof and let the paralytic down in front of Jesus.

One of the things that is so striking about examples like this is that one can observe Matthew and Luke writing especially characteristically at the beginning of the pericopae in question. The docile reproduction occurs at points later in the pericopae in places where the evangelists appear to be moving into the wording of their source material. Inconcinnities[52] are generated by the evangelists making changes in the early part of the narrative that they are unable to sustain throughout. There are, in other words, some elements that give the game away, vestiges of Matthew's and Luke's literary source, Mark, telltale signs of their dependence on that Gospel.

Concluding Thoughts

In a book devoted to the attempt to dispense with Q, it may seem odd to spend so much time reflecting on the plausibility of the Priority of Mark. Perhaps, if the Farrer theory were widely perceived as placing Markan Priority at its heart, this would not have been necessary. But since contemporary scholarship tends to group together all alternatives to the two-source theory, stressing what is different about the Farrer theory rather than what is similar, and since adherents of the Farrer theory have devoted almost all their energy to the business of dispensing with Q, it has been necessary to make sure that this key building block, Matthew's and Luke's use of Mark, is set firmly in place. For the case against Q only has any chance of success if this most important witness for the prosecution is allowed to speak. Frequently, the Priority of Mark will provide us with not only the key presupposition for the case against Q, but also the best illustrations of its plausibility.

It is one of the more unfortunate elements in some discussions of the Synoptic Problem that so much energy has been devoted to the question of the Priority of Mark when, as we will see in the rest of this book, it is Q that is the more vulnerable partner in the two-source theory. While many of the arguments commonly advanced for the existence of Q are

---

52. This is the term preferred by Davies and Allison, *Matthew*, 1:106–8.

overstated, problematic, or flawed, Markan Priority remains plausible because it continues to make such good sense not only of the origin of the Gospel genre, but also of the existence of Matthew's and Luke's Gospels. Indeed one cannot help suspecting that scholars have been reluctant to jettison Markan Priority because of the explanatory power of the hypothesis. It is not merely an element in the solution to the Synoptic Problem. Its strength lies in the role it plays in illuminating Christian origins. Mark generates a new kind of book in which traditions of the life of Jesus are subordinated to the theology of Christ Crucified in a narrative that combines the mysterious with the profound, insisting that "the reader" takes care to understand what is at stake.

The strength of the standard understanding of Mark is not only that this kind of origin is more plausible than the conflation theory of Griesbach, but also that it makes such good sense of the existence of both Matthew and Luke. Both are simultaneously enthralled and concerned by Mark. While inspired by the notion of writing this kind of narrative of Jesus' life culminating in the Passion, they nevertheless see it as only "the beginning of the Gospel of Jesus Christ" and want to fill it out with stories of Jesus' origin at one end and his resurrection at the other, adding much material in between focusing on Jesus' teaching, correcting what they perceive to be its rough literary style and, more important, its theological idiosyncrasies. The only remarkable thing is that they should both have hit upon such a similar plan at, apparently, much the same time. Once Markan Priority has been granted, the question of whether Matthew and Luke used Mark independently of one another becomes irresistible. This theory of independence is, of course, the premise for the Q hypothesis and next we will begin to explore its plausibility.

As far as the key tenet of Markan Priority is concerned, however, there can be no turning back. Adherents of both the two-source theory and the Farrer theory rightly build on this secure foundation. The vigorous challenge by the late William Farmer and other neo-Griesbachians, while encouraging us to think about the Synoptic Problem in fresh ways, and helping us to clarify our thoughts, methods, and arguments, is not, in the end, likely to prove persuasive.[53] Although fundamentally correct

---

53. One other element in the revival of the Griesbach hypothesis has been a fresh emphasis on the external evidence. W. R. Farmer, for example, begins his "Systematic Overview of the Two-Gospel Hypothesis" (Chapter 2 in *The Gospel of Jesus*) with the claim that Church tradition supports Griesbach's proposed order (pp. 15–18). However, the only clear example that is offered for the order Matthew–Luke–Mark is Clement of Alexandria (in Eusebius, *Ecclesiastical History* 6.14.5–7), which is in contradiction with virtually every other patristic witness, which

to have been suspicious about elements in the standard solution, their mistake has been to reject one of the great achievements of historical scholarship, the theory of Markan Priority. For the stone that they have rejected may turn out to be the head of the corner.

give the order Matthew–Mark–Luke; Stephen Carlson has convincingly argued that προγράφω should here be taken not as "written before" but as "to set forth publicly," so that Clement is not claiming that Matthew and Luke "were written first" but rather that they were written for public consumption in contrast to Mark which had a different origin. See Stephen C. Carlson, "Clement of Alexandria on the 'Order' of the Gospels," *NTS* 47 (2001): 118–25.

Chapter Three

REASONS AND RHETORIC

Of course the dominance of the Q hypothesis does not result solely from the kinds of general impressions discussed in Chapter 1. Many scholars defending the Q hypothesis have rightly earned their reputations on the basis of brilliant and insightful yet meticulous and painstaking research. In this chapter I will begin to explore their arguments for the existence of Q.

Focusing on recent Q scholarship, I will examine critically the central arguments of several scholars. The arguments broadly fall into two categories — negative ones, which argue the case against Luke's use of Matthew (the first four below), and positive ones, which argue from the distinctive character of Q and the plausibility of redaction-critical studies which assume Q. While the positive arguments need to be taken seriously, they are essentially secondary in character. They would not be strong enough to stand on their own without the negative ones. Those using these arguments tend to speak of them as "corroborating" and "supporting" the Q hypothesis rather than establishing it. The most important arguments have been those in the first category, and the foundation of the Q hypothesis remains the independence of Matthew and Luke.

Both of the most recent full-scale explorations of the Q hypothesis, Christopher Tuckett's *Q and the History of Early Christianity* and John Kloppenborg Verbin's *Excavating Q* rightly emphasize the origin of the Q hypothesis as a derivative hypothesis. It is, essentially, the logical corollary of the postulate that Matthew and Luke both used Mark independently of one another. For as soon as one has theorized that they used Mark independently of one another, the extensive verbatim agreement in the double tradition material necessitates the thesis of a common literary ancestor, not least given the fact that in the double tradition material Matthew and Luke are, if anything, more similar than they are in the triple tradition material. Kloppenborg explains it like this:

46

Stated succinctly, the Two Document hypothesis proposes that the gospels of Matthew and Luke independently used Mark as a source. Since Matthew and Luke share about 235 verses that they did not get from Mark, the 2DH requires that they had independent access to a second source consisting mainly of sayings of Jesus. This, for want of a better term, is the "Sayings Gospel," or, "Q."[1]

Tuckett observes, when introducing "Traditional Arguments for Q," that "the standard arguments used to defend the Q hypothesis" are "mostly of a negative form, claiming that Luke's use of Matthew seems very improbable."[2] This is the heart of the disagreement between Q theorists, on the one side, and Q skeptics, on the other. While there is agreement on the question of Matthew's and Luke's use of Mark, paths divide when it comes to asking whether this use of Mark was independent or not. In this chapter we will begin to look at the arguments adduced for the lack of contact between Matthew and Luke, the lack of contact that necessitates Q.[3] Such arguments are far from conclusive.

Before proceeding to these arguments, however, it is worth considering the *prima facie* case for some contact between Matthew and Luke. This is an issue seldom if ever taken seriously in studies that take Q for granted, which all too quickly proceed to stress differences at the micro level between Matthew and Luke without first thinking about the quite striking similarity at the macro level. Even the most casual reader of the Gospels cannot help noticing that Matthew and Luke have a remarkably similar literary plan. On the assumption that both Matthew and Luke knew Mark's Gospel, it is interesting that both decided to write

---

1. John S. Kloppenborg Verbin, *Excavating Q*, 12–13.

2. Christopher Tuckett, *Q and the History of Early Christianity*, 7; cf. 4: "At one level, the Q hypothesis is simply a negative theory, denying the possibility that one evangelist made direct use of the work of another."

3. It is theoretically possible to postulate Q notwithstanding Lukan knowledge of Matthew, a view that has had three important adherents, E. Simons, *Hat der dritte Evangelist den kanonischen Matthäus benutzt?* (Bonn: Universitäts-Buchdruckerei von Carl Georgi, 1880); R. Morgenthaler, *Statistische Synopse* (Zürich: Gotthelf Verlag, 1971), 301–5; and R. H. Gundry, *Matthew: A Commentary on His Literary and Theological Art* (Grand Rapids: Eerdmans, 1982), 4–5; cf. also the second edition, published as *Matthew: A Commentary on His Handbook for a Mixed Church Under Persecution* (Grand Rapids: Eerdmans, 1994), xv–xvi for a later comment. For discussion of this possibility, see F. Neirynck, "Recent Developments in the Study of Q," in *Logia. Les paroles de Jésus — The Sayings of Jesus.* Mémorial J. Coppens (ed. J. Delobel; BETL 59; Leuven: Leuven University Press — Peeters, 1982), 29–75 (esp. 34–35), reprinted in F. Neirynck, *Evangelica II 1982–1991* (ed. F. Van Segbroeck; BETL 99; Leuven: Leuven University Press, 1991), 409–64 (esp. 414–15); and M. D. Goulder, *Luke*, 10–11; and see further below.

a similar book at around the same time, the latter part of the first century, in which Mark's perceived shortcomings are overcome by major improvements in Greek style, the addition of a prologue dealing with Jesus' infancy, an epilogue providing resurrection appearances, and a great deal of new teaching material in between. Perhaps, one might say, books looking like Matthew and Luke are the inevitable and obvious reaction to the production of a book looking like Mark. But if so, one wonders why no one else in early Christianity to our knowledge tried to do the same thing. The fact that Matthew and Luke are such similar books makes good sense on the assumption that Luke, already familiar with Mark's Gospel, subsequently came across a copy of Matthew and could see straight away what the latter had done with Mark. Thus it makes good sense to think of Matthew as the direct catalyst for Luke's own reworking of Mark, and not only a catalyst but also a source, providing Luke with much material — mainly teaching material — to use in his book. Without Luke's use of Matthew, we have to assume that both evangelists, independently of one another and at about the same time, came upon a very similar plan. The general plausibility of this view is further undermined by the narrow window available for Matthew and Luke to be writing in independence of one another. The greater the gap in time between Matthew and Luke, the less likely it becomes that Luke did not possess a copy of Matthew's Gospel.[4]

In other words there is at least a *prima facie* case for a direct connection between Matthew and Luke outside of the one that is mediated through Mark.[5] However, this only presses us to pay all the more attention to arguments against this kind of scenario. What is it about the detailed evidence of those two Gospels that apparently continues to persuade many of the existence of Q?

---

4. This comes into focus quite starkly in the work of Burton Mack, who dates Matthew in the late 80s and Luke in 120, *Who Wrote the New Testament: The Making of the Christian Myth* (San Francisco: HarperSanFrancisco, 1995), 161 and 167. Given the popularity of Matthew's Gospel already by the early to mid second century, it seems odd that Luke is held not to have had a copy when he does own a copy of Q, which was now, according to Mack, "all but passé in Christian circles" (169).

5. While it is the thesis of this book that Luke knew Matthew, in this context (the *prima facie* case) it would of course also make sense for a thesis of Matthew's knowledge of Luke. However, it is unlikely that the case could be persuasive for reasons that I hope will be obvious from the detailed argumentation in this book. Though it has rarely been argued in the literature, see Martin Hengel and Anna Maria Schwemer who recently proposed the view that Matthew postdates Luke and had come across the latter, which he disliked, *Paul Between Damascus and Antioch: The Unknown Years* (ET, London: SCM, 1997).

Luke's Ignorance of Matthew's Modifications of Mark[6]

One of the most common arguments for the existence of Q is that Luke does not show any knowledge of Matthew's additions to Mark within the triple tradition. "Is it conceivable," Kümmel asks, "that Luke would have taken over none of the Matthean additions to the Markan text?"[7] Similarly Christopher Tuckett, having given several examples (Matt 12:5–7; 14:28–31; 16:16–19; 27:19, 24), asks:

> If Luke knew Matthew, why does he never show any knowledge of Matthew's redaction of Mark? It seems easiest to presume that Luke did not know of these Matthean additions to Mark and hence did not know Matthew.[8]

Likewise, Fitzmyer writes:

> Luke is never seen to reproduce the typically Matthean additions within the triple tradition. By "additions" I mean the fuller Matthean formulations of parallels in Mark, such as the exceptive phrases in the prohibition of divorce (Matt 19:9; cf. Mark 10:11ff.); Jesus' promise to Peter (Matt 16:16b–19; cf. Mark 8:29); Peter's walking on the waters (Matt 14:28–31; cf. Mark 6:50); and the peculiarly Matthean episodes in the passion narrative (especially the dream of Pilate's wife [Matt 27:19] or Pilate washing his hands [Matt 27:24]) . . . the real issue here is to explain Luke's failure to adopt the extra Matthean materials in his parallels, or at least some of them, if he has written in dependence on Matthew.[9]

---

6. This section is an expanded and revised version of my "A Monopoly on Marcan Priority," 592–99.

7. W. G. Kümmel, *Introduction to the New Testament* (ET, London: SCM, 1966; rev. ed., 1975), 50. Page numbers in this and subsequent references will be to the 1966 edition.

8. Christopher M. Tuckett, "The Existence of Q" in R. A. Piper, ed., *The Gospel Behind the Gospels*, 19–47, esp. 25 (=*Q and the History of Early Christianity*, 8).

9. *The Gospel According to Luke I–IX: Introduction, Translation, and Notes* (Anchor Bible 28; New York: Doubleday, 1981), 73–74. Notice that Fitzmyer also gives eight examples of Luke's failure to include "smaller Matthean additions to Mark," e.g., Matt 9:9, "who is called Peter" (74). This is essentially a complaint that there are not more minor agreements between Matthew and Luke against Mark than we do in fact find. But given the number and weight of the minor agreements (see Chapter 8, below), an admitted difficulty for the two-source theory, this point is limited in force. This is the first of several references in this chapter to Fitzmyer's arguments for Q. See also his "The Priority of Mark and the Q Source in Luke" in David A. Buttrick, ed., *Jesus and Man's Hope, Perspective* 2/1 (1970): 131–70. Howard Clark Kee finds Fitzmyer's arguments persuasive, "Synoptic Studies," Chapter 9 in Eldon Jay Epp and George W. MacRae, eds., *The New Testament and Its Modern Interpreters* (Atlanta: Scholars Press, 1989), 245–69 (esp. 249–50).

And, more recently, Kloppenborg writes:

> It has been observed that Luke fails to reproduce Matthew's "additions" to Mark and fails to adopt the more obvious Mattheanisms in the first gospel. Or, to put it more neutrally, in Lukan material for which there are Matthean and Markan parallels, Luke rarely reflects what is distinctive of Matthew when it is compared with Mark. For example, Luke lacks the conversation between John the Baptist and Jesus in Matt 3:14–15 (contrast Mark 1:9–11 / Luke 3:21–22) and Matthew's extension of the quotation of Isa 6:9–10 (contrast Mark 4:12 / Luke 8:10).... For Luke to have so consistently avoided what Matthew added to Mark... requires an idiosyncratic view of Lukan editorializing; obviously, it is far simpler to conclude that Luke lacks these Mattheanisms because he has edited Mark independently of Matthew.[10]

There are major difficulties with this oft-repeated argument.[11] To begin with, the examples given are not strong enough to make the case. Matt 14:28–31, an example given by both Fitzmyer and Tuckett, is a Matthean addition in the middle of the story of the Walking on the Water (Mark 6:45–52 // Matthew 14:22–33), a story that is wholly absent from Luke, in either its Markan or Matthean form. It is in no way surprising that Luke lacks the Matthean additions to a story that does not feature at all in his Gospel. Matt 3:14–15, one of only two examples given by Kloppenborg, is also a weak example. This is the conversation between John the Baptist and Jesus about whether or not John should baptize Jesus. Its absence from Luke is unremarkable given the context (Luke 3:21–22). Famously, Luke has already narrated John's arrest (Luke 3:18–20) and goes on to narrate Jesus' baptism without any

---

10. John S. Kloppenborg Verbin, *Excavating Q*, 41.

11. See also Davies and Allison, *Matthew*, 1:116, "If Luke drew upon the First Gospel it is remarkable that he betrays no knowledge of the obvious Matthean additions to the Markan material (e.g., Mt. 3.14–15; 9.13a.; 12.5–7; 16.2b–3, 17–19; 19.9; 21.10–11; 26.52–54; 27.19, 24, 52b–53). In other words, Luke seems to have known Mark, not Mark as revised by Matthew." The latter statement rests on a misunderstanding. To speak of Luke's knowledge of "Mark" or of "Mark as revised by Matthew" is to present a false alternative. The Farrer theory supposes that Luke knows *both* Mark *and* Mark as revised by Matthew. See too Robert Stein, *The Synoptic Problem: An Introduction* (Grand Rapids: Baker Book House, 1987), 91, "One of the strongest arguments against the use of Matthew by Luke is the fact that when Matthew has additional material in the triple tradition ("Matthean additions to the narrative"), it is 'never' found in Luke." Stein's inverted commas around "never" are presumably used because he is conscious of exceptions. In other words, "never" means "not often."

mention of John. Matthew's conversation between John and Jesus would have been inappropriate in Luke's very differently framed narrative.

The issue that comes into focus here is the importance of paying careful attention to the character of these Matthean additions to Mark. Not only do they tend to have a strikingly Matthean stamp but also they appear to be uncongenial to what we know of Luke's interests. In other words, it is easy to imagine why, on each of these occasions, Luke might have preferred the Markan version. On each occasion, the exegete needs to ask whether it is plausible that Luke has behaved in the way suggested by the Farrer theory. The difficulty is that scholars tend simply to list alleged examples and not to think about the redaction-critical consequences. There is a difference between an argument and a list.

When we use redaction criticism in analyzing Luke's use of Mark, we work on the assumption that, on the whole, Luke will include those passages he finds congenial. When we work on the assumption of Luke's use of Matthew, suspending redaction-critical practice should not be a realistic option. We will expect to find, to use Austin Farrer's phrase, only the "Luke-pleasing" elements of Matthew in the third Gospel.[12] In particular, it is unsurprising that Luke's version of Peter's Confession (Luke 9:22-26) does not feature Matthew's additions about the ascendancy of Peter (Matt 16:16b-19). After all, Luke is not as positive about Peter overall as Matthew, and the narrative development in Acts of the Apostles — in which Peter progressively recedes further and further into the background — would seem to exclude the possibility of Luke's inclusion of the Matthean statement. It is exactly the kind of Matthean addition to Mark that we would expect Luke to omit.

Moreover, if Luke had already known Mark for some time when he came into contact with Matthew,[13] that very familiarity with Mark might have made the Matthean additions clear to him. Under these circumstances, each time Luke sees one of these Matthean additions, he is confronted with a decision: should he include the addition or not?

---

12. Austin Farrer, "On Dispensing," 57.

13. Cf. H. Benedict Green, "The Credibility of Luke's Transformation of Matthew" in C. M. Tuckett, ed., *Synoptic Studies,* 130–55: "If the literary and chronological relationship between Mark and Matthew is what the majority take it to be (and I have indicated that I am with the majority here), then Luke will have known Mark for a great deal longer than he has known Matthew — will have used it week by week in the worship of the Church, preached from it, taught from it, and lived with it as the only written gospel; and if his project of a new and enlarged gospel was forming in his mind for any length of time, it will have been in terms of Mark that it was originally conceived" (133). See also Eric Franklin, *Luke,* Chapter 13, especially 313–15. And see further on this below.

Where the additions are not conducive to Luke's interests, one will not, on balance, find it strange that he avoids them.

There is, however, a far more serious problem with the argument from Luke's lack of Matthew's additions to Mark in triple tradition material. Its premise, that Luke does not feature any of Matthew's modifications of Mark, is flawed. On the assumption that Luke knows Matthew as well as Mark, Luke prefers Matthew's version to Mark's in several triple tradition incidents: the whole John the Baptist complex (Matt 3, Mark 1, Luke 3); the Temptation (Matt 4:1–11 // Mark 1:12–13 // Luke 4:1–13), the Beelzebub Controversy (Matt 12:22–30 // Mark 3:20–27 // Luke 11:14–23) and the Mustard Seed (Matt 13:18–19 // Mark 4:30–32 // Luke 13:18–19) among them. On all of these occasions, the parallels between Matthew and Luke are more extensive than those between Mark and Luke. Indeed the early parts of each Gospel are particularly rich in examples of Luke apparently following Matthew's modified versions of the shorter Markan pericopae. John the Baptist's prophecy about Jesus, shown on the following page, provides a good example.

The underlined words represent substantial addition to Mark by Matthew, material that is paralleled in Luke, contradicting the claim that such material never occurs. The same is true in the nearby story of the Temptation of Jesus. Mark's version (Mark 1:12–13) is only two verses long whereas Matthew (Matt 4:1–11) and Luke (Luke 4:1–13) both have an extended story featuring a major dialogue between Jesus and the Satan with the three famous temptations and rebuttals. To use Kloppenborg's terminology, these are clear cases of "Lukan material for which there are Matthean and Markan parallels" in which Luke "reflects what is distinctive of Matthew when it is compared with Mark."[14] Or, to put it another way, Luke has here preferred to use Matthew's substantial modification of the Markan story. The argument from Luke's lack of Matthew's modifications of Mark seems to be refuted by a simple glance at the Synopsis.

This material is of course familiar to scholars using the argument about Luke's lack of Matthew's additions to Mark, but the force of this evidence, and the fact that it contradicts one of the standard arguments is not felt. The primary reason for this[15] is that examples of this kind

---

14. John S. Kloppenborg Verbin, *Excavating Q*, 41.

15. Notice also that some of the most impressive examples of this feature come in Luke 3–4, covering material like John the Baptist and the Temptation. This is precisely the material that tends to be allowed an honorary exception to the rule when one is discussing the related

Matthew 3:11–12	Mark 1:7–8	Luke 3:16–17
11. ἐγὼ μὲν ὑμᾶς <u>βαπτίζω</u> ἐν ὕδατι εἰς μετάνοιαν· ὁ δὲ ὀπίσω μου ἐρχόμενος ἰσχυρότερός μού ἐστιν, οὗ οὐκ εἰμὶ ἱκανὸς τὰ ὑποδήματα βαστάσαι· αὐτὸς ὑμᾶς βαπτίσει ἐν πνεύματι ἁγίῳ <u>καὶ</u> <u>πυρί</u>. 12. <u>οὗ τὸ πτύον</u> <u>ἐν τῇ χειρὶ αὐτοῦ</u>, <u>καὶ</u> <u>διακαθαριεῖ</u> <u>τὴν ἅλωνα</u> <u>αὐτοῦ</u>, <u>καὶ</u> <u>συνάξει</u> <u>τὸν σῖτον αὐτοῦ εἰς</u> <u>τὴν ἀποθήκην</u>, <u>τὸ δὲ</u> <u>ἄχυρον κατακαύσει</u> <u>πυρὶ ἀσβέστῳ</u>.	[cf. Mark 1:8a] ἔρχεται ὁ ἰσχυρότερός μου ὀπίσω μου, οὗ οὐκ εἰμὶ ἱκανὸς κύψας λῦσαι τὸν ἱμάντα τῶν ὑποδημάτων αὐτοῦ. 8. ἐγὼ ἐβάπτισα ὑμᾶς ὕδατι, αὐτὸς δὲ βαπτίσει ὑμᾶς ἐν πνεύματι ἁγίῳ	ἐγὼ μὲν ὕδατι <u>βαπτίζω</u> ὑμᾶς· ἔρχεται δὲ ὁ ἰσχυρότερός μου, οὗ οὐκ εἰμὶ ἱκανὸς λῦσαι τὸν ἱμάντα τῶν ὑποδημάτων αὐτοῦ· αὐτὸς ὑμᾶς βαπτίσει ἐν πνεύματι ἁγίῳ <u>καὶ</u> <u>πυρί</u>. 17. <u>οὗ τὸ πτύον</u> <u>ἐν τῇ χειρὶ αὐτοῦ</u>, <u>διακαθᾶραι</u> <u>τὴν ἅλωνα</u> <u>αὐτοῦ</u>, <u>καὶ</u> <u>συναγαγεῖν</u> <u>τὸν σῖτον εἰς τὴν</u> <u>ἀποθήκην αὐτοῦ</u>, <u>τὸ δὲ</u> <u>ἄχυρον κατακαύσει</u> <u>πυρὶ ἀσβέστῳ</u>.
	7. "And he preached, saying,	16. "And John answered, saying to all,
11. " 'I, <u>on the one hand,</u> baptize you in water for repentance, <u>but</u> the one who is coming after me is stronger than me, the shoes of whom I am not worthy to untie.	'The one who is stronger than me comes after me, the thong of whose sandals I am not worthy, having stooped down, to loose. 8. I baptized you in water (cf. Matt 3:11//Luke 3:16), but he will baptize you in holy spirit.' "	'I, <u>on the one hand,</u> baptize you in water <u>but</u> the one who is stronger than me comes after me, the thong of whose sandals I am not worthy to loose.
He will baptize you in holy spirit <u>and fire. 12.</u> <u>His winnowing fork is in</u> <u>his hand and he will clear</u> <u>his threshing floor and he</u> <u>will gather his wheat into</u> <u>his granary, but the chaff</u> <u>he will burn with</u> <u>unquenchable fire.' "</u>		He will baptize you in holy spirit <u>and fire. 17.</u> <u>His winnowing fork is in</u> <u>his hand to clear</u> <u>his threshing floor and to</u> <u>gather the wheat into his</u> <u>granary, but the chaff he</u> <u>will burn with</u> <u>unquenchable fire.' "</u>

are placed in the special category of "Mark-Q overlap," those passages occurring in all three Synoptics in which Mark is not clearly the middle term, which blur the usually more straightforward distinction between "triple tradition" and "double tradition." In other words, there is effectively a fallacy at the base of this argument for Q in that it invokes a category that assumes the truth of the matter under discussion, namely the existence of Q. Thus where Luke, on the assumption of Markan Priority without Q, prefers the Matthean version of a pericope shared with Mark, this automatically goes into the category "Mark-Q overlap." Places where Luke prefers the Markan version of a pericope shared with Matthew are held to demonstrate his lack of knowledge of the Matthean versions of Markan pericopae. In other words, Q skeptics are placed in a "no-win" situation here. The apparent persuasiveness of the argument dissolves on closer examination.

Luke's Lack of "M" Material

This argument is related to the previous one, but where that one focuses on Luke's lack of Matthean material within triple tradition pericopae, this one focuses on his lack of Matthean material outside of triple tradition pericopae. In other words, it is about Luke's failure to include any of Matthew's special material ("M," or *Sondergut*). Fitzmyer, for example, asks: "If Luke depended on Matthew, why did he constantly omit Matthean material in episodes lacking Markan parallels, e.g., in the infancy and resurrection narratives?"[16]

This kind of argument is not very persuasive. On an abstract level, there is obvious circularity here. Luke does not include M material by definition. On the assumption that he used Matthew, any of Matthew's special material taken over by Luke would of course cease to be Matthew's special material. Any substantive non-Markan material taken over from Matthew would automatically have become Q material. On this abstract level, the point will appear so obvious to some that it is a little

---

phenomenon of Luke's order — Luke never, it is said, places double tradition material in the same triple tradition context as Matthew, except in Chapters 3–4. Although this exception is not specifically invoked in the context of Luke's alleged lack of Matthean additions to Mark, it may be that the same exception is thought to apply here. The Q skeptic's concern is that this is just the kind of rather bulky exception that tests a rule and finds it wanting. Further, much of Luke's agreement with Matthew's additions to Mark actually occurs outside of Luke 3–4.

16. Fitzmyer, *Luke I–IX,* 75.

embarrassing to have to draw attention to it. Perhaps this is why some treatments of Q do not use this argument at all.

But the more detailed exposition of the point is also unpersuasive. This is how Robert Stein puts it:

> If we assume that Luke used Matthew, how are we to explain his great omission of all the narrative material outside of the triple tradition found in Matthew? Why would Luke have omitted such material as the coming of the wise men (Matt 2:1–12)? Would not the presence of such Gentiles at the birth of Jesus have been meaningful for Luke's Gentile-oriented Gospel? Why would he have omitted the flight to Egypt and the return to Nazareth (Matt 2:13–23); the story of the guards at the tomb (Matt 27:62–66) and their report (Matt 28:11–15); the unique Matthean material concerning the resurrection (Matt 28:9–10, 16–20); and so on? ... It would therefore appear that Luke's use of Matthew is improbable, due to the lack of his incorporation of the M material into his Gospel.[17]

This argument is problematic in several ways. First, it is inaccurate to speak of Luke's "great omission of all the narrative material outside of the triple tradition found in Matthew." Of the relatively limited number of fresh narrative incidents outside of the triple tradition in Matthew, Luke includes a significant proportion including the Temptation Narrative (Matt 4:1–11 // Luke 4:1–13; cf. Mark 1:12–13), the Centurion's Boy (Matt 8:5–13 // Luke 7:1–11) and the Messengers from John the Baptist (Matt 11:2–19 // Luke 7:18–35). In other words, this simply brings us back to the question of circularity and the importance of describing the evidence accurately. If Luke knew Matthew's Gospel, he does include a considerable amount of Luke-pleasing narrative material from Matthew. There is no use in saying, "But these narratives are from Q," because that simply begs the question. The constraints imposed by describing the data according to the demands of the two-source theory can all too easily cause the interpreter to lose sight of all of the evidence.

Second, it is worth taking a closer look at some of the actual examples given by Stein. They are all located in the Birth Narratives and the Resurrection Story. Stein provides a list couched in rhetorical questions but draws special attention to the omission by Luke of Matthew's Gentile Magi (Matt 2:1–12), which he finds striking in so Gentile-friendly a

---

17. Robert Stein, *The Synoptic Problem*, 102.

Gospel. While Stein is on the right lines in looking for elements in Matthew that might appear congenial to Luke, he is mistaken in finding such an element in, of all stories, the Magi. Luke is the only writer other than Matthew in the New Testament to give us a hint of his view of magi and it is negative — a certain Simon Magus is one of the villains in Acts of the Apostles (8:9–24).[18] Moreover, at least since Conzelmann[19] scholars have been sensitive to Luke's apparent reticence to have Jesus coming into contact with Gentiles in the Gospel. One only has to witness the lengths to which Luke has gone to keep the Centurion out of Jesus' sight to see the point (Matt 8:5–13 // Luke 7:1–11).

Further, knowledge of a source is not the same as direct use of a source, and one of the key questions is whether there are any signs of Luke's knowledge of Matthew in the Birth Narrative. After all, Luke may well have been inspired by Matthew's account to write his own somewhat different account. If this possibility is taken seriously, the focus shifts away from the lack of extensive parallels between Matthew 1–2 and Luke 1–2 toward the more nuanced question of evidence for Luke's knowledge of Matthew. In other words, rather than looking at the obvious points of divergence between the accounts, we might ask whether any of the points of contact are sufficiently marked to suggest that Luke may have known Matthew.

Though it is not often appreciated, there are indeed signs that Luke knows Matthew's Birth Narrative.[20] Not only do they agree on matters unique to the two of them within the New Testament, like Jesus' birth in Bethlehem, the name of Jesus' father (Joseph) and, most importantly, the Virginal Conception,[21] they even share words in common, including the following key sentence:

---

18. Although Luke does not specifically call Simon a μάγος, he speaks of him as μαγεύων καὶ ἐξιστάνων τὸ ἔθνος τῆς Σαμαρείας (8:9) and διὰ τὸ ἱκανῷ χρόνῳ ταῖς μαγείαις ἐξεστακέναι αὐτούς (8:11). Cf. Acts 13:6, 8 where Luke uses the word μάγος negatively in relation to Elymas; and cf. Acts 19:19 of the burning of the books of sorcery.

19. Hans Conzelmann, *Die Mitte der Zeit: Studien zur Theologie des Lukas* (BhT 17; Tübingen: Mohr, 1954); ET, *The Theology of St Luke* (London: Faber, 1960).

20. See John Drury, *Tradition and Design*, 122–27; Austin Farrer, "On Dispensing," 79–80; Michael Goulder, *Luke*, 205–64; H. Benedict Green, "Credibility," 143–45 and Eric Franklin, *Luke*, 353–66.

21. For the case that a "virginal conception" is intended by neither evangelist, see Jane Schaberg, *The Illegitimacy of Jesus: a Feminist Theological Interpretation of the Infancy Narratives* (Sheffield: Sheffield Academic Press, 1995). For Schaberg's reflections on the possibility of a literary link between Matthew and Luke, see pp. 80–82, though in the end she accepts the two-source theory.

Matt 1:21	Luke 1:31
τέξεται δὲ υἱὸν καὶ καλέσεις τὸ ὄνομα αὐτοῦ Ἰησοῦν.	καὶ τέξῃ υἱὸν καὶ καλέσεις τὸ ὄνομα αὐτοῦ Ἰησοῦν.
She will give birth to a son and you shall call him Jesus.	You will give birth to a son and you shall call him Jesus

The passage[22] is striking not least because of the verbatim agreement in a sentence that is much more consonant with Matthew's narrative than it is with Luke's. In Matthew καλέσεις ("you shall call," singular) is addressed appropriately to Joseph who, as Matthew will make clear later in the same passage, will name the child, καὶ οὐκ ἐγίνωσκεν αὐτὴν ἕως οὗ ἔτεκεν υἱόν· καὶ ἐκάλεσεν τὸ ὄνομα αὐτοῦ Ἰησοῦν ("And he did not know her until she bore a son; and he called his name Jesus," Matt 1:25). In Luke, by contrast, καλέσεις ("you shall call," singular) is addressed less appropriately to Mary who will not be solely responsible for the naming of the child. As Luke elsewhere makes clear, the naming of the child is either the sole responsibility of the father (1:13) or, at best, of both parents (1:59–66; cf. 2:21). In other words, this close parallel between Matthew and Luke points in the direction of Luke's familiarity with Matthew, from whom Luke has taken over a clause that was more appropriate in its original context in Matthew.

The theory that Luke could not have known Matthew because he does not copy wholesale from his Birth Narrative is not, therefore, especially convincing. Indeed like many arguments for Q, reflection on the evidence can lead in quite the opposite direction, in favor of Luke's familiarity with Matthew. Perhaps Matthew's Birth Narrative gave Luke the idea of writing a Birth Narrative of his own; perhaps it was the catalyst for Luke's identical decision to preface Mark's Gospel with an account featuring both prenatal (Matt 1 // Luke 1) and postnatal (Matt 2 // Luke 2) stories about Jesus. Because many readers are so familiar with the Birth Narratives, it is easy to assume that prefacing a Gospel with a Birth Narrative is a natural step to take, but neither Mark nor John thought that it was such an obvious thing to do and, all things considered, the presence of a Birth Narrative in Luke is probably a sign that Luke knows Matthew. Moreover if, as seems likely, Luke thought that he could improve on Matthew's account, then subsequent history, devotion, and liturgy have agreed with him. It is from Luke that we get our shepherds, our choir of angels, and our manger; it is from Luke that

---

22. I am grateful to Jeff Peterson for drawing my attention to this important parallel.

we derive our picture of Mary; and it is from Luke that we take our canticles, the Benedictus, the Magnificat, and the Nunc Dimittis.

The same is true of Matthew 28 and Luke 24. Just as Luke has the fuller, richer opening to his Gospel, so too he has the fuller close to his Gospel. In out-Matthewing Matthew, Luke takes Matthew's lead but makes his own, newer material far more appropriate for his rather different purposes. Just as context is important in judging Luke 1–2 — Luke's attempt to segue from the Hebrew Bible to his version of the life of Jesus — so too context determines Luke 24, Luke's attempt to prepare the way for his second volume.

When looking at the end of the Gospel, we should, once again, try to avoid becoming fatigued in exercising redaction criticism. Stein expresses surprise that Luke does not include Matt 28:9–10, but what author, whose second volume plots events "beginning from Jerusalem" (Luke 24:47; cf. Acts 1:8) could plausibly have included an account of an announcement in Galilee? As with the Birth Narratives, the discussion does not need to focus on the extent of the parallels between the two but rather on the issue of whether Luke shows any knowledge of the Matthean narrative, and whether it seems plausible that he has attempted to improve on it. As there, so here. It is worth asking what in Matthew's Great Commission (Matt 28:16–20) would have been most likely to have appealed to Luke, and whether we can see any sign of it at the end of Luke's Gospel. Perhaps the most Lukan-friendly element here in Matthew would be Jesus' universalistic commission, πορευθέντες οὖν μαθητεύσατε πάντα τὰ ἔθνη, βαπτίζοντες αὐτοὺς εἰς τὸ ὄνομα τοῦ πατρὸς καὶ τοῦ υἱοῦ καὶ τοῦ ἁγίου πνεύματος ("Go, therefore, making disciples of *all the nations,* baptizing them *in the name of* the father and of the son and of the holy spirit," Matt 28:19). And it is exactly this element in the commission that is echoed in Luke's own version of it, κηρυχθῆναι ἐπὶ τῷ ὀνόματι αὐτοῦ μετάνοιαν εἰς ἄφεσιν ἁμαρτιῶν εἰς πάντα τὰ ἔθνη ("proclaiming *in his name* repentance and forgiveness of sins to *all the nations,*" Luke 24:47). To speak, then, of Luke omitting this material won't do. A clear echo of Matthew's resurrection story is present in Luke, and it is striking that the echo is at the most Luke-friendly juncture, the command to disciple (Matthew) or preach (Luke) to all the nations.

Overall, the argument from Luke's lack of M material does not have the persuasive force necessary to establish the Q theory. Indeed, as with the previous category (Luke's alleged lack of Matthean additions to

Mark in the triple tradition), it is a category that actually makes more sense on the assumption that Luke knew Matthew. As well as the hints of Luke's knowledge of Matthew's Birth Narrative and Matthew's Resurrection Narrative, it is revealing that Luke parallels Matthew's desire to expand the parameters of Mark's gospel story, taking the narrative not from John the Baptist to the empty tomb but from prebirth annunciation to postresurrection commission.

It is striking, moreover, that neither Stein nor Fitzmyer provides a single example of M material lacking in Luke outside of the birth and resurrection accounts. If one looks at the M material appearing in the main body of Matthew, one of the most remarkable things is that it is characterized by particularly Matthean interests. There is scarcely a pericope there that one could imagine Luke finding congenial to his interests. On the Farrer theory, this is precisely what one would expect, for on this theory M is constituted by those parts of Matthew's non-Markan material that Luke chose not to use. Q, on the other hand, is constituted by those parts Luke found useful. In other words, far from being a problem for Q skeptics, this category is one in which the Farrer theory is put to the test. One will expect Luke to include only the "Luke-pleasing" elements from Matthew and the more one looks at the M material, the more one notices just how little it fits with Luke's literary and theological interests. Luke's lack of M material is not, then, a fact that forwards the Q hypothesis.

Luke's Order

Many argue that Luke's arrangement of double tradition material is inexplicable on the assumption that he has used Matthew. Matthew's order is seen as logical, structured, clear, coherent; Luke's is regarded as only making sense on the assumption that he is, on the whole, following the order of Q.[23] Holtzmann asked whether it was likely "that Luke should so wantonly have broken up the great structures, and scattered the ruins to the four winds?"[24] More recently, Graham Stanton observes that if

---

23. Cf. G. M. Styler, "If Matthew is Luke's source, there seems to be no common-sense explanation for his order and procedure" ("Synoptic Problem" in *The Oxford Companion to the Bible* [eds. Bruce M. Metzger and Michael D. Coogan; Oxford: Oxford University Press, 1993], 724–27, esp. 726).

24. H. J. Holtzmann, *Die synoptischen Evangelien, Ihr Ursprung und geschichtlicher Charakter* (Leipzig: Engelmann, 1863), 130, quoted by Michael Goulder, *Luke*, 38.

Luke read Matthew, he "has virtually demolished Matthew's carefully constructed discourses"[25] and Christopher Tuckett writes:

> If Luke knew Matthew, why has he changed the Matthean order so thoroughly, disrupting Matthew's clear and concise arrangement of the teaching material into five blocks, each concerned with a particular theme?[26]

An important aspect of this argument is that Matthew consistently seems to find the appropriate Markan context for double tradition material and Luke almost never does. The John the Baptist material and the Temptations, which feature both Markan and Q elements, occur in the same context in all three Synoptics, but after this, Matthew and Luke usually diverge in their placement of Q pericopae. Matthew, according to this argument, seems to have the double tradition material in appropriate Markan contexts and Luke does not.[27]

The discussion focuses explicitly on Matthew's Sermon on the Mount and the alleged problems with accepting Luke's apparent redactional procedure. For if Luke used Matthew, he cut the length of his Sermon considerably, writing the less memorable Sermon on the Plain (Luke 6:17–49), omitting much and distributing the remainder at many different points in the Gospel. Since Matthew's Sermon is widely regarded as one of the finest pieces of religious writing of all time, many have felt it to be unlikely that Luke would have disturbed and rewritten his source. These critics argue that it is more plausible that Matthew composed the Sermon using the shorter discourse in Q, best represented now by Luke's Sermon on the Plain, at the same time incorporating elements from elsewhere in Q as well as adding fresh material.

This argument is felt to be persuasive. Robert Gundry, who has argued at length that Luke is familiar with Matthew's Gospel,[28] nevertheless remains persuaded of the existence of Q on the grounds of Luke's arrangement of pericopae.[29] Along with the argument from mu-

25. Graham N. Stanton, "Matthew, Gospel of" in *DBI*, ad loc.

26. Christopher M. Tuckett, "Synoptic Problem" in *ABD*, VI, 263–70 (esp. 268).

27. Cf. also Arland Jacobson, *The First Gospel*, 18.

28. Robert Gundry, "Matthean Foreign Bodies in Agreements of Luke with Matthew against Mark: Evidence That Luke used Matthew" in F. Van Segbroeck et al., eds., *The Four Gospels*, vol. 2, 1467–95.

29. Robert Gundry, *Matthew* (2d ed.), xvi, "Still another question — viz., whether the similarities between Matthew and Luke which I attribute to Matthew's borrowing from Q might have a better explanation in Luke's borrowing from Matthew if he borrowed from Matthew at all — would seem to press me toward eliminating Q in favor of Luke's borrowing whole-

tual primitivity, this one remains one of the major pillars supporting the Q hypothesis and it will require a little time to take it seriously and tease it out. For this reason, the next three chapters of the book will investigate the question of Luke's order in a little more detail and from several different perspectives. For the reader who wants to know some more at this stage, a summary will have to suffice. The argument from order depends on misstatements of the evidence, a dubious value judgment, and failures in both the application of redaction criticism and the appreciation of Luke's literary ability or narrative agenda.

Alternating Primitivity

Many argue that if Luke read Matthew, his versions of double tradition material ought always to be secondary since on this theory he is writing after Matthew, with the earlier versions of sayings in front of him. This, according to Q theorists, is manifestly not the case. Rather, "again and again," Davies and Allison say, one notices that:

> Sometimes it is the First Evangelist who seems to preserve the more original form of saying appearing in the double tradition, at other times it is Luke. This is inexplicable if one evangelist is following the other.[30]

The point is illustrated in a variety of ways, but perhaps the most popular examples of supposed Lukan priority in Q material are the Lord's Prayer (Luke 11:2–4, contrast Matt 6:9–13), the Beatitudes (Luke 6:20–23, contrast Matt 5:3–12) and the doom oracle (Luke 11:49–51, contrast Matt 23:34–36).[31] In these and other cases, it is felt that the Lukan version appears less likely to be the product of his redaction than the Matthean version appears to be of his redaction. In other words, the situation is easily explicable if both are independently redacting an unknown source, Q, but it is inexplicable if Luke is redacting Matthew.

---

sale from Matthew. But the consequent problem of Luke's equally wholesale disarrangement of Matthew's materials — a problem which not even latter-day Griesbachians or the likes of M. Goulder . . . have convincingly solved — stands in the way. The neatness of Matthew's arrangement worsens the problem."

30. Davies and Allison, *Matthew*, 1:116.

31. Cf. Arland Jacobson, *The First Gospel*, 18, who lists Matt 5:3–12 // Luke 6:20–23; Matt 11:19 // Luke 7:35; Matt 6:9–13 // Luke 11:2–4; Matt 12:28 // Luke 11:20; Matt 12:40 // Luke 11:30; Matt 23:34 // Luke 11:49; Matt 5:32 // Luke 16:18.

This argument, like the previous one from Luke's arrangement of pericopae, is of major importance, a real pillar supporting the Q hypothesis.
But close inspection of the evidence and careful reflection on the circumstances surrounding the composition of the Gospels will show the
argument to be much less secure than it is normally assumed to be. At
the heart of the issue is the question of how one calculates the greater
primitivity in double tradition material.

One of the assumptions in the reconstruction of Q is that where
language characteristic of Matthew occurs, this provides an important
indication that his wording is unlikely to have belonged to the original
wording of Q.[32] So where Matthew and Luke have different wording
in the same double tradition passage, and where Matthew's wording is
particularly characteristic of his writing, theorists often conclude that
Matthew and not Q is responsible for those Matthean elements. The
end result is that the Lukan version, on such occasions, will appear to
be more primitive than the Matthean version.

Michael Goulder has pointed to a major problem for this principle by
drawing attention to double tradition material in which characteristic
Matthean expressions are present in both the Matthean and the Lukan
versions, including famously Matthean expressions like ὀλιγόπιστοι ("Ye
of little faith," Matt 8:26 R; 16:8 R, 14:31 M; Matt 6:30 // Luke 12:28
QC[33]); ἐκεῖ ἔσται ὁ κλαυθμὸς καὶ ὁ βρυγμὸς τῶν ὀδόντων ("there there
will be weeping and gnashing of teeth," Matt 13:42, 50; 22:13; 24:51;
25:30; Matt 8:12 // Luke 13:28 QC) and "And when Jesus had finished
[these sayings]..." (Matt 11:1; 13:53; 19:1; 26:1; Matt 7:28 // Luke
7:1). Since such distinctively Matthean expressions occur in this bedrock
"QC" material, a major question mark is placed over one of the standard principles used in the reconstruction of Q. Since Q's style is clearly
Matthean on these occasions, reconstructing Q elsewhere by eliminating
the Matthean elements, the standard practice, becomes problematic. We
cannot assume that the Matthean expressions occurring in his versions

---

32. Among many examples that could be provided from the IQP evaluations in *Documenta
Q*, see Shawn Carruth and James M. Robinson, *Q 4:1–13, 16, 32* on Q 4:1–2, "Matthew's
preference for τότε is good reason to exclude it as reflecting Q here" (Carruth); or p. 106
on Q 4:3, "Since the verb in this construction is so distinctively Matthean, it can safely be
ascribed to Matthean redaction" (James M. Robinson on whether or not to read προσελθών
with Matthew); or p. 126 on Q 4:4, "Matthew's entire introduction to the words of Jesus
is phrased in a typically Matthean way, so that his wording most likely reflects a redactional
preference" (Carruth).

33. R=Redactional addition by Matthew on the assumption of Markan Priority; M=only in
Matthew; QC=common to Matthew and Luke.

of double tradition material, but absent in the Lukan parallels, are due to Matthean redaction rather than to Q. In other words, the notion that Luke often features the more original Q wording is based in part on a fallacy in the way that this "original wording" is calculated. If we accept the existence of Q, we know that its style was at least sometimes Matthean in nature. This deprives us of one of the main grounds for concluding that Matthean language in Q passages where Matthew and Luke differ is secondary.[34]

There is a related problem. The calculation that Lukan forms of Q sayings are sometimes more original than their Matthean counterparts is also based on a feature of Luke's style. Luke is a subtle and versatile writer with a large vocabulary and a tendency to vary his synonyms. Matthew, on the other hand, has a more pronounced, easily recognizable style, and he does not have so rich a vocabulary. It is consequently much less straightforward to judge Lukan redactional activity than it is to pick out where Matthew has edited sources, and it is correspondingly easy to jump to the conclusion that an apparently "un-Lukan" form is a "pre-Lukan," Q form. Again and again one sees in the literature claims that a given word is "un-Lukan and therefore pre-Lukan," claims that artificially reinforce the notion that Luke's version is more primitive than Matthew's.[35]

Further, an important observation needs to be made about the logic of this general argument for Q. This is how Graham Stanton frames the argument:

> Scholars who claim that Luke has used Matthew must accept that it is always Luke who has changed Matthew's earlier form of the tradition. Their attempts to defend this view often look like special pleading.[36]

---

34. For the original argument on the "Matthean Vocabulary Fallacy," see Michael Goulder, *Luke: A New Paradigm*, particularly 11–15. For a critique, see my *Goulder and the Gospels*, Chapter 2, especially 83–85. Goulder modified the argument, partly in response to my critique, in "Self-Contradiction in the IQP," *JBL* 118 (1999): 506–17. This statement is stronger than the earlier version of the argument, partly because it focuses primarily on telling Matthean expressions and partly because it focuses specifically on the issue of the reconstruction of Q and not more generally (as before) on the supposed prevalence of Matthean vocabulary in Q. A full-length response to Goulder's article appeared late in the production of this manuscript, Robert A. Derrenbacker, Jr. and John S. Kloppenborg Verbin, "Self-Contradiction in the IQP: A Reply to Michael Goulder," *JBL* 120 (2001): 57–76. Since I cannot do justice to this in a footnote, I will publish a full response in due course.

35. Goulder, *Luke*, 15–17.

36. Graham Stanton, *Gospel Truth? New Light on Jesus and the Gospels* (London: HarperCollins, 1995), 70–71.

When the argument is put as starkly as this, it does sound like Luke's use of Matthew is a hopeless theory. But is it so hopeless? What if we were to find a Lukan form of a Q saying that appeared on solid grounds to be more original than its Matthean counterpart? Would this offer a witness to the existence of Q? While it is universally assumed that the answer to this question is affirmative, this is not actually the case. Occasional signs of greater primitivity are only a difficulty for Luke's literary knowledge of Matthew if we are prepared to deny the role of oral tradition in Gospel relationships,[37] if we assume oral traditions of the Jesus story died out as soon as each evangelist committed them to papyrus, or if we think that oral traditions each traveled down their own individual, exclusive pipelines, one for Mark, one for Q, one for L and so on.

The situation, in other words, is like this. If we grant Luke's literary dependence on both Matthew and Mark, it is inherently plausible to imagine this literary dependence interacting with Luke's knowledge of oral traditions of some of the same material. This makes it inevitable that, on occasion, Luke will show knowledge of some more primitive traditions. Take, for example, the Lord's Prayer (Matt 6:9–13 // Luke 11:2–4), one of the key examples of a supposedly more primitive Lukan form, and, as a liturgical text, the kind of passage that we will expect to have been particularly prone to local variation in oral tradition. Even today, where the Lord's Prayer is often known primarily orally and not in dependence on a written text, one finds local variation. The same kind of thing seems highly likely to have been the case when Luke came to write his version of the prayer in 11:2–4. He looks at the Matthean version but rewrites it in line with the version more familiar to him from frequent recitation in his own tradition. Just as many Catholics today end the prayer where Matthew ends it, at "Deliver us from evil," without adding "Thine be the kingdom, the glory and the power, for ever and ever Amen," so Luke ends his prayer with "Lead us not into temptation" and not with "But deliver us from evil," in spite of the fact that the latter is present in his text of Matthew. Just as Catholics today know of the existence of the "Thine is the kingdom" clause, but choose not to use it

37. This is effectively Michael Goulder's position but see Mark Goodacre, *Goulder and the Gospels*, Part 2, especially 284–87. John Drury, *Tradition and Design in Luke's Gospel* and *Parables in the Gospels* follows Goulder but contrast Austin Farrer, "On Dispensing," 85; H. Benedict Green, "Credibility," 149; E. P. Sanders and M. Davies, *Studying the Synoptic Gospels*, especially 117; John Muddiman, Review of Michael Goulder, *Luke* in *JTS* 43 (1992): 176–80; and Eric Franklin, *Luke*, especially 346–52.

because of familiarity and loyalty to tradition, so too it is hardly difficult to think of Luke knowing the clause "But deliver us from evil," but not using it for the same kinds of reason.

We can see the same principle at work in Luke's use of Mark. We do not always automatically accord priority to the Markan version of traditions they share. In the case of the Eucharistic tradition, for example (Matt 26:26–29 // Mark 14:22–25 // Luke 22:15–20), Luke appears to have different, arguably "more original" elements over against Mark— indeed we are lucky enough to have an independent witness to this in 1 Corinthians 11:23–26.[38] Given that most of us are happy to grant that there are, on occasions, some more primitive elements in Luke's triple tradition passages, not withstanding Luke's agreed literary dependence on Mark, we should not be surprised to see the same thing from time to time in the double tradition material that Luke shares with Matthew.

The difficulty is that scholars have routinely confused issues of literary priority with issues over the relative age of traditions. The theory of Luke's literary dependence on Mark and Matthew does not necessitate the assumption that his material is always and inevitably secondary to Matthew's and Mark's. Few scholars today would deny the likelihood that Luke creatively and critically interacted with the living stream of oral tradition when he was working with Mark, so too we should not think it odd that he might have interacted with Matthew in the light of his knowledge of similar material in oral tradition.[39]

Luke himself gives us a strong hint of what is going on in his preface, 1:1–4, in which he implies that he has been engaging carefully not only with those who have undertaken to write narratives (πολλοὶ ἐπεχείρησαν ἀνατάξασθαι διήγησιν, 1:1), but also with the things that have been "handed down by those who from the first were eyewitnesses and servants of the word" (καθὼς παρέδοσαν ἡμῖν οἱ ἀπ᾽ ἀρχῆς αὐτόπται καὶ ὑπηρέται γενόμενοι τοῦ λόγου, 1:2). If we take this seriously, we have a picture of an evangelist who is critically and creatively interacting with both oral traditions and writings of "the events that have been fulfilled

---

38. See, however, Bart Ehrman, *The Orthodox Corruption of Scripture: The Effect of Early Christological Controversies on the Text of the New Testament* (Oxford: Oxford University Press, 1993), 197–209 for the theory that Luke 22:19–20, the verses that closely parallel 1 Cor 11:24–25, are a later "orthodox corruption" of the more original shorter text. If correct, this actually reinforces the point, whereby "earlier" material (traditions derived from or paralleling 1 Cor 11:23–26) appears in the later text (versions of Luke featuring the longer text).

39. Cf. especially the works by John Muddiman, Eric Franklin, and Mark Goodacre cited in n. 37, above.

among us." The time has come to distinguish properly between direct literary use of a prior text and knowledge of oral traditions, both of which are key in the composition of Luke's Gospel. Since practically all scholars accept that Luke was familiar with oral traditions of Jesus material, it is quite reasonable to assume that some of these traditions will have overlapped and interacted with his direct knowledge of his written sources. It is quite reasonable, in other words, to call into question the premise behind this argument for the existence of Q.

The number of such passages is probably not large. Other factors, the means by which original forms of Q are calculated and the under-estimation of strong arguments for Luke's secondary nature, account for many of the allegedly more primitive Lukan forms. Sometimes it is simply the case that strong arguments for the secondary nature of some Lukan versions have been overlooked. In Chapter 7 below, we will take a careful look at one such case, a textbook example of alleged greater primitivity in Luke, the first beatitude, "Blessed are the poor." But that said, scholars would be mistaken to be afraid of plausible appeals to oral tradition in the discussion of Luke's use of Matthew when, after all, they are using the very same appeals in their discussions of Matthew's and Luke's use of Mark.

The Distinctive Character of Q

Forms of these four arguments — from Luke's alleged lack of Matthean additions to Mark in triple tradition material, Luke's lack of M, his arrangement of incidents, and alternating primitivity — have been used with different degrees of emphasis on repeated occasions over the last century or so.[40] All these are essentially negative arguments, pressing the case for Q by attempting to eliminate the primary alternative, Luke's use of Matthew. But now, two fresh arguments for Q based less on negative reasoning have begun to emerge. These arguments do not yet have a high profile in the literature, but it would be a mistake not to pay some attention to them.

The first is based on the notion that Q makes its presence felt in the Gospels. It distinguishes itself from the other material in the Synoptics

---

40. Christopher Tuckett, "Existence," 24–27, chronicles three of these arguments (omitting Luke's lack of M material) and adds another, that from the presence of doublets in Matthew and Luke, which, he says, "is perhaps one of the weakest arguments for the existence of a Q source" (27). It does not appear to be used as an argument for Q in any of the recent literature. Cf. W. G. Kümmel, *Introduction*, 51–53.

not purely because it provides a preferable explanation for the phenomenon of the double tradition but also because it is held to have a special
theology, vocabulary, history, structure, and style. Q is not the same as
Matthew and it is distinct from Luke.[41] David Catchpole focuses on distinctive themes in Q, against Michael Goulder's claim that the theology
of Matthew and the theology of Q are indistinguishable:[42]

> I shall argue that space is indeed visible between the two on key
> issues such as poverty, the Gentiles, the debate about the status of
> the law, the kingship and Davidic lineage of Jesus, the relationship
> of Jesus to Wisdom, and the gift of the Spirit.[43]

Others like John Kloppenborg are beginning to draw attention to
evidence of a distinctive genre for Q as an argument for its existence:

> Evidence of design and deliberate structure serves not only to ex-
> pose the distinctive theology of Q; it turns out to be relevant to a yet
> more basic issue, that of the very existence of Q.... For it is exceed-
> ingly unlikely that a subset of materials mechanically abstracted
> from two Gospels would display an inherent genre and structure
> unless in fact that subset substantially represented a discrete and
> independent document.[44]

The use of this kind of argument for the existence of Q can, however,
generate problems. Perhaps the closest analogy to this approach in the
twentieth century would be the discovery of "Proto-Luke" from the
isolation of the Q and L material in Luke's Gospel, a process that appeared to confirm the existence of a discrete, independent, early version

---

41. Arland Jacobson notes that the attempt to discover Q's integrity is in one way the beginning point of Q research, *The First Gospel*, 18, "In particular, it must be shown that the
disparate units of text where Matthew and Luke agree against Mark really belong together as
parts of a single document whose structure and coherence can be demonstrated."

42. This thesis is a major element in *Midrash and Lection in Matthew* but is most clearly
spelled out in *Luke*, 52–71.

43. David Catchpole, *The Quest for Q* (Edinburgh: T & T Clark, 1993), 7. Cf. Ulrich Luz,
Matthew 1–7 (ET, Edinburgh: T & T Clark, 1990), 74–76 and 82–83, who draws attention
to apparent discrepancies between the views of Q and Matthew. Unlike Catchpole, however,
Luz does not use this as an argument against Luke's use of Matthew.

44. "Introduction" in John S. Kloppenborg, ed., *The Shape Of Q: Signal Essays on The Sayings Gospel* (Minneapolis: Fortress, 1994), 2; cf. *Excavating Q*, 163–64 (on which see further
below) and Robert A. Derrenbacker, Jr. and John Kloppenborg Verbin, "Self-Contradiction,"
73–76. For a similar example, see Alan Kirk, *The Composition of the Sayings Source: Genre,
Synchrony, and Wisdom Redaction in Q* (NovTSup, 91; Leiden: E. J. Brill, 1998), 85–86.
See also Michael Steinhauser's comment in the introduction to John S. Kloppenborg et al., *Q
Thomas Reader*, 13.

of Luke's Gospel that responded to genre and structural analysis. Once Markan material had been mechanically removed, the remaining sections still appeared to conform to the expectations of a narrative gospel framework.[45] The fact that now no one adheres to Streeter's and Taylor's Proto-Luke might suggest caution in using any robust form of this kind of argument.

It should perhaps be added that Kloppenborg's reference to "a subset of materials mechanically abstracted from two Gospels" is an oversimplification of what goes on in Q research, as of course Kloppenborg, one of the editors of the International Q Project, realizes as much as anyone. The very reason that such painstaking labor has to go into the reconstruction of Q is that it is not a simple task to abstract its contents mechanically from Matthew and Luke. The issue of whether to include triple tradition pericopae featuring major agreements between Matthew and Luke against Mark is not the only difficult decision that has to be made.

What, though, of David Catchpole's more broadly thematic argument? His case is built up on the assumption that the observable space between the theology of Matthew and the alleged theology of Q points clearly to the existence of Q. The argument proceeds on the assumption that if Luke knew Matthew as well as Mark, such distance does not exist. The difficulty with Catchpole's argument, however, is that on the Farrer theory one would indeed expect to see space between Q and Matthew since, on this theory, Q is constituted by the parts of Matthew's non-Markan material that are extracted, reproduced, and reworked by Luke. Or, to oversimplify a little for the sake of making the point, they are the "Luke-pleasing" elements in Matthew's extra material.[46] If one wanted to put this into an equation, it would look something like this:

---

45. The two major exponents of Proto-Luke were B. H. Streeter, *The Four Gospels*, Chapter 8 and Vincent Taylor, *Behind the Third Gospel: A Study of the Proto-Luke Hypothesis* (Oxford: Clarendon, 1926). Taylor's text of Proto-Luke can be found in *The First Draft of St Luke's Gospel* (London: SPCK, 1927). Perhaps the most recent defense of Proto-Luke in the Streeter-Taylor form was G. B. Caird, *Saint Luke* (Pelican Gospel Commentaries; Harmondsworth: Penguin, 1963), 23–27. For an early critique of it, see J. M. Creed, *The Gospel According to St Luke: The Greek Text With Introduction, Notes and Indices* (London: Macmillan, 1930), especially lviii. The hypothesis is criticized repeatedly in (the footnotes of) Hans Conzelmann's *Die Mitte der Zeit* (ET, *The Theology of St Luke*).

46. This needs to be stressed as a partial corrective to Goulder's exposition of the identity between Q and Matthew, *Luke*, 52–71. Goulder's brilliant observations are relevant insofar that they demonstrate the decisive role played by Matthew in generating what we call Q, but it needs to be added that there will be major contrasts because of the reworking and recontextualizing of this material in Luke, alongside the fact that — on this theory — Luke has made Luke-pleasing selections from Matthew.

Q = (Matthew *minus* Mark) *divided by* "Luke-pleasingness"

Since it is not commonly seen that Q will also have a distinctive profile on the Farrer theory, let us take the first of the elements on Catchpole's list quoted above, poverty, by way of illustration. One of the most characteristic elements in the alleged profile of Q concerns its attitude to the poor. But for Catchpole, such a concern is not evident in Matthew. He summarizes:

> It should not be forgotten that on the matter of poverty a gap has been found separating the outlook of Q from the outlook of Matthew. Q was concerned about the poor: the position of the trio of beatitudes (Q 6:20b, 21) at the start of the inaugural discourse puts that beyond doubt. But where is there any sign of Matthean energy and commitment in this area? True, he adopts here a tradition, there a tradition, on poverty. But he does nothing constructive with any of them and is clearly happier with piety than with poverty. He even slides past Jesus' own words, "Whenever you will, you can do good to them."[47]

On the standard reconstructions, there are two references to the poor in Q, at Q 6:20, μακάριοι οἱ πτωχοί ("blessed are the poor") and Q 7:22, πτωχοὶ εὐαγγελίζονται ("the poor are evangelized"). While Matthew retains the second of these references to the poor in this quotation from Isaiah 61:1 LXX (Matt 11:5), the distance between Matthew and Q is effectively generated by the first of these references in which the unambiguous blessing on the poor in Q 6:20 is qualified in Matthew, μακάριοι οἱ πτωχοὶ τῷ πνεύματι ("Blessed are the poor *in spirit,*" Matt 5:3).

But let us assume that the literary relationship here is not Matthew's and Luke's mutual dependence on a discrete hypothetical document but is rather Luke's dependence directly on Matthew. On this scenario, too, some distance between the hypothetical Q and Matthew should be expected. Matthew 11:5, with its obvious allusion to Isaiah 61:1, will be exactly the kind of passage that we will expect Luke to have found congenial or "Luke-pleasing." If we can judge from the importance given to Isaiah 61 in Jesus' first public preaching (Luke 4:16–30), this is one of Luke's favorite texts for summing up the identity of Jesus, the one who is anointed to evangelize the poor, εὐαγγελίσασθαι πτωχοῖς (Luke

---

47. *The Quest for Q*, 23. The quotation at the end is the phrase in Mark 14:7 absent in the parallel Matthew 26:11.

4:18). Given the importance of this text to Luke, it would be equally
unsurprising if he were to redact Matthew's "Blessed are the poor in
spirit" to produce "Blessed are the poor" in Luke 6:20, not least given
the fact that others of Luke's favorite redactional strategies are in evidence in the same passage.[48] Not only is this just the kind of move
we might have expected Luke to make, but also such a move will have
inevitably generated some distance between Q as reconstructed on the
basis of Luke, and Matthew's Gospel.[49] In short, Q's concern for the
poor does indeed contrast with Matthew's much less strident concern,
but Q's concern for the poor is something that has been generated by
scholarly reconstruction of Q, a reconstruction made notwithstanding
Luke's even more well-known preference for the poor.

The general point is confirmed by an important observation concerning
entire Matthean pericopae absent in Luke. If Q is indeed the result of a
"Luke-pleasing" reworking of Matthew's non-Markan material, then we
will expect the material he left behind to be in some way uncongenial,
either in terms of its general theme or its literary framing.[50] Now the
material that, on the Farrer theory, Luke left behind is the M material. And
it is striking that whereas the Q material generally has a "Luke-pleasing"
profile, the M material tends to have a "Luke-displeasing" profile. The

---

48. See further Chapter 7 below.

49. In addition to this, Catchpole's focus is specifically directed at Goulder's case (see especially *Midrash and Lection in Matthew*) for the identity of Matthew and Q, a case that
involves the somewhat singular view that Matthew himself composed the non-Markan material in his Gospel without recourse to substantial extra-Markan sources. Catchpole comments,
for example, that "the Q hypothesis does more justice to the data than the theory of Matthean
creativity" (*The Quest for Q*, 16). Catchpole's emphasis is entirely natural — Goulder is the
leading and most recent exponent of the theory of Markan Priority without Q and one would
expect Catchpole to engage with the specific exponent of the theory rather than the general
theory. But now, once rid of this idiosyncratic and unnecessary element in the Farrer theory,
Catchpole's argument loses much of its force. The question of Matthew's source material for
the Beatitudes remains, of course, but for the purposes of discussing the Synoptic Problem this
is a secondary issue, rather like the issues of the source material for Mark on the assumption of
Markan Priority or the sources for Q on the assumption of the Q hypothesis. The point in this
context is that the case for Luke's literary dependence on Matthew should not be obscured by
Goulder's undue emphasis on Matthean creativity, just as Markan Priorists often have radically
differing views on the origin of Mark's source material.

50. I here stress whole pericopae since within individual pericopae it will sometimes be the
case that elements will be eliminated or reworked by Luke. The Beatitudes themselves are a case
in point. As Catchpole points out in *The Quest for Q* (16–23), some of Matthew's additional
beatitudes overlap with themes Luke may have liked, for example meekness and mercy (21).
Yet in a Lukan literary reworking into a series of beatitudes and woes connected with poverty
and persecution, in a major Lukan schema of eschatological reversal, the additional Matthean
beatitudes inevitably drop out. Sometimes it is not enough simply to count up congenial themes;
it is also important to look at literary context and framing. See further below, pp. 143–46.

Q pericopae are precisely the ones we would expect Luke to take over from a book like Matthew, selections from the Sermon on the Mount, the Centurion's Boy, the Lost Sheep, teachings about discipleship and the rest; and there is not a pericope in M that looks like it might have been congenial to Luke: several have an oddly "legendary" character (e.g., Matt 17:24–27, Coin in the Fish's Mouth) and others are in direct conflict with Luke's theology (e.g., Matt 25:31–46, the Sheep and the Goats). Indeed it has long been recognized that the Q material has a more clearly pro-Gentile profile than does the M material, which tends to be inspired by and focused on the Jewish-Christian mission and Jewish-Christian interests.

Moreover, the argument from Q's distinctiveness is a beneficiary of the fact that the Q theory is the status quo position. Studies that assume Q inevitably cause a reentrenchment of the notion that Q is distinctive. The repeated analysis of the double tradition material in isolation from its Matthean and Lukan contexts generates a momentum of its own, the tendency of which is to reinforce the starting point, which was the isolation of the double tradition material from its contexts in Matthew and Luke. It is rare to see Q scholars pausing to reflect on how the same evidence appears on a Q-skeptical theory, and ultimately this is the kind of thing that is needed in order to test claims that the distinctiveness of the Q material implies the existence of a Q document.

Kloppenborg concludes his recent discussion of the character of the main redaction of Q with the following reflections on its relevance to the Synoptic Problem:

> There is a very broad consensus among specialists in regard to the character of what I have called the main redaction of Q: it is marked thematically by repetitive elements — the announcement of judgment and the employment of a deuteronomistic view of history. I would add that the main redaction evokes the story of Lot and the destruction of Sodom. What is especially significant from the standpoint of the Synoptic Problem is that the "double tradition," once extracted from Matthew and Luke, displays a strong thematic coherence and organization that do not derive from the main redactional themes of either Matthew or Luke.[51]

These reflections illustrate the problem. One will not expect the main redactional characteristics of Q, as they are calculated by those assum-

---

51. Kloppenborg, *Excavating Q,* 163–64.

ing its existence, to "derive from the main redactional themes of either
Matthew or Luke." The expectation will rather be simply that we will
be able to see points of contact between the alleged "main redactional
themes" of Q and elements that play a role in both Matthew and Luke.
For the postulation of Q, and the isolation of non-Markan material common to Matthew and Luke, inevitably tends towards the diminishing of
characteristically or distinctively Matthean or Lukan elements within the
standard reconstructions of Q.[52]

The point is best made by means of illustration. One element in the
"main redaction of Q" is said to be the announcement of judgment
(found at Q 3:7–9; 6:46; 10:13–15; 11:31–32, 42–44, 46–47, 52, 49–
51; 12:8–9, 54–56; 13:26–27, 28–29, 34–35; 17:26–27, 34–35). The
first question here for the Q skeptic will be whether or not there are
points of contact between the double tradition and elements that are
present in Matthew alone, a question that will help establish whether
the general theme is at least an element in Matthew's thinking. The signs
are that there are indeed important points of contact between Q and
non-Q material in Matthew. Q 3:7–9, for example, is the first speech in
Q, and a speech characterized by the announcement of judgment:

> You brood of vipers! Who warned you to escape from the coming
> wrath? Bear fruit worthy of repentance and do not begin[53] to say
> to yourselves, "We have Abraham as our father," for I say to you
> that God is able from these stones to raise up children to Abraham.
> Even now the axe is lying at the root of the tree; therefore every tree
> not producing good fruit will be cut down and thrown into the fire.

The language and form of the announcement has a close parallel in the
non-Q verse Matthew 23:33:

> Snakes! Brood of vipers! How can you flee from the judgment of
> Gehenna?

The same term is used, γεννήματα ἐχιδνῶν ("brood of vipers")[54] and it
is also the same form, offensive vocative followed by a rhetorical ques-

---

52. In spite of this, there are nevertheless signs of Matthean redaction in Q in passages in
which there is verbatim or near-verbatim agreement between Matthew and Luke. These signs
may point to Luke's use of Matthew—see further above, p. 62.

53. Matt 3:9 δόξητε; Luke 3:8 ἄρξησθε.

54. The term also occurs in a similar form in Matthew 12:34, another non-Q sentence in
Matthew.

tion,[55] a form common elsewhere in Matthew and Q.[56] And just as the language is congenial to Matthew, so too is the theme of the announcement of judgment and the way in which the concept is framed. The trees not producing good fruit are cut down and thrown into the fire, and fire is often the image of impending judgment for the impenitent throughout Matthew's Gospel, not only here in the Q material (Matt 3:10 // Luke 3:9; Matt 3:12 // Luke 3:17), but also in non-Q material (Matt 5:22, 7:19,[57] 13:40, 25:41). The announcement of judgment in Q is indeed a key element in Matthew's thinking; there is overlap here between the interests of Matthew and the alleged interests of Q.

But likewise, the announcement of judgment appears to be congenial to Luke. Bultmann listed fifteen *Drohworte* or "prophetic threats" in the Synoptic tradition,[58] two of which appear in Mark, one at 8:38 and one at 12:38–40. Since Luke retains both (Luke 9:26 and 20:45–47), in spite of the fact that he has other versions of the same sayings elsewhere,[59] the signs are that this theme was important to Luke. On the basis of his use of Mark, we might have expected Luke to take over the announcements of judgment from Matthew. Further, it is Luke alone who has the damning woes following from his beatitudes (Luke 6:24–26), as searing an announcement of judgment as one can imagine.[60] On this theme, therefore, one cannot help thinking that the evidence is at least as conducive to the Farrer theory as it is to the Q hypothesis. Matthew's interest in the announcement of judgment is reflected in the language in which 3:7–9 (and other passages) is framed and there are clear signs that the theme would have proved congenial to Luke. The evidence is just as

---

55. Michael Goulder labels this form an *echidnic* after its threefold presence in connection with snakes in Matthew 3:7, 12:34 and 23:33 (*Midrash and Lection in Matthew,* 79); cf. my *Goulder and the Gospels,* 49 for other examples of the form in the Synoptics.

56. It is sometimes observed by Q scholars that rhetorical questions are common in Q's announcements of judgment, e.g., Arland Jacobson, "The Literary Unity of Q," *JBL* 101 (1982): 365–89 (375), partially reproduced in J. S. Kloppenborg, ed., *The Shape of Q,* 98–115 (102).

57. Matt 7:19 (πᾶν δένδρον μὴ ποιοῦν καρπὸν καλὸν ἐκκόπτεται καὶ εἰς πῦρ βάλλεται) is a good case in point — it is almost identical to Matt 3:10 // Luke 3:9 but is absent from Luke's version of this passage, Luke 6:43–45.

58. Rudolf Bultmann, *History of the Synoptic Tradition* (2d ed.; ET, Oxford: Blackwell, 1968), 111–18.

59. Parallels to the Mark 8:38 saying are found at Matt 10:33 // Luke 12:9. The Mark 12:38–40 material overlaps with Matt 23:1–36 and Luke 11:37–54.

60. The passage is, of course, assigned by some to Q, e.g., Heinz Schürmann, *Das Lukasevangelium. 1: Kommentar zu Kap. 1,1–9,50* (HTKNT 3/1; Freiburg: Herder, 1969), 336–41; David Catchpole, *Quest for Q,* 87–90; but contrast the International Q Project who do not read the Woes in Q, James M. Robinson et al., eds., *The Critical Edition of Q,* 54–55. See further below, pp. 136–38.

we might have expected it to be and does not provide any real difficulty for dispensing with Q.

Finally, in many respects Q seems not to be distinctive enough for the case to be made with any degree of confidence. For one thing, there is rather too much overlap between the style of Q and the style of M. The predominantly M section Matt 5:17–20,[61] for example, bears all the stylistic traits common to many of the adjacent and related Q passages.[62] Furthermore, it is sometimes said that Luke must have used some pericopae from Q which were not used by Matthew. In other words, the document Q overlaps the double tradition but is not identical with it. It is a notorious difficulty, however, to isolate alleged Q pericopae in Luke outside of the double tradition,[63] something that is perhaps surprising given the claims about the distinctiveness of Q's thought and style. Indeed the candidates most commonly suggested, like Luke 11:27–28 (Woman in the Crowd),[64] Luke 12:15–21 (Parable of the Rich Fool) or Luke 15:8–10 (Lost Coin), all have an uncannily Lukan ring about them — their Lukan style is, if anything, as marked here as anywhere.[65]

These observations are intended to go some way towards pointing to the difficulties involved with the argument from the distinctiveness of Q. Although at the moment scholars rarely stress that argument in the literature, these thoughts focus on some of the problems involved for those who might be inclined in the future to give it a higher profile. The

61. Matt 5:18 has a loose parallel in Luke 16:17. Cf. James M. Robinson et al., eds., *The Critical Edition of Q*, 468–69 for the International Q Project's reconstruction of Q 16:17.

62. Cf. Michael Goulder, *Midrash and Lection in Matthew*, 285.

63. See Tuckett, *Q*, 93–96, "The identification of specific *Sondergut* passages which may have been part of Q has never commanded anything approaching a scholarly consensus" (95). Tuckett himself argues for the inclusion of Luke 4:16–18 in Q (see *Q*, 226–28 and literature cited there). For discussion of method and of candidates, see further Petros Vassiliadis, "The Nature and Extent of the Q Document," *NovT* 20 (1978): 49–73; Kloppenborg, *Excavating Q*, 91–101; and *Formation of Q*, 82–84. One of the most expansive editions of Q is Heinz Schürmann's, in various publications, helpfully summarized in Frans Neirynck, "Recent Developments in the Study of Q" in *LOGIA. Les Paroles de Jésus — The Sayings of Jesus* (ed. J. Delobel; BETL 59; Leuven: Leuven University Press, 1982), 29–75 (esp. 38–39)=Franz Neirynck, *Evangelica II* (BETL 99; Leuven: Leuven University Press, 1991), 409–64 (esp. 418–19).

64. The Lukan nature of this unit is overwhelming: the foil comment with τίς; the gynecological detail; the theology of hearing the word of God and doing it. See further my "Luke 11.27–28 // Thomas 79: A Case of Thomasine Dependence," forthcoming.

65. Kloppenborg, *Excavating Q*, 96–99, argues strongly in favor of the inclusion of Luke 15:8–10 in Q. Indeed this is one of the few pieces of *Sondergut* that is included in the IQP's *Critical Edition of Q*, with a {C} rating. Yet the case for some measure of Lukan creativity remains strong — it is structured around the typically Lukan 10:1 ratio (on which see Michael Goulder, *Luke*, 104–5 and Mark Goodacre, *Goulder and the Gospels*, 267–70), and the gender coupling that is an alleged characteristic of Q here is just as much an obvious characteristic of Luke.

distinctiveness of Q as it is reconstructed from Matthew and Luke is a function of the way in which Q is reconstructed; it is a distinctiveness that makes sense for Q skeptics too. One thought, however, remains and we have hardly begun to touch on it. What of the alleged distinctiveness over Q's structure and genre? Does the Q material respond well to genre-comparative analysis? In Chapter 9 below, there will be an investigation of Q alongside its closest alleged relation, the Gospel of Thomas.

The Redaction-Critical Argument

Graham Stanton succinctly summarizes the argument from redaction criticism:

> The success of redaction criticism in clarifying the literary methods and distinctive theological emphases of Matthew and Luke on the assumption of dependence on Mark and Q is an important argument in favour of the two-source hypothesis.[66]

This argument states strongly a consideration that may well be weighty in the minds of many. What it amounts to is a *laissez-faire* argument in favor of a conservative position: one ought to maintain the status quo in the light of the fine scholarship that the consensus has produced or, to put it another way, "If it ain't broke, don't fix it."[67]

Although the explicit statement of this argument is a relatively recent phenomenon, it would be a mistake to play down its importance, for while many believe in Q, there are still few who write books about it, and even fewer who state clearly their reasons for accepting the hypothesis. This large, Q-believing majority, takes the hypothesis for granted in both books and everyday teaching on the New Testament, and every time it is presupposed, Q can seem to gain more ground. In other words, if Q consistently makes sense in so many different studies on the New

---

66. Stanton, *Gospel*, 35. Cf. J. Fitzmyer, *Luke I–IX*, 65, "the modified Two-Source Theory has at least led to all sorts of advances in gospel interpretation and has pragmatically established its utility'; Arland Jacobson, *The First Gospel*, 5: "to the extent that a hypothesis may be judged by its fruitfulness, the Two Document Hypothesis has certainly made a good case for itself"; Davies and Allison, *Matthew*, 1:98.

67. Observe in particular here Ulrich Luz, *Matthew 1–7: A Commentary* (ET, Edinburgh: T & T Clark, 1989), 46, "To question this hypothesis is to refute a large part of the post-1945 redaction-critical research in the Synoptics, a truly daring undertaking which seems to me to be neither necessary nor possible." The term "possible" is odd, for there is no doubt that it is possible to challenge the consensus — many have done so. The question surely revolves around the matter of plausibility — how convincing are the attempts to refute the consensus?

Testament, it might seem to be a workable hypothesis. And a workable hypothesis can look like a plausible hypothesis.

There are, however, major problems with taking this seriously as an argument in favor of the Q hypothesis. Once again, the issue of entrenchment is relevant. Repeated studies of Matthew and Luke assume Q and this assumption then becomes a normative element in such studies. Indeed one of the very tools for the study of Matthew and Luke is Q, little more than a reflex of working within the consensus. There is, of course, no problem with this in itself. Scholars cannot continually question every assumption at every stage of their analyses or progress would never get made — everyone works within the general consensus until a cogent, well-argued and plausible alternative becomes available. The point rather is that is it is illegitimate to use the fact that there is a general consensus on an issue as an argument in favor of that general consensus. The argument from the status quo is effectively little more than an assertion that there is a status quo, and if scholars across all academic disciplines decided only to work within established consensus frameworks, we would never see interesting challenges to the bigger pictures that have been constructed.

A second and key difficulty with this argument is that it does not distinguish clearly between Markan Priority specifically and the two-source theory generally. As an argument it is far more relevant, therefore, to the Griesbach hypothesis than it is to Farrer. The Farrer theory shares with the two-source theory the appeal to Matthew's and Luke's use of Mark, and equally, at least, to Luke's subsidiary use of another written document in addition to Mark for the double tradition. Moreover, while an argument of this kind might legitimately be used in favor of Markan Priority, for which we have an extant text with which we can compare Matthew and Luke, it is much less straightforward to use it in favor of Q, which is hypothetical.[68] Thus the interpreter can consistently ask the question: does redaction criticism of Luke's use of Mark here, or of Matthew's use of Mark there, make good sense? But before one is able

---

68. John Dominic Crossan, *The Birth of Christianity: Discovering What Happened in the Years Immediately After the Execution of Jesus* (Edinburgh: T & T Clark, 1999), 107, in my view correctly focuses specifically on Markan Priority when he is using this argument: "If . . . you postulate Matthean and Lukan dependence on Mark, you should be able to explain every omission, addition, or alteration in Matthew and Luke over their Markan source. *Because, of course, we still have Mark.* For many scholars, including myself, it was the success of such endeavors in redaction-criticism that served retroactively to confirm the historical primacy of Mark" (emphasis added).

to ask the same question of Matthew's and Luke's alleged use of Q, one has to reconstruct Q, or, at the very least, to suggest in general terms what was in Q. And the difficulty in this context is not only that Q, a hypothetical document, has a far greater degree of potential flexibility than does Mark, which is an extant document, but also that the primary means by which Q is reconstructed is by means of redaction criticism. If one were to lean too strongly, therefore, on this as an argument specifically for the existence of Q, there would be an unavoidable circularity — a tool that has been used to generate a document is said to corroborate the existence of the document that has been generated.[69]

Rhetoric in the Case for Q

It is something of a truism that the arguments given in defense of a theory are seldom identical to the reasons its proponents actually hold that theory. Thus, naturally and inevitably, several of the arguments for Q — as for other elements taken for granted in Gospel studies — have the character of secondary rationalizations of a thesis already held on other grounds. One of the most interesting things about the last of the arguments used above is that it appears to come closest to the reason that many scholars, quite legitimately, continue to believe in Q. They think that on a hard-working day-by-day, year-on-year basis, it's the hypothesis that provides the best working model for understanding the double tradition material in Matthew and Luke. It makes good sense of Matthew, good sense of Luke and offers real help in reconstructing the history of Christian origins. Yet Q, as an element in the working model, has an inherent vulnerability to Occam's Razor in a way that its sometime sister postulate Markan Priority does not. The question we need to ask is whether the alternative model, retaining Markan Priority but dispensing with Q, might be able to offer scholarship something that is as plausible and potentially useful in explaining the Gospels and Christian origins. The attempt to establish the viability of an alternative is, however, no mean task. While some ignore the option of Markan

---

69. Since the argument is, as stated above, currently framed in terms of the two-source theory generally, this argument should not trouble Q skeptics as much as skeptics of Markan Priority. However, the potential circularity of using Q in redaction criticism of Matthew and Luke is already beginning to make its presence felt in the literature. James M. Robinson, for example, speaks of a time when "the reconstruction of a critical text of Q" will make redaction criticism of Matthew and Luke on the basis of this text a possibility ("The Jesus of Q as Liberation Theologian," 260).

Priority without Q, those who do pay it any attention often use the most strident language in their arguments against it.

It seems that scholars are unable to talk about the hypothesis of Luke's use of Matthew without resorting to strings of rhetorical questions, with exclamation marks, joke quotation marks, humorous imagery and, at times, even ridicule. In most of the examples above, especially in the first four arguments, the rhetoric of the argument is forceful. Kümmel and Tuckett ask questions that do not require answers ("Is it conceivable...?"; "what could have moved Luke...?") and Stanton has exclamations as asides and speaks of "tortuous explanations." Matters do not seem to be implausible, unlikely, or improbable. Rather, they are "untenable," "inexplicable," and "incomprehensible." Likewise, Luke does not disturb or alter Matthew's arrangements; he "destroys" or "demolishes" them.

We might speculate on what causes such strong language. It may be that it is largely a function of its context. The arguments for the existence of Q often occur in introductory pieces, Bible dictionaries, introductions to commentaries and similar works, in which the scholar has word-limits to worry about and readers' patience at stake. Here, with limited space, rhetorical questions and overstatement sometimes have to stand in for detailed argumentation. But this is not the whole picture.

A second reason for the inflated rhetoric is probably the conscious imitation and unconscious influence of the most marked use of such language, B. H. Streeter's famous attempt to dispose of the theory that Luke used Matthew:

> If then Luke derived this material from Matthew, he must have gone through both Matthew and Mark so as to discriminate with meticulous precision between Marcan and non-Marcan material; he must then have proceeded with the utmost care to tear every little piece of non-Marcan material he desired to use from the context of Mark in which it appeared in Matthew — in spite of the fact that contexts in Matthew are always exceedingly appropriate — in order to re-insert it into a different context of Mark having no special appropriateness. A theory which would make an author capable of such a proceeding would only be tenable if, on other grounds, we had reason to believe he was a crank.[70]

---

70. B. H. Streeter, *The Four Gospels: A Study of Origins* (London: Macmillan, 1924), 183.

This statement is often quoted and frequently echoed. Its influence has been overwhelming. This is not surprising since the wonderful rhetoric is instantly memorable. No one wants to believe that Luke is a "crank": they want neither to slander Luke nor to risk the charge of being stupid themselves. Nor does anyone who has the slightest acquaintance with Luke's Gospel want to feel that it could have been made up of a perverse combing, tearing-up, and inappropriate restructuring of Matthew. Streeter wins the day before the reader has even opened up the Synopsis.

One might guess at a further reason for the excessive rhetoric. I suspect that for many there is a certain feeling of frustration that debates over the Synoptic Problem continue to rage on from year to year, that Q skeptics obstinately refuse to acknowledge the supposed triumph of the two-source theory. There is the attitude that these are issues that were settled long ago — the foundations were laid successfully and scholars have been building on them without trouble ever since. Not only are Q skeptics a nuisance, but also they appear to have a certain arrogance, the surprising and implausible notion that they might be able to overturn the consensus of a century.

Conversely, it is easy for Q skeptics to underestimate the sheer persuasive force that the consensus, simply by virtue of its being the consensus, continues to exert. This is particularly the case in relation to the redaction-critical argument. In book after book and article after article, reasonable sense seems to be made of Matthew and Luke on the assumption that they used Mark independently of one another. What are a handful of books, however erudite, however inspired, against an avalanche of books making good literary, theological, and historical sense of Matthew and Luke, to say nothing of Christian Origins more broadly, on the assumption of Q?

It is worth seeing, though, that the rhetoric does communicate something important. While caricature and overstatement may not be the way to truth, the language used in the standard arguments for Q is not empty rhetoric but is attempting to show the student in an instant just how implausible the thesis of Luke's knowledge of Matthew is held to be. It is saying, in effect, "Can you really believe this?" This is why the rhetoric is most strident when one is dealing with the negative arguments. There is less reason for it when stating positive reasons for believing in Q.

I hope that it is already clear that the strength of the reaction against Luke's use of Matthew is sometimes misplaced. But a little more time will be needed for investigation of the argument that generates the strongest language, the argument from order. If Luke indeed knew Matthew as well as Mark, was he a crank? Is his reordering of Matthew wanton? Is it tantamount to a demolition? In the next three chapters, I will explore the question of Luke's order from a variety of perspectives. I will gently suggest that Luke's creative reworking of his source material, far from "unscrambling the egg with a vengeance," makes best sense when we dispense with Q.

Chapter Four

"UNSCRAMBLING THE EGG WITH A VENGEANCE"?
Luke's Order and the Sermon on the Mount

For many, the argument from order is highly persuasive. They allege that if Luke knows Matthew, his arrangement of double tradition material is inexplicable. This is one of the pillars of the Q hypothesis and it will be worth spending some time looking carefully at how the argument works, examining its implied premises, inquiring into the way the evidence is stated and reflecting on the plausibility of the alternative. There are several problems with the standard argument from order, beginning with the mischaracterizing of the evidence and continuing with a dubious value judgment and lack of attention to Luke's redactional tendencies and literary preferences. This chapter will examine these difficulties carefully and will begin to explore the plausibility of Luke's reworking of the Sermon on the Mount, a task that will be continued in Chapters 5 and 6.

Mischaracterizing the Evidence

One of the starkest examples of the oft-repeated argument from order is R. H. Fuller's summary dismissal of Farrer's attempt to dispense with Q, following Streeter in finding Luke's knowledge of Matthew untenable:

> Simple and attractive though this last theory is, it is open to a fatal objection. Matthew has tidily collected the Q material into great blocks. Luke, we must then suppose, has broken up this tidy arrangement and scattered the Q material without rhyme or reason all over his gospel — a case of unscrambling the egg with a vengeance![1]

Fuller's formulation of this argument provides a simple example of what is most problematic about this kind of reasoning. Not only is there the

---

1. Reginald H. Fuller, *The New Testament in Current Study* (London: SCM, 1963), 87.

same surplus of rhetoric that is common in arguments for Q, but the very framing of the argument detracts from any serious engagement with the position that is being criticized. The argument is stated not in the terms of the hypothesis that Luke has read Matthew but rather in the terms of the Q hypothesis itself. "Matthew has tidily collected the Q material into great blocks," Fuller says, speaking, of course, about Matthew's five "blocks" of teaching material, each of which is marked off with the formula, "When Jesus had finished . . . " (Matt 7:28; 11:1; 13:53; 19:1; 26:1). But this is no more than a description of Matthew's procedure on the assumption of Q. "Luke," he goes on, "has broken up this tidy arrangement and scattered the Q material without rhyme or reason all over his gospel" but, once more, this does not begin the task of attempting to imagine what Luke's approach to Matthew might have been like. To state the argument against one hypothesis using the presuppositions and terminology of the competing hypothesis involves a circularity that undermines any hope for a fair assessment of the evidence.

Furthermore, the emphasis on the five Matthean blocks generates a misleading impression. The casual reader, who does not check the secondary literature by paying careful attention to an open Synopsis, might assume that all of the Q material appears in those five Matthean blocks. Fuller is not the only person to state this unambiguously but Robert Stein, in his much-used introduction to *The Synoptic Problem*, says:

> Matthew's handling of his source, however, was far more thorough-going [than Luke's], for he has arranged this material into five "books." The result is a masterful organization whose artistry is well-recognized.[2]

Even those who do not state this explicitly tend to connect the Q material so closely with Matthew's five discourses that they imply a connection that is stronger than is actually the case.[3] The fact is that the double tradition material is often located in Matthew outside of his five major discourses, in Chapters 3–4 (John the Baptist; Temptation); 8:5–13 (Centurion's Boy); 8:19–22 (Foxes); 9:37–38 (Laborers); 11:2–27 (Messengers from John; Woes; Thanksgiving); 12:22–45 (Beelzebub; Fruit;

---

2. Stein, *The Synoptic Problem*, 95; cf. also, "Within Matthew this material is found in five (or six) sections, all of which end with something like 'And when Jesus finished these sayings. . . . ' These five sections (5–7; 10; 13; 18; 23–25 [or 23; 24–25]) are artistically arranged within Matthew's Gospel . . . " (ibid.).

3. See above, pp. 59–60 for examples of this in Holtzmann, Stanton and Tuckett.

House Swept Clean); 22:1–10 (Banquet); and Chapter 23 (Woes against Pharisees).[4]

Further, large parts of the five major blocks are made up of Markan and other non-Q material. The third discourse (Matthew 13), for example, has only three verses of Q material (13:16–17, Blessings; cf. 13:31–32, Mustard Seed; 13:33, Leaven). And similarly the fourth (Matthew 18) has only four verses of Q material (18:12–13, Lost Sheep; 18:21–22, Seven Times Seventy). To put it mildly, the double tradition material is at least as widely distributed in Matthew as it is in Luke. In other words, it is useful to be wary of the assumption that Luke, on the Farrer theory, is primarily unraveling Matthew's five discourses when he is reproducing double tradition material. This is a major oversimplification of the evidence, and one which detracts from a proper appreciation of what might have been involved in a reworking of Matthew by Luke.

There are further difficulties, however, with the way the evidence is often presented in the argument from order. In a recent, short statement of the grounds for accepting Q, Bart Ehrman writes the following:

> It is unlikely that one of the authors [Matthew or Luke] used Mark, added several stories of his own, and that his account then served as the source for the other. If this were the case, we would not be able to explain the phenomenon noted above, that these stories found in Matthew and Luke but not in Mark are almost always inserted by these authors into a different sequence of Mark's narrative. Why would an author follow the sequence of one of his sources, except for stories that are not found in his other one? It is more likely that these stories were drawn from another source that no longer exists, the source that scholars have designated as Q.[5]

Ehrman's comments are strange not least given the fact that the double tradition is primarily made up of sayings material and not "stories," as Ehrman recognizes elsewhere in the same discussion, mentioning the Temptation Narrative (Matt 4:1–11 // Luke 4:1–13) and the Centurion's

---

4. Stein acknowledges that much Q material occurs in Matthew 23 but tends to treat it as part of the fifth discourse (see n. 2 above).

5. Bart Ehrman, *The New Testament: A Historical Introduction to the Early Christian Writings* (2d ed.; New York; Oxford: Oxford University Press, 2000), 79.

Servant as the exceptions to this general rule (Matt 8:5–13 // Luke 7:1–
10).[6] And since the first of these two stories, the Temptation, occurs
in the identical sequence in the Markan narrative and the other, the
Centurion's Servant, occurs in a similar context, one begins to wonder
whether the evidence adduced by Ehrman can really make the point he
is intending to make.[7]

But the more troubling element in Ehrman's statement is the comment
"these stories found in Matthew and Luke but not in Mark are almost
always inserted by these authors into a different sequence of Mark's
narrative," a statement that is no doubt influenced by Streeter's similar
comments concerning the thesis of Luke's reworking of Matthew, with
its caricature of Luke as having "proceeded with the utmost care to
tear every little piece of non-Markan material he desired to use from the
context of Mark in which it appeared in Matthew . . . in order to re-insert
it into a different context of Mark having no special appropriateness."[8]
As it stands, the statement might appear to be convincing because the
process described would indeed be somewhat peculiar, but the difficulty
with the caricature is that Streeter is misrepresenting an important fact.[9]
As he well knew,[10] most of the pieces of Luke's double tradition do
not appear in a "different context of Mark," whether appropriate or
otherwise, because hardly any of Luke's double tradition occurs in a
Markan context at all.[11] That is, whereas Matthew often features Q
in Markan contexts, Luke rarely does, for most of Luke's Q material
occurs in 6:20–8:3 and 9:51–18:14, and there is famously little use of

---

6. Ibid. "It is indeed striking that almost all of this material comprises sayings of Jesus.
But there are at least two narratives involved: the full story of Jesus' three temptations in the
wilderness . . . and the story of the healing of the Centurion's Servant" (79).

7. The Temptation, indeed the whole of Matt 3:7–4:11 // Luke 3:7–4:13, is usually cited
solely as an exception to the rule. Cf. John Drury, *Tradition and Design,* 128–29, "Streeter's
'subsequent to the temptation story' shows him choosing his ground with more care than justice
and tacitly allowing that there is no need of the Q theory up to the end of the temptation story.
Here is a substantial stretch where Matthew and Luke agree in inserting the same sayings at
the same point in the Markan outline." The Centurion's Servant occurs in Luke straight after
the Sermon on the Plain (Luke 6:20–49) and in Matthew with only the Leper intervening
(Matt 8:1–4), a story Luke has already recounted in its Markan setting (Mark 1:40–45 // Luke
5:12–16).

8. B. H. Streeter, *The Four Gospels,* 183.

9. For this point, cf. Michael Goulder, *Luke,* 39 and Sanders and Davies, *Studying,* 114–15.

10. See, for example, B. H. Streeter, *Four Gospels,* 201: "There are two large tracts, viz.
Luke 6:20–8:3 and Luke 9:51–18:14, in which he makes no use of Mark at all, or, at most,
derives from him a few odd verses."

11. For the observation see H. G. Jameson, *The Origin of the Synoptic Gospels: A Revision of
the Synoptic Problem* (Oxford: Basil Blackwell, 1922), 15–16; Austin Farrer, "On Dispensing,"
66 and 82 and H. Benedict Green, "Luke's Transformation," 135.

Mark in these sections.[12] The point here is that in order to have any hope of providing plausible answers to the basic question, it is essential first to make sure that the evidence is stated as accurately as possible. Misstatement of the evidence, to say nothing of caricature and sarcasm, rarely contributes to useful debate.

The Value Judgment

There is a more troubling difficulty, however, with the way that the argument from order tends to be framed. Fuller speaks of Luke, on the assumption of his knowledge of Matthew, acting "without rhyme or reason," a sentiment that echoes B. H. Streeter's well-known comment that Luke's activity, on this thesis, would be that of a "crank."[13] According to Streeter, the contexts for double tradition material in Matthew are "always exceedingly appropriate" whereas Luke's have "no special appropriateness,"[14] a judgment that is echoed frequently, as for example by Styler, in another celebrated article, speaking of the impossibility of Luke's "violently and frequently" disturbing Matthew's order.[15] Again, the thinking is spelled out explicitly by Robert Stein:

> The thesis that Luke obtained the Q material from Matthew cannot explain why Luke would have rearranged this material in a totally different and "artistically inferior" format.[16]

These scholars take it for granted, then, that Matthew's general arrangement is artistically superior to Luke's. The reader should not feel obliged, however, to agree with what amounts to a simple subjective statement of preference. In spite of the confidence with which this position is repeatedly asserted, it is by no means self-evident that Matthew's order is superior to Luke's. All that can be said is that Luke's order is indeed different from Matthew's. Whether or not one believes that Luke

---

12. The only exceptions are the John the Baptist — Temptations material in Luke 3–4 and the Parable of the Pounds in Luke 19:11–27, the former incidents in the same Markan context and the latter a different one (from Matthew).

13. See above, p. 78, for the full quotation.

14. Streeter, *Four Gospels,* 183.

15. G. M. Styler, Excursus 4 in C. F. D. Moule, *The Birth of the New Testament* (3d ed.; London: Black, 1981), 285–316 (288).

16. Robert Stein, *The Synoptic Problem,* 95. Cf. also 96: "The arrangement of the material in Matthew is extremely well done. The Sermon on the Mount (Matt 5–7) ranks as one of the greatest works of literature ever written. Why would Luke, who was by no means an inept writer, choose to break up this masterpiece and scatter its material in a far less artistic fashion throughout his Gospel?"

read Matthew, all agree that these two evangelists had different aims, different perspectives, different theological tendencies and different literary techniques. Naturally they order their material differently — this is, after all, one of the things that makes a work distinctive.

But if the comments on the difference amount simply to a questionable value judgment, how might the Q skeptic begin to formulate a case against it and how might the uncommitted reader decide between Q and Luke's use of Matthew? Arguments about degrees of artistry and literary skill can only, inevitably, be of the most subjective kind. I propose, therefore, to enlist the support of two partners in Chapters 5 and 6. First, narrative criticism will be brought in to engage in a dialogue with source criticism to see if it too might be able to help out with the question over Luke's literary work. Second, we will examine the use of the Sermon on the Mount in twentieth-century cinema with a view to answering the question about Matthew's and Luke's artistry. Could it be that the filmmakers help to shed some light on the standard scholarly perspective? Before joining hands with these new friends, however, it will be worth asking whether old friends like redaction criticism might yet have more to say on the question.

Luke's Use of Mark

It has become a generally received truth that Q's order is closest to Luke's order.[17] No current Q theorist, to my knowledge, dissents from this view.[18] The difficulty with generally received truths is that it is easy to forget why the view was adopted in the first place. The simple repetition of an established point of consensus often suffices without the need for extra argument. But if the view does have an origin outside of the generally stated preference for Matthew's order over Luke's,[19] it is to be found in an observation combined with an inference. The observation

---

17. For example F. Neirynck, "Q" in *IDBSupp.*, 715, "It is generally held that the original order of Q is preserved more faithfully in Luke," or G. N. Stanton, *The Gospels and Jesus* (Oxford: Oxford University Press, 1989), 89: "Most scholars accept that on the whole Luke has retained the order and content of Q more fully than Matthew, so reconstructions of Q are usually based on Luke."

18. Adolph von Harnack saw Matthew as better representing Q, *New Testament Studies II: The Sayings of Jesus. The Second Source of St. Matthew and St. Luke* (trans. J. R. Wilkinson; New York: G. P. Putnam's Sons; London: Williams & Norgate, 1908).

19. Cf. also the occasional appeal to "Matthew's penchant to collect and organize sayings" (John S. Kloppenborg Verbin, *Excavating Q*, 41). But this is the converse of Luke's penchant to avoid excessively long monologues — see further below.

is that Luke preserves Mark's order more faithfully than does Matthew; the inference is that he is likely therefore also to be preserving Q's order more faithfully than does Matthew. J. M. Creed, for example, says: "It is reasonable to conjecture that Luke has, on the whole, preserved the original order of Q, as he has, on the whole, preserved the original order of Mark."[20] Or, more recently, Christopher Tuckett says:

> Insofar as this [double] tradition may come from a single source Q, the fact that Luke has preserved the order of his Markan source almost unaltered, whereas Matthew has rearranged the Markan material in the interests of his thematic arrangement, suggests that the same has probably happened in the case of Q. Thus, most today assume that Luke has preserved the order of Q more faithfully than Matthew.[21]

This may sound like a strong argument based on a reasonable inference. There are, however, some difficulties here. First, the observation concerning Luke's use of Mark is overstated, for there are several Markan incidents that are transposed by Luke.[22] While most of the incidents related in the earlier "Galilee" section of Luke, in 4:14–6:16 and 8:4–9:50, broadly follow Mark's order, there is a good deal of material that is out of sequence: Jesus' Rejection at Nazareth (Luke 4:16–30) comes much earlier on (cf. Mark 6:1–6); the Call of the Disciples (Luke 5:1–11) comes later (cf. Mark 1:16–20); the Naming of the Twelve (Luke 6:12–16) and the Ministering to Multitudes (Luke 6:17–19) are inverted (cf. Mark 3:13–19 and 3:7–12); the Anointing is brought forward (Luke 7:36–50; cf. Mark 14:3–9); and the Mother and Brothers pericope is kept for later (Luke 8:19–21; cf. Mark 3:31–35). On nearly all of these occasions, Matthew's order is closer to Mark's. Moreover, it is well-known that Luke's Passion Narrative makes significant departures from Mark whereas Matthew's is much more faithful to Mark.[23]

---

20. J. M. Creed, *The Gospel According to St Luke*, lxv.

21. C. M. Tuckett, "Synoptic Problem," *ABD*, 268.

22. One of the best examples of overstatement concerning Luke's policy is J. Jeremias who speaks of Luke as "the enemy of rearrangement," *The Eucharistic Words of Jesus* (ET, London: SCM, 1966), 161.

23. Fitzmyer, *Luke I–IX*, 71–72, speaks of the "seven well-known transpositions of Markan episodes in Luke." Fitzmyer rightly points out, like Tuckett, that these changes are easily explicable on the assumption that Luke has used Mark. My point here is simply to dispute the overstatement concerning Luke's faithfulness to Mark which is made in the context of discussions concerning his alleged faithfulness to Q.

It is an exaggeration to speak of this as "scarcely changing" Mark's order "at all," as Tuckett does.[24] Further, it is easy to overestimate the extent of Matthew's reordering of Mark, which is not as radical as sometimes claimed. Nearly all the changes in the Markan order come in the earlier part of his Gospel. From at least Chapter 13 onward, the order of Matthew is very similar to Mark; there are only the occasional pauses for the insertion of non-Markan material. The most balanced statement of the evidence would be that Matthew and Luke both depart, at times, from Mark's order, though in different ways.[25]

But even if the notion that Luke preserves Mark's order very carefully were accurate, the inference based on it — that he will have preserved his second source equally faithfully — does not necessarily follow. Christopher Tuckett spells the argument out in this way:

> Luke generally preserves Mark's order closely. Thus many have concluded that Luke cannot have proceeded in such a radically different way in relation to his two alleged sources. Rather, Luke's use of Mark suggests that he cannot have used Matthew as well in such a completely different way.[26]

While it is of course a possible inference that Luke would have treated each source in the same way, it is by no means a necessary inference. The two-source theory allows Luke to treat Mark and Q in similar ways because of the difference in content between the two alleged sources, largely narrative triple tradition material in Mark and largely sayings double tradition material in Q, with only some overlap between them. But the difficulty of treating sources in precisely the same way becomes acute if one of a writer's two major sources might be recognized as a

---

24. Tuckett, "Existence," 45 (=*Q*, 31). In other contexts, Tuckett's statements about Luke's departures from Mark's order are more nuanced, especially "Arguments from Order: Definition and Evaluation" in C. M. Tuckett, ed., *Synoptic Studies: The Ampleforth Conferences of 1982 and 1983* (JSNTSup, 7; Sheffield: JSOT Press, 1984), 197–219 (see for example pp. 204 and 211–12). See also "Synoptic Problem," *ABD*, 265. Even here, though, the number of departures from Mark is lessened by Tuckett's decision not to count passages like Luke 7:36–50, 10:25–28 and 13:18–19 because they may be dependent on alternative traditions in addition to / instead of Mark. But even if Luke is dependent on alternative traditions in these cases, he has still made a decision to depart from the order of the parallel Markan versions of the incidents.

25. Cf. W. G. Kümmel, *Introduction,* 46–48 features diagrams of Matthew's order and Luke's order in relation to Mark 1–6:6. He observes that "Luke shows only four divergences from the Markan sequence" and that "Matthew diverges from the Markan sequence only in two ways." On Kümmel's reckoning, Matthew and Luke diverge from the Markan sequence to a similar, limited extent.

26. C. M. Tuckett, *Q*, 9. This is part of an addition to the earlier version of the chapter "Existence."

version of the other one. If Luke knew Matthew as well as Mark, treating these sources on a par with one another would not have been a realistic option.

Our first thought, therefore, that Luke would have attempted to harmonize Mark and Matthew, conflating and reconciling as he is best able, is unlikely.[27] For one thing, it is anachronistic. As far as we can tell, the attempt to harmonize Gospel accounts in the second century was an apologetically motivated response to the difficulty faced by the emergence of four authoritative Gospels. Luke, and the churches of his day, have no such crisis. Further, whereas Tatian, the first known harmonist,[28] had no doubt known all four Gospels together for as long as he could remember, Luke's situation is very different. Writing toward the end of the first century, we might theorize that he has had a copy of Mark for much longer than he has had a copy of Matthew. He has known Mark for perhaps twenty years whereas Matthew is a much more recent discovery. His greater familiarity with the Markan structure has already fixed itself in his mind in such a way that the appearance of the new Gospel of Matthew demands a decision. In writing his own Gospel, how is he to proceed?

Thus, before Matthew is even written, Luke is used to interacting with Mark, reading from Mark, preaching on Mark, steadily getting Mark by heart. When a copy of Matthew comes into his possession, Luke begins to interact with the new Gospel too, quickly noticing, because of his familiarity with Mark, that much of the same ground is covered in Matthew. Luke soon gets into the habit, in such circumstances, of giving priority to the Markan Gospel that has long been at the heart of his understanding of the Jesus story, and using Matthew in a secondary way. Indeed, the process that began here perhaps gave birth to the idea of

---

27. Notice, however, that Michael Goulder does draw analogies between Luke and harmonists, "The Order of a Crank" in C. M. Tuckett, ed., *Synoptic Studies*, 111–30 (esp. 112), and he speaks of Luke as "harmonizing" in *Luke*, 382. Although Goulder is careful to make distinctions between Luke and modern harmonists ("Order of a Crank," 112), the danger of even using the language of "harmonizing" is evident in F. Gerald Downing's somewhat strident reaction to this in "A Paradigm Perplex: Luke, Matthew and Mark," *NTS* 38 (1992): 15–36, reproduced in F. Gerald Downing, *Doing Things With Words in the First Christian Century* (JSNTSup, 200; Sheffield: Sheffield Academic Press, 2000), Chapter 9.

28. That is, unless Justin wrote a harmony, evidence of which might be his "mixed" quotations of Jesus-sayings. There is also evidence of a non-Tatianic Gospel harmony dating from at least the late second century in the fragment of a Gospel harmony found at Dura-Europos, on which see David Parker, David Taylor and Mark Goodacre, "The Dura-Europos Gospel Harmony" in *Studies in the Early Text of the Gospels and Acts*, Texts and Studies: Contributions to Biblical and Patristic Literature (Third Series), vol. 1 (ed. David Taylor; Birmingham: University of Birmingham Press, 1999), 192–228.

writing for Theophilus his own Gospel, with the appearance of Matthew as the immediate catalyst.

The advantage of this scenario is that it makes sense of the redaction-critical insight that both Matthew and Luke are attempts to improve on Mark's Gospel, to provide what they saw to be lacking in it. As many have recognized, Matthew and Luke stand in a similar relationship to Mark's Gospel in that they are both influenced by it yet apparently critical of it. Both fill out the gospel story along the same lines, adding birth narratives and genealogy, adding resurrection appearances and commissioning, adding a substantial amount of teaching material, yet playing down the secrecy motifs and the negative portrait of the disciples. While it is possible that they coincided in doing this independently of one another, it is more likely that Matthew's attempt to fix Mark, when it first came into Luke's hands, suggested to him the possibility that he could fix Mark himself; indeed that he might be able to do it better than Matthew, both by incorporating the best of Matthew and by dispensing with much of Matthew's restructuring of Mark, and especially Matthew's rather imposing, lengthy, unbroken monologues.

Of first importance, then, in understanding Luke's reordering of Matthew is recognizing the priority of Mark.[29] Scholars are accustomed to seeing Mark as prior to Matthew. Perhaps Luke is even more sure of Markan Priority than we are; he has known Mark for longer and it has had time to enter into his bloodstream before there is any question of contamination from its interpretation by and absorption into Matthew. In this way, Luke stands at a unique moment in Christian origins, a moment when Matthew's importance is beginning to be felt, but when Mark is still in many ways valued more highly.

Narratives and Sayings

Any decision to grant Mark priority in matters of order would have been reinforced by the fact that much of the fresh, non-Markan material in Matthew was constituted by sayings material, a fact that has itself in a different way always been fundamental to studies on Q. Although the double tradition does contain narrative material, the bulk of it is made

---

29. Cf. Eric Franklin, *Luke*, 369–70. Franklin acknowledges the importance of recognizing Mark's priority in Luke's handling of his two sources but adds that "More than priority is involved: if Luke knew Matthew, he handled it with a freedom which shows that he gave to it a value which was wholly at variance with that which he gave to Mark" (370).

up of sayings. We might imagine that Luke was happy to take greater liberties with sayings material than he does with narrative material. In this way he is able to keep to the basic Markan framework, with which he is so familiar, subsequently finding fresh settings for much of the sayings material that he draws from Matthew.[30]

Indeed, when it comes to the small amount of narrative material in Q, Luke broadly keeps to Matthew's order. Thus both Matthew and Luke place the John the Baptist material in the same Markan context (Mark 1, Matt 3, Luke 3) and, equally, go on to place the Temptations in the same Markan context (Mark 1:12–13 // Matt 4:1–11 // Luke 4:1–13), matters that Q theorists have always accepted only to use as exceptions which prove the rule.[31] But further, given that Luke places his version of the Sermon a little later than does Matthew in the relative Markan framework, it is striking that the Q story of the Centurion's Boy (Matt 8:5–13 // Luke 7:1–10) occurs almost immediately afterwards, with just the Leper intervening in Matthew (8:1–4), which pericope Luke has already related (5:12–16).

There is, however, a great deal more narrative material in Mark than there is in the Q material which Luke took over from Matthew and thus, broadly, the pattern develops from quite early on: Luke keeps to the Markan narrative framework, using Matthean sayings material with greater freedom. But given the standard argument that Luke would not have broken up Matthew's fine discourses, and especially the Sermon on the Mount, and thus that he would not have acted with such freedom when it came to sayings material, some further investigation of Luke's general attitude to lengthy discourses is required.

Although Mark's Gospel does not contain any materials that are anywhere near as long as the Sermon on the Mount, there are some fairly sizeable discourses, one of which is the "Parable Chapter" (Mark 4:1–34). Where Matthew, typically, increases the length of the chapter

---

30. Cf. Austin Farrer, "On Dispensing," 67; John Drury, *Tradition and Design*, 121; and Michael Goulder, "The Order of a Crank," 112. See also the minor corrective to this viewpoint in H. Benedict Green, "Luke's Transformation," 134.

31. See further above, pp. 52–54. It may be significant that the most marked agreement between Matthew and Luke against Mark does come at this early point in Luke's Gospel. Cf. John Drury, *Tradition and Design*, 128–31, especially 129, "Every writer knows that at the outset of his work, with hopes and energy running high, he expects to achieve something more than, and different from, that which the exigencies of the task produce in the end. So at the beginning of his work Luke labors for a more equally blended synthesis of Mark and Matthew than he finds possible in the final outcome. He is helped by the historical character of Matthew's contribution here, the teaching being more pointedly related to the Markan story than in Matthew's longer discourses."

(Matt 13:1–52), Luke, equally typically, shortens it. Mark's discourse consists of the Sower (4:1–9), its interpretation (4:13–20), the Purpose of Parables (4:10–12), the Lamp under a Bushel (4:21–25), the Seed Growing Secretly (4:26–29), the Mustard Seed (4:30–32) and a summary (4:33–34). Matthew 13 contains all this[32] and much more. Luke, on the other hand, treats it in just the same way that he treats the Sermon on the Mount. Some of it is retained, the Sower and its Interpretation (Luke 8:4–8, 11–15), the Purpose of Parables (8:9–10) and the Lamp (8:16–18); some of it is omitted, the Seed Growing Secretly and the summary; and some of it is redistributed, such as the Mustard Seed (Luke 13:18–19). In summary, it looks like this:

Mark 4:1–9: Parable of the Sower	*Paralleled in* Luke 8:4–8
Mark 4:10–12: Purpose of Parables	*Paralleled in* Luke 8:9–10
Mark 4:13–20: Interpretation of the Sower	*Paralleled in* Luke 8:11–15
Mark 4:21–25: Lamp Under a Bushel	*Paralleled in* Luke 8:16–18
Mark 4:26–29: Seed Growing Secretly	*Omitted in Luke*
Mark 4:30–32: Mustard Seed	*Redistributed:* Luke 13:18–19
Mark 4:33–34: Summary	*Omitted in Luke*

Furthermore, the same happens with Luke's treatment of the discourse in Mark 9:33–50. Luke's parallel in context is a great deal shorter, only five verses (Luke 9:46–48: Dispute about Greatness; 9:49–50: Strange Exorcist), and, as with the Parable Chapter, Luke either omits (Mark 9:43–48: Scandals) or redistributes (Mark 9:42 // Luke 17:1–2: Little Ones; Mark 9:49–50 // Luke 14:34–35) the rest.[33]

Luke regularly shortens Mark's discourses, retaining some material, omitting other material and relocating the rest. Turning to Luke's alleged use of Matthew, we find the same behavior. Matthew 5–7 is treated in the same way that Mark 4 is treated; some is retained, some is omitted, and the rest is redistributed. The scale is different[34] but the redactional procedure is the same. Nor is it just the Sermon that is treated in this

---

32. On the Wheat and the Tares (Matt 13:24–30), cf. p. 32, n. 28 above.

33. In these latter two cases there are also important parallels in Matthew, 18:6–7 on Scandals and 5:13–16 on Salt, respectively. I am aware that on the Q theory, Luke has these two sections in their Q contexts and so he omits them in the parallel to Mark. My purpose here, however, is to illustrate that Luke's procedure, on the assumption of his knowledge of both Matthew and Mark, is consistent and that there is therefore no difficulty in understanding his treatment of the Sermon on the Mount.

34. Luke's Sermon is 739 words of English text in the RSV; Matthew's is 2,325, so the Sermon on the Mount is of course far longer than Mark's parable chapter. No doubt this would have only exacerbated Luke's desire to do something radical with the Sermon. See further on these figures below, pp. 125–26.

way. Luke's attitude is consistent and thus *prima facie* coherent; if Luke has used Matthew, he has consistently shortened the five great Matthean edifices (Matt 5–7; 10; 13; 18; 24–25) — Luke's parallel is in each case shorter; some material is kept in place, some is omitted, some is redistributed to other contexts.

Thus, Luke's procedure with Matthew is not only explicable, it is consistent with his established behavior with respect to Mark. Goulder makes this argument clearly in response to the standard argument from order:

> [Luke] has indeed embodied part of it [the Sermon on the Mount] in his own Sermon on the Plain, scattered part, and omitted part; but his action has not been wanton, nor to the four winds, and the question of what moved him is not beyond resolution if it is taken seriously....Luke treats it just as he treats long discourses in Mark. He regularly likes teaching pericopes of about twelve to twenty verses, which he regards as the amount a congregation (or reader) can assimilate at one time; and he sets them apart with a proper introduction apiece.[35]

This is a strong argument and its force is not yet being felt in literature supporting Q. Kloppenborg is dismissive:

> Goulder...asserts that Luke knew Matthew's lengthy Sermon on the Mount but reduced it in size because Luke "does not like long units." This is not an argument. It is only the *observation* that Luke's Sermon on the Plain is shorter than Matthew's Sermon on the Mount converted into a statement about Luke's aesthetic preferences with the help of the *presupposition* of Luke's use of Matthew. Since it presupposes precisely what is to be proven, it is not an argument at all. In order to create a plausible argument, one would have to show, for example, that elsewhere in Luke-Acts, the author tends to favor short speeches or that other writers of Luke's caliber preferred short, pithy speeches. Only in this way would it be plausible to claim that if Luke encountered a long speech in a source, he would reduce it in length. Parenthetically, it can be observed that both Luke and Acts have rather long speeches, longer

---

35. Goulder, *Luke*, 40–41.

than the twenty-nine verses of Luke's Sermon on the Plain. Thus, at least this line of defense of Luke's procedure fails to convince. In order for an explanation to be at all plausible, it must appeal to some data external to the matter under examination.[36]

Kloppenborg's objections here are a little baffling since he appears not to have noticed that Goulder's case is based on observing Luke's agreed practice in relation to Mark and proceeding to making a case for his alleged practice in relation to Matthew. This is, of course, exactly the same way that Q theorists proceed, from Luke's agreed practice in relation to Mark to his alleged practice in relation to Q. The one is taken as a guide to the other; it is at the heart of standard redaction criticism of the Gospels. To show "that elsewhere in Luke-Acts, the author tends to favor short speeches," using the consensus ground of Markan Priority, is just what Goulder has attempted.

Christopher Tuckett attempts to answer Goulder by offering several counter-examples.[37] He observes that Luke 12:22–53 "constitutes a sustained piece of teaching with no real break at all"; he also mentions Luke 15 but he lays most stress on Luke 21, the eschatological discourse paralleled in Mark 13. Goulder had said that the latter "cannot be broken up,"[38] and Tuckett replies that this is "patently false" given that Matthew does break up the chapter, placing part of it (13:9–13) in his Chapter 10.

Tuckett adds that there are several long discourses in Acts, Peter's speech in Acts 2, "Stephen's 52–verse oration in Acts 7" and the story of Cornelius's conversion in Acts 10. He sums up and asks another rhetorical question: "The appeal to Luke's desire for brevity thus seems unconvincing. The problem therefore remains: why does Luke split up all his material in the way he has?"[39] It is actually Tuckett's objections, however, that do not convince. Neither Luke 12:22–53 (32 verses), nor Luke 15:3–32 (30 verses), nor Luke 21:5–36 (31 verses), nor Acts 2:14–36 (23 verses) is substantially longer than the twelve to twenty or so verses that Goulder suggests as a rule of thumb for Luke. And Acts 10, the story of Cornelius's conversion, features at most ten verses of direct speech at a time (10:34–43).

---

36. Kloppenborg, *Excavating Q*, 16–17, emphasis original.
37. Surprisingly, he says that it is a "very fragile" argument, *Q*, 26–27 ("Existence," 41).
38. Goulder, *Luke*, 39.
39. Tuckett, *Q*, 27 ("Existence," 41).

In any case, though, Goulder is not simply focusing narrowly on "Luke's desire for brevity," as Tuckett puts it, but rather he is discussing Luke's attitude to source material, arguing against all those Q theorists who say that Luke's proposed procedure with Matthew's Sermon on the Mount would have been inexplicable. Goulder is making his case by pointing out that Luke does just the same thing with Mark on at least two clearly observable occasions, Mark 4:1–34 and Mark 9:33–50. Two of Tuckett's counter-examples, Luke 12:22–53 and Luke 15, and perhaps all of the examples from Acts, do not address this point. These passages are certainly a little longer than the twelve to twenty verses that Goulder suggests for Luke's "rule of thumb," but they are not cases of Luke retaining long discourses from source material.

Tuckett's counterexamples are useful in one way, however, in reminding us that Luke does not dislike lengthy discourses *per se*. They point to the necessity of refining Goulder's argument in the following way: although Luke's tendency is to reduce lengthy discourse, he has no ideological objection to long discourses in themselves but will use them, where necessary, in the interests of plausibility and good story line. Aspects of the Sermon, and for that matter Mark 4, can be made to serve Luke's greater purpose to write a plausible sequential narrative, some in the same position, other parts redistributed or omitted. At times it suits Luke to feature a longer discourse, but it will only be when the flow of the story demands it.

Stephen's speech in Acts 7, for example, has to be where it is in its entirety. It tells a story, the story of Israel and the Temple, and it could not reasonably be broken up. It is this very speech that leads to Stephen's death (7:54: "Now when they heard these things they were enraged ... "), partly because of its length, with its great sweeping claims that seem so arrogant to his disputants. Likewise, Luke's Chapter 15 is linked together thematically in a way that much of Matthew's Sermon is not. This chapter arguably constitutes the very heart of the Lukan Gospel: forgiveness, grace, repentance, all couched in Luke's splendidly creative parables of the Lost. Of course he will allow himself thirty verses together in such circumstances, and even then Luke 15 is less than a quarter of the length of Matthew's sermon.[40] Nor can Luke 21 really be urged in this context against Luke's use of Matthew. This is not an

---

40. And again there is a brief narrator's interlude at 15:11, εἶπεν δέ, the kind of interlude absent from the whole of Matthew's Sermon.

exceptionally long discourse — it is at most 29 verses (vv. 8–36, with breaks at vv. 10 and 29), again not a great deal longer than the suggested average of twelve to twenty verses. But in addition, like Stephen's Speech the material has a certain order. As Goulder says, Mark 13 is a "serial description of the future"[41] and does not easily lend itself to being broken up. Of course, as Tuckett points out, Matthew relocates part of it (Mark 13:9–13) to his Chapter 10 (Matt 10:17–22), but as Tuckett also admits, Matthew repeats its substance in its proper context in his Chapter 24 (Matt 24:9–13), and this is the key point, that the discourse of Mark 13 belongs together.[42] Matthew apparently does not feel at liberty in his version of the eschatological discourse to omit the section he had recounted earlier in his mission discourse.

The Sermon on the Mount is manifestly unlike this and lends itself happily to being epitomized, broken up, reworked and redistributed. This is, after all, the way that the Sermon has often been taken.

The Matthean Nature of the Sermon

Luke's attitude to the Sermon is, in any case, dictated by a further consideration which has long been self-evident to Q theorists, that Matthew's Sermon on the Mount is exactly that, Matthew's Sermon, and it is its very Matthean character that no doubt encouraged Luke to make his radical revisions. Nearly all scholars, after all, recognize the Sermon's thoroughly Matthean nature.[43] Stanton, for example, claims that here "Matthew has sought to meet the needs of Christians in his own day," adding that "Matthew's first discourse contains many of his own distinctive emphases."[44]

---

41. *Luke*, 39.

42. This issue of the relationship between Mark 13 and parallels is, of course, a complex one. Here, I am merely concerned to press the point that Luke's keeping of Mark 13 intact in Luke 21 need not tell against his not having kept Matthew's Sermon on the Mount intact in Luke 6.

43. The main exception is Hans Dieter Betz, who sees it as a pre-Matthean epitome of Jesus' teaching. See his *The Sermon on the Mount: A Commentary on the Sermon on the Mount including the Sermon on the Plain* (Minneapolis: Fortress, 1995). Though widely praised for its excellence on the exegetical level, its thesis that the Sermon as we have it in Matthew is essentially pre-Matthean has won no support. See, for example, the review by Dale Allison, *JBL* 117 (1998): 136–38.

44. G. Stanton, *Gospel for a New People*, 286. Cf. John Riches, *Matthew* (New Testament Guides; Sheffield: Sheffield Academic Press, 1996), 68: "What we have here is not just a set of rules but the foundation document of a new religious community which sees itself as children of a heavenly father who will forgive and reward the 'righteous.'"

But this is a crucial observation. On the standard theory, it is assumed that the Matthean nature of the Sermon results from the evangelist's having adapted and arranged Q and other material.[45] It is then held to follow from this that Luke's version of the Sermon is closer to the original Q version, especially as the Sermon on the Plain is less distinctively Lukan than the Sermon on the Mount is distinctively Matthean. Yet the theory of Luke's use of Matthew makes equally as good an account of the data as does the Q theory. For Q skeptics, material in the Sermon becomes "distinctively Matthean" not because of what Matthew has added to Q but rather because of what Luke has left out of Matthew. That is, Luke does not feature, practically by definition, those parts of Matthew's Sermon that are distinctive of the first evangelist.

For if we imagine, for a moment, Luke with a copy of Matthew's very Matthean Sermon in front of him, how is it likely that he would have proceeded?[46] First, he will have seen the need to shorten it, for it is distinctive of Matthew to feature such enormous discourses, and characteristic of Luke to prefer shorter ones, since anything so long will rupture the flow of his story.[47] But what should one leave out? What parts would make good sense elsewhere? Well, what is least congenial to Luke is the heavy emphasis on the Law which dominates Matthew 5 and, not surprisingly, this is largely left on one side by Luke. Indeed some Q theorists such as Fitzmyer can see this very principle at work:

> Luke seems also to have eliminated some material that was in the nucleus sermon (and in "Q"?) because it was more suited to Jewish-Christian concerns and less suited to the Gentile Christians for whom he has primarily destined his account.[48]

Not for Luke either is the stereotyped, repeated formula, "You have heard....But I say to you" of the so-called antitheses (Matt 5:21, 27, 31, 33, 38, 43). Outside of this mechanical structure, though, much of

---

45. For example Stanton, *Gospel for a New People*, 286. Incidentally, I have no objection to this argument, that Matthew has creatively molded traditional materials in the light of his own situation and theology. My disagreement with the consensus concerns the attempt to gain access to the traditional materials by analyzing the parallels in Luke since the latter are better understood as Luke's reworkings of material found in Matthew.

46. See Mark Matson, "Luke's Rewriting of the Sermon on the Mount," *Society of Biblical Literature Seminar Papers 2000* (Society of Biblical Literature Seminar Paper Series, 39; Atlanta: Society of Biblical Literature, 2000), 623–50, for a recent, well-argued case for the plausibility of Luke's reworking of the Sermon.

47. Notice that Stanton himself admits as much even for Matthew: "the five discourses may break up the flow of the narrative..." (*Gospel for a New People*, 319).

48. J. Fitzmyer, *Luke I–IX*, 628.

this material is redeemable and some will be used in appropriate contexts when they crop up later (Matt 5:25–26 in Luke 12:58–59, for example). And one part will lend itself to exposition here, the matter on loving enemies (Matt 5:43–48 // Luke 6:27–36).

Love Your Enemies

Why does Luke focus on the material about loving enemies? The answer may be that already in Matthew this pericope is concerned with persecution, "Love your enemies *and pray for those who persecute you*" (5:44). In Luke this is made more explicit by the fourfold parallelism: "Love your enemies, do good to those who hate you, bless those who curse you, pray for those who abuse you" (6:27). This stress in Luke should give us the clue; he wants to focus on persecution, the strident theme on which both his Blessings and his Woes conclude. For just as Matthew's Beatitudes finish with the blessing on "those who are persecuted for righteousness' sake" (5:10) with a connected exposition (5:11–12),[49] so too Luke's last beatitude is a fourfold blessing: "Blessed are you when people hate you and when they exclude you and revile you and cast out your name as evil for the sake of the Son of Man" (Luke 6:22). But the persecution theme is brought out in Luke not just in the fresh rhetoric but also in the final, contrasting woe on those who are not persecuted: "Woe to you, when all people speak well of you, for in the same way their fathers did to the false prophets" (Luke 6:26).

But whereas in Matthew the theme of persecution ends here until it reappears in the loving of enemies material at the end of the chapter, in Luke the theme is reinforced straight away by the loving of enemies material which follows straight on from this (6:27–36). Luke has, in other words, in shortening the discourse and omitting and redistributing Matthean matter about the Law, seized on and exploited an important theme present in Matthew 5, that of persecution, by drawing together Blessings, Woes, and the Love of Enemies.

---

49. The standard appeal to Matthew's "nine" beatitudes is unduly influenced by the parallel between Matt 5:11–12 and Luke 6:22–23. The so-called "ninth" is quite different in form from the previous eight and is identical in substance with the eighth, thus 5:11–12 is best seen as expounding the eighth beatitude, just as 6:14–15 is an exposition of the petition "forgive us our debts ..." (6:12) in the Lord's Prayer, and not part of that prayer itself. Cf. Michael Goulder, *Midrash,* 254–56; *Luke,* 350–51.

The Second Half of Matthew's Sermon

But what of the rest of Luke's version of the Sermon? To see how he has proceeded, it is important to bear in mind another feature of Matthew's Sermon that has, like its markedly Matthean character, long been evident to Q theorists, and that is the question of the structure of its second half. Fitzmyer speaks of Matt 6:19–7:27 as "a series of loosely related sayings"[50] and Stanton echoes this:

> What about the structure of the second half of the Sermon? Matt 6:19–7:11 has long puzzled interpreters. This part of the Sermon seems to be a "rag-bag" of sayings, only some of which are loosely related to others.[51]

This accurate observation is illuminating for the theory that Luke has read Matthew, for if interpreters have long been puzzled about the arrangement of these sayings, it would not be surprising if one of its earliest interpreters, Luke, shared their view. It is worth asking, therefore, how one might relate this observation to the standard objections to Luke's having known Matthew's Sermon. Stanton, a few pages earlier, had dispensed with the view that Luke knew Matthew's Sermon on the Mount with the following comment:

> Opponents of this view claim, surely correctly, that if Luke did use Matthew, he acted in a quite arbitrary way. He has failed to include numerous sayings at any point in his gospel . . . he has placed the remainder in six different places with little regard for Matthew's order.[52]

If Stanton and others are right here, that there is a relatively loose structure in the latter part of the Sermon, then the argument from the inexplicability of Luke's editorial behavior is compromised. Perhaps Luke too thought of it as a "rag-bag" and selected from it what he thought most appropriate to the occasion. It is quite right to think of Luke here

---

50. Fitzmyer, *Luke I–IX*, 629; cf. K. Grayston, "Sermon on the Mount" in *IDB*, "7.1–12 is an oddly assorted group of sayings"; cf. John Riches, *Matthew*, 67–68.

51. G. Stanton, *Gospel for a New People*, 298; repeated in G. Stanton, "The Sermon on the Mount" in *DBI*, 625–28 (esp. 628).

52. G. Stanton, *Gospel for a New People*, 288. The question of Luke not having included some matter from Matthew's Sermon anywhere in his Gospel is only problematic if one assumes that no evangelist would ever leave out anything substantial from his source, an assumption which is both unhelpful and, on the assumption of Markan priority, patently false, for Luke has omitted much from Mark.

having "little regard for Matthew's order"; the mistake is to assume that that is the same thing as "act[ing] in a quite arbitrary way."[53]

This straightforward point is generally missed in the scholarship. The difficulty for those who want to challenge Q is that the issue has usually been dismissed before one actually looks at the Sermon. Frequent repetition of this aspect of the argument from the order has numbed scholars to noticing the contradiction inherent in it. There is a simple choice: either one apologizes for the clearly observable lack of order in the second half, or abandons this tenet of the case for Q.

Luke has, then, taken the "rag bag" of sayings and has placed them in appropriate contexts in his Gospel. In our next chapter we will look at the ideal literary context provided by Luke for Matt 6:25–34 (Luke 12:22–31, "Consider the lilies"), which falls in the heart of this section in Matthew. Furthermore, Luke moves Matt 6:19–21 (Treasures on Earth) into place just after "Consider the lilies," in Luke 12:33–34, providing an ideal linking verse in 12:32, "Do not fear, little flock...." Likewise, Matt 6:24 (Two Masters) is moved appropriately to the material that follows on from the odd Unjust Steward parable (Luke 16:1–13), and Matt 7:7–11 (Asking and Receiving) functions ideally in Luke's section on prayer (11:1–13) where it comments most effectively on the Friend at Midnight that precedes it (11:5–8).

The same is not true throughout. Matthew 6:22–23 (the Single Eye) is reproduced in Luke 11:34–36, in connection with the Lamp Under a Bushel (11:33; cf. 8:16 and par.) and following on from the Sign of Jonah (11:29–32), and the flow of thought is not as clear as we might like it to be. Nevertheless, since the context for this material in Matthew is no easier to understand, even in this instance there is no difficulty for the case against Q. There is no question of Luke "destroying Matthew's fine order,"[54] only of his working with something that is already problematic in Matthew.

When the matter from the latter part of the Sermon has been redistributed, then, most of it to appropriate contexts, what remains? First,

53. G. Stanton, *Gospel for a New People*, 288. The contradiction is explicit in Fitzmyer too, who makes both points, that Luke's reordering of the Sermon is inexplicable on the basis of his knowledge of Matthew (see p. 110, n. 12 below), and that the structure of the latter part of the Sermon is loose (see p. 99 above)."

54. I do not have the space to comment on every single aspect of the Sermon but I hope that the general point is clear. Matt 7:6 is probably omitted by Luke as a detail of Jewish practice of less practical interest to Luke than to Matthew, just as he also omits Matt 5:22 and 18:17. Matt 7:13–14 (the Narrow Gate) is given an excellent new context in Luke 13:24, part of the section 13:22–35.

there is Matt 7:1–5, reproduced in Luke 6:37–42, often labeled in both Matthew and Luke "On Judging"[55] or "Judging Others."[56] This label, though quite accurate, does obscure an important theme in the material, that of reciprocity, or "doing unto others." This is a theme already present in Matthew's Sermon, most notably, of course, in Matt 7:12, "Therefore whatsoever you wish that people would do to you, likewise also do unto them," but it becomes even more prominent in Luke. He has already reproduced Matt 7:12 in Luke 6:31, and the theme overlaps with and illustrates the theme of persecution that is prominent in the first part of Luke's sermon. Individuals are to love their enemies, to do good to those who hate them, and to expect nothing in return.

But now Luke has the opportunity to develop this theme further by using Matt 7:1–5 in juxtaposition with the material already gleaned from Matt 5. Indeed, he expands Matt 7:1–5 with alacrity and is inspired to the finest poetic moment in his Gospel:

> Give and it will be given to you; good measure, pressed down, shaken together, running over, will be put into your lap.
>
> (Luke 6:38)

The importance of this for the case against Q is to notice that Matt 7:1–5, unlike its parallel in Luke 6:37–42, does not have any clear connection with what goes before it (in Matthew this is 6:25–34, "Consider the lilies"). The material here comes rather as a surprise. Luke, by contrast, has crafted this aspect of his Sermon carefully.

Luke has, therefore, dealt most appropriately with the "rag bag" section Matt 6:19–7:11. What then remains? 7:12 (the Golden Rule) is, as we saw above, in place in the Lukan sermon (Luke 6:31), and 7:13–14 (Narrow Gate) is relocated in Luke 13:22–30 with other similar material on the judgment of those who are outside of the kingdom, some of it (13:25–27) from Matt 7:21–23.

This leaves us with most of Matt 7:15–27, on False Prophets, those who say "Lord, Lord" and the parable of the Two Builders. There is here a clear thread of thought,[57] focused especially on hearing, saying, and doing. One will be judged by what one does — otherwise words will be hollow and hypocritical — in this way both Matthew's and Luke's

---

55. So Huck-Greeven, *Synopse,* Pericope 48, 40.
56. So UBS3 for both Matt 7:1–5 and Luke 6:37–42.
57. Cf. Stanton, *Gospel for a New People,* 297, "The Sermon is rounded off by an epilogue, 7.13–27, in which, as we shall see, there is considerable coherence."

sermons end with the theme of reciprocity not far away. Luke keeps
Matthew's material intact here with relatively minor changes and omissions (Luke 6:43–49), one of them, as we have just seen, the relocation
of most of the "Lord, Lord" matter to 13:25–27. This same conclusion
to both sermons, Matt 7:15–27 and Luke 6:43–49, provides no problems, of course, for the thesis that Luke has derived his Sermon from
Matthew's.

The Less Lukan Sermon on the Plain

The difficulty with this survey, however, is that it runs the risk of sound-
ing superficial and unconvincing to the Q theorist who is used to seeing
the Lukan Sermon as the one that best represents the Q sermon.[58] For it
is not only that Matthew's Sermon is very Matthean, it is also that Luke's
Sermon is not, apparently, very Lukan, a state of affairs easily explicable,
at first sight, on the Q hypothesis. As Stanton says: "Matthew's first discourse contains many of his own distinctive emphases. Luke's Sermon is
also related to his overall purposes, though much less clearly."[59] Several
points need to be made in response to this.

1. It is a question of what one is looking for. The Q hypothesis is
   generally assumed before one begins looking at the Lukan Sermon,
   which is then taken as best representing the Q Sermon which has
   been transformed by Matthew. The emphasis in the scholarship
   is naturally, under such circumstances, twofold — first, to discover
   the underlying Q Sermon and second, to analyze just how Matthew
   has redacted it to produce his distinctive piece. The extent to which
   the Lukan Sermon might be distinctively Lukan thus gets largely
   bypassed.

2. The Sermon is actually Lukan in several important respects. We
   have already seen how Luke draws out his peculiarly unique themes
   of persecution and reciprocity, focusing them by stressing the love
   of enemies in quite characteristic vein; one only has to think of the
   Good Samaritan (10:25–37) to confirm just how important a theme
   this is to the third evangelist. Furthermore, the whole Sermon in

---

58. Streeter is insistent on this point — the Q Sermon is "practically identical with Luke's
Sermon on the Plain," *Four Gospels*, 251. Catchpole agrees with this consensus with some
reservations (*Quest*, 79, etc.).

59. Stanton, *Gospel for a New People*, 286.

Luke begins in the most distinctive Lukan mode imaginable, with a blessing on the poor (6:20), with its corresponding woe to the rich (6:24). No theme resonates through the Gospel as clearly as this one, the reversal of fortunes for the poor and rich, from the Magnificat (1:46–55), to Jesus' inaugural sermon in Nazara (4:16–30), to the parable of the Rich Man and Lazarus (16:19–31). It is quite surprising, in the light of all this, to see the extent to which the Lukan "Blessed are the poor" has been regarded as due to Q and not Luke.[60]

3. Perhaps most importantly, one needs to realize what the evidence looks like from the perspective of Luke's knowledge of Matthew. Q theorists rarely pause to consider that the data that they assume supports their theory can often be explained just as effectively by the competing one. Luke, on the Farrer theory, has made "Luke-pleasing" selections from Matthew's Sermon and so, if Luke is using Matthew, we would expect to find a characteristically Matthean Sermon and a less characteristically Lukan Sermon. We thus have a situation that makes as much sense on Luke's use of Matthew as it does on the Q hypothesis. Luke's Sermon is indeed Lukan, but it is a Lukan crafting of material taken over from Matthew. The character and tone of the respective Sermons, Matthew's and Luke's, is as conducive to the Farrer theory as it is to the Q hypothesis.

Conclusion

The consensus view has always had difficulty with one of the most important pieces of evidence, Luke's preface, in which the third evangelist tells Theophilus what he believes he is doing: he is writing *in order* (καθεξῆς, Luke 1:3).[61] The mystery for two-source theorists has been why Luke should so stress this writing in order, alongside a mention of the "many"

---

60. See further Chapter 7, below.
61. See here the excellent discussion in Goulder, *Luke*, 198–204. See also the comments by John Drury, *Tradition and Design*, 82, "The adverb καθεξῆς lets the reader into Luke's reason for writing and his way of going about it. At Luke 8:1 and Acts 18:23 he uses it of Jesus and Paul travelling from place to place, at Acts 3:24 of a succession of prophecy beginning with Samuel which foretold the events he narrates, and at Acts 11:4 of Peter telling in orderly succession the events which led him to support the admission of the Gentiles. Its meaning emerges as 'in succession,' 'connectedly' or 'in historical order.' It testifies to Luke's enthusiasm for temporal succession as his vehicle for theology, a conviction inherited from the Old Testament and, above all, from the Deuteronomistic historian whose Succession Narrative, well so called, deployed it on an equally epic scale."

(πολλοί, Luke 1:1) who have undertaken to write before him, for on this standard theory Luke's order is, essentially, simply Mark's order plus Q's order; there is little special about it, and certainly nothing to justify the rather marked emphasis.

The Q theory has, however, become a mind-set, and many have got used to the idea that Luke faithfully preserves the order of both Mark and Q, so much so that this supposition gets bound into the arguments against the opposing positions. But analogies from Luke's use of Mark, attention to the distinction between narrative and sayings, and recognition of the role the priority of Mark may have played for Luke himself, go a long way toward clarifying and explaining Luke's reordering of Matthew. Streeter misleads the reader in speaking of "meticulous precision," "utmost care," "tear[ing] every little piece" and so on.[62] As soon as Luke is committed to following the Markan order, there is simply no question of attempting to follow the Matthean order in the same way. The one excludes the possibility of the other: Matthew's double tradition material appears in the context of a reordered Mark, a reordering that is not congenial to Luke. In any case, such a perverse,[63] scissors-and-paste Luke, anachronistic and implausible enough to have convinced many of the existence of Q, is not at all necessary to seeing how Luke might have used Matthew. More important than anything else discussed so far is the observation that Luke is one of the great literary artists of the New Testament, an observation all too easily lost when one spends too long dwelling on the old-fashioned, narrowly source-critical focus of Streeter and those in his legacy. For Luke's purposes, as everyone acknowledges, were quite different from Matthew's. If Luke is attempting to write a connected narrative with plausible biographical development, then it follows that Matthew's structure with its five great thematically linked edifices, built into his restructuring of Mark, will simply not do. One might almost say that the real perversity is not this believable Luke, who skillfully and creatively incorporated elements of Matthew and Mark into the first volume of a grand-scale, sequential narrative, but the Luke of the Q theory, who is criticized for writing a Gospel with a different order from Matthew, and then excused for doing so by allowing him the defense of loyalty to a source that no one has ever seen.

---

62. B. H. Streeter, *Four Gospels*, 183.
63. Cf. Streeter's review of H. G. Jameson, *The Origin of the Synoptic Gospels* in *Theology* 7/37 (July 1923): 60: "Luke also, then, on this theory, is a perverse crank." The review is given in full in Neville, *Arguments from Order*, 137.

Chapter Five

LUKE, NARRATIVE CRITICISM, AND THE SERMON ON THE MOUNT

It is a commonly held view that study of the Synoptic Problem is complex, irrelevant, and boring.[1] One will do well to avoid entering this corner of New Testament study and to steer clear of those who practice it. For one thing, it is dated. Obsession with the minutiae of the Greek texts in synopsis — the counting of words, the location of "minor agreements," the compilation of intricate charts — this is the stuff of yesteryear, the concern of bookish scholars whose world was their study. For another thing, the solution to the problem is pretty well established. It has been tried and tested and found to be both workable and plausible. Ninety-five percent of scholars accept it, most of whom have sensibly moved on to other, more profitable areas of study.

In this chapter I would like to depart from the redaction-critical base of most of the discussion so far to propose something different. Among the many newer approaches to the New Testament is one that might inject some fresh life into the study of the Synoptic Problem — narrative criticism of the Gospels. At first, this might sound most unlikely. The one discipline is wedded to the historical-critical approach; the other is in large part a reaction against it. The Synoptic Problem is all about the search for sources with which narrative criticism has no concern.

Yet a moment's pause for thought confirms that something exciting might happen when these two unlikely partners are introduced to one another. The ground has been prepared by those scholars who are calling for a rapprochement between older, historical-critical perspectives and the newer methodologies in the hope that the diversity of approaches will generate lively, new dialogues and not cacophony.[2] And narrative

---

1. R. E. Brown, *An Introduction to the New Testament* (The Anchor Bible Reference Library; New York: Doubleday, 1997), 111. "Most readers," Brown claims, will find the Synoptic Problem "complex, irrelevant to their interests and boring."

2. Cf. David B. Gowler, "Heteroglossic Trends in Biblical Studies: Polyphonic Dialogues

criticism has received a cautious welcome from several scholars who want to see it acting as a handmaiden of more traditional models of doing exegesis. Raymond Brown, for example, in his recent *Introduction to the New Testament,* showed an overall antipathy to newer methodologies, yet admitted some sympathy for the fruits of recent narrative-critical work.[3] Likewise, M. C. de Boer speaks of the potential for narrative criticism as "a useful first tool in the repertoire of the historical critic" even if "the real work of interpretation has only begun when the work of the narrative critic is finished."[4]

But there is indeed a problem with the proposed discussion. Not only are Synoptic Problem experts, on the whole, ignorant of or uninterested in narrative criticism, but narrative criticism is rarely, if ever, thought to have direct relevance to the Synoptic Problem. Insofar as it is even mentioned in narrative-critical studies, it is only brought up with a view to explaining the difference between the concerns of the historical critic and the concerns of the narrative critic. Mark Allan Powell, for example, explains:

> For narrative critics, then, questions concerning whether Luke's Gospel was written by a companion of Paul or whether the Evangelist drew some of his material from the Gospel of Mark or from a now lost Q document are irrelevant. These questions are significant for historical critics who wish to make judgments concerning the historical reliability of Luke's work or who want to determine the theological agenda of the Gospel's redactor. But they are not significant for appreciating and understanding Luke's Gospel as a completed work of literature that must, in any case, be interpreted from the perspective of its implied author.[5]

---

or Clanging Cymbals?" *Review and Exposition* 97/4 (2000): 443–66, and Anthony Thiselton, "New Testament Interpretation in Historical Perspective," in *Hearing the New Testament: Strategies for Interpretation* (ed. Joel B. Green; Grand Rapids: Eerdmans; Carlisle: Paternoster, 1995), 10–36, especially 36. For some introductory reflections on the possibilities of dialogue between the historical-critical approach and newer methods, see my " 'Drawing from the Treasure Both New and Old': Current Trends in New Testament Studies," *Scripture Bulletin* 27/2 (July 1997): 66–77.

    3. R. E. Brown, *Introduction to the New Testament,* 25–26.

    4. M. C. de Boer, "Narrative Criticism, Historical Criticism, and the Gospel of John," *JSNT* 45 (1992): 35–48; reproduced in *The Interpretation of John* (ed. John Ashton; 2d ed.; Studies in New Testament Interpretation; Edinburgh: T & T Clark, 1997), 301–14, 309.

    5. Mark Allan Powell, "Narrative Criticism" in *Hearing the New Testament: Strategies for Interpretation* (ed. Joel B. Green; Grand Rapids: Eerdmans; Carlisle: Paternoster, 1995), 239–55 (241). My choice of quotation here only attempts to illustrate the way in which the relationship between the historical-critical approach and narrative criticism is generally con-

Powell is, of course, quite right. It is essential for any reader who wants to take narrative criticism seriously to be clear about the differences between this, as an approach focused on the text, its implied author and its implied readers, and an historical-critical approach focused on reconstructions of sources, communities and an historical author. Nevertheless, it is worth asking whether there might be other reasons for looking at narrative criticism and the Synoptic Problem together. Given the essential difference between the approaches, might there be grounds for dialogue between them, and might this dialogue shed some fresh light on the Gospels?

The potential scope for dialogue might be illustrated by looking at the issue of "intertextuality," a key concern in narrative criticism. The term is seldom applied to the interrelationship between the Gospels, but is regularly used of the interplay between the Gospels and the Hebrew Bible. When narrative critics focus on Luke, intertextuality tends to be about Luke and Isaiah, Luke and Deuteronomy, Luke and Genesis and never Luke and Mark, or Luke and Matthew. Narrative critics might reasonably reply that the implied reader knows about the Hebrew Scriptures and is expected to engage with Luke's references to them and development of favorite themes in the light of them. This is true of course. But the implied reader is familiar not only with the Hebrew Bible but also, apparently, with something similar in kind to the third Gospel. Luke's preface (1:1–4) famously tells us about the πολλοί ("many") who have drawn up a διήγησις ("narrative") of their own. While the implied reader is not necessarily familiar with these, s/he has at least been "instructed" (κατηχήθης) in something closely resembling them, and on the topic of which Luke's Gospel is now going to give the truth (ἀσφαλεῖα).

The tendency to bypass the interrelationships of the Gospels when dealing with the question of intertextuality is symptomatic of a concern over the way narrative criticism is currently practiced. The desire to look each of the Gospels (or in the case of Luke, Luke-Acts) as a unity can be overplayed. In looking at texts in isolation from each other, it becomes all too easy to forget that these are texts that have, and have always been perceived as having, an intimate interrelationship, an interrelationship

---

ceived. In many ways this has been a necessary stage in the evolution of biblical criticism, which often first stresses a method's essential difference from existing methods, before in due course looking towards the possibilities of dialogue between the new and the old. It is worth adding that Powell is in fact one of those who has written excellent pieces from both a narrative-critical and an historical-critical viewpoint.

that — when it is submitted to scrutiny — could inject fresh energy into narrative-critical approaches. There are several ways in which this might happen. One might be able to shed light on the literary structure of one Gospel, for example, by comparing it with the literary structure of one or more of the others. Or the narrative critic might be able to illustrate the aptness of the placing of an incident or saying in the narrative of one Gospel by comparing the location of one of its parallels in the narrative of another Gospel. The same might apply to other elements in narrative criticism like characterization, the role of the narrator, narrative devices, and so on. In other words, there may well be potential for the Synopsis to help rather than hinder the work of the narrative critic.

One of the problems, however, is that the Synopsis is thought of as a tool that has relevance exclusively to those working with an historical-critical approach. It does not, on the whole, occur to narrative critics that there could be any other reason for comparing, say, Luke to Mark than a source-critical or a redaction-critical one. Narrative critics have allowed themselves, in other words, to be seduced by the assumption that one uses a Synopsis solely with a view to using the text as a window onto Jesus and Christian origins.

Joel Green's otherwise refreshing commentary on Luke is typical of this perspective.[6] In over 850 pages of thorough, detailed narrative-critical commentary, he studiously avoids bringing up a single synoptic parallel. For Green's implied readers, who know both Matthew and Mark (and who may know Thomas, the Didache and other early Christian texts too), there is an inevitable artificiality in discussing passages like the Lord's Prayer without a sideways glance across the Synopsis, or flicking over a few pages in the New Testament, especially given that Green is careful to find comparison between this prayer and the Eighteen Benedictions.[7] The narrative critic sheds light on Luke's Gospel by appealing to its mother, the Hebrew Bible, but construes the Gospel as an only child. Perhaps now its siblings, Matthew, Mark, and John, should be called upon for help too.

The value of narrative criticism for the study of the Synoptics more broadly is its potential to free scholars of some of the standard assumptions made by source criticism and so to test them. In particular, we might ask the question: do the kinds of things that get taken for granted

---

6. Joel Green, *The Gospel of Luke* (The New International Commentary on the New Testament; Grand Rapids: Eerdmans, 1997).

7. Ibid., 439.

by Synoptic scholars stand up to narrative-critical scrutiny? Or, to turn the question on its head, might a reading of Luke's Gospel sensitive to narrative-critical concerns help the source critic in his or her task? Specifically, it will be useful to bring some of the discussions of the order of Luke's Gospel into narrative-critical focus.

As we have seen already,[8] the commonly held view is that Luke's ordering of events in his Gospel, and especially his Central Section, is inexplicable on the assumption of his use of Matthew. It is one of the chief planks on which the Q theory rests. Matthew's order is seen as logical, structured, clear, coherent; Luke's is regarded as only making sense on the assumption that it follows, on the whole, the order of Q. Graham Stanton, for example, says that if Luke read Matthew, he "has virtually demolished Matthew's carefully constructed discourses"[9] and Christopher Tuckett echoes:

> If Luke knew Matthew, why has he changed the Matthean order so thoroughly, disrupting Matthew's clear and concise arrangement of the teaching material into five blocks, each concerned with a particular theme?[10]

Both statements go back to the classic, highly influential statement by Streeter:

> If then Luke derived this material from Matthew, he must have gone through both Matthew and Mark so as to discriminate with meticulous precision between Marcan and non-Marcan material; he must then have proceeded with the utmost care to tear every little piece of non-Marcan material he desired to use from the context of Mark in which it appeared in Matthew — in spite of the fact that contexts in Matthew are always exceedingly appropriate — in order to re-insert it into a different context of Mark having no special appropriateness. A theory which would make an author capable of such a proceeding would only be tenable if, on other grounds, we had reason to believe he was a crank.[11]

---

8. See above, pp. 59–61 and Chapter 4, throughout.
9. Graham N. Stanton, "Matthew, Gospel of" in *DBI*, ad loc.
10. Christopher M. Tuckett, "Synoptic Problem" in *ABD*, VI, 263–70 (esp. 268).
11. Streeter, *The Four Gospels*, 183. Cf. also the earlier, similar statement by H. J. Holtzmann, *Die synoptischen Evangelien*, 130; and later statements by G. M. Styler, "If Matthew is Luke's source, there seems to be no common-sense explanation for his order and procedure." "Synoptic Problem" in *The Oxford Companion to the Bible* (ed. Bruce M. Metzger and Michael D. Coogan; Oxford: Oxford University Press, 1993): 724–27 (esp. 726); cf.

Let us be clear about what is being claimed here. Contemporary synoptic scholars like Stanton and Tuckett are, in the tradition of Streeter, pointing out the absurdity of the idea that Luke read Matthew *because of the order of material in Luke.* The Q theory is a necessity; without it we cannot make sense of Luke's order.

The focus for this question is usually on the supposed reordering of the Sermon on the Mount in Luke, with specific reference to its parallels in Luke's Central Section. Holtzmann, Kümmel, and Fitzmyer all make it clear that this would be especially absurd. They think that Luke is far too sensitive and literary an artist to have been capable of a reworking of the Sermon on the Mount that is usually lampooned using the imagery of "violence" and "destruction."[12] What I propose, therefore, in this section of the chapter, is to undertake a brief narrative-critical survey of some of the relevant material in order to see if the extravagant claims bear scrutiny. Let us focus on two parts of the Central Section which parallel material from the Sermon on the Mount.

Luke 11:1–13

Narrative-critical reading

The first part of Luke's Central Section to feature parallels to the Sermon on the Mount is Luke 11:1–13. This unit is made up of three parts:

Luke 11:1–4	Parallel Matt 6:9–13	Lord's Prayer
Luke 11:5–8	No parallel	Parable of the Friend at Midnight
Luke 11:9–13	Parallel Matt 7:7–11	"Ask and you shall receive"

First we need to ask whether there is any sign of unity of theme here. Indeed there is. Luke 11:1–13 is made up, as has long been recognized, of three sections on prayer. This is not, though, just a compilation of loosely related material on prayer. It is linked at a deeper level in that

---

Reginald H. Fuller, *The New Testament in Current Study,* 87; Arland Jacobson, *The First Gospel,* 18.

12. Kümmel, *Introduction to the New Testament,* 50: "This hypothesis [viz. Luke's use of Matthew] is completely untenable. What could have moved Luke to break up Matthew's Sermon on the Mount and to embody part of it in his Sermon on the Plain, to distribute part over the various chapters of his Gospel, and to omit part?" J. Fitzmyer: "Why would so literary an artist as Luke want to destroy the Matthean masterpiece of the Sermon on the Mount?" *Luke I–IX,* 74. It is the thesis of this chapter that it is precisely because Luke is "so literary an artist" that he would have wanted creatively to rework the Sermon on the Mount.

each segment deals with an aspect of the Fatherhood of God.[13] It begins and ends with the affirmation of a relationship to God that is constituted by the imagery of Father and Son, from the first line of the prayer, πάτερ ("Father," 11:2) to the last line of the exhortation, πόσῳ μᾶλλον ὁ πατὴρ [ὁ] ἐξ οὐρανοῦ δώσει πνεῦμα ἅγιον τοῖς αἰτοῦσιν αὐτόν ("how much more will the heavenly Father give the Holy Spirit to those who ask him," 11:13).

The narrative critic will be alert to several other factors in this section. For one thing, the disciples' request in 11:1, κύριε, δίδαξον ἡμᾶς προσεύχεσθαι ("Lord, teach us to pray"), is entirely expected, both from the immediate context, in which Jesus is depicted as ἐν τόπῳ τινὶ προσευχόμενον ("praying in a certain place," 11:1) and the broader context which features several accounts of prayer, 3:21–22; 6:12; 9:18, 28; 10:21–22 and especially 5:16 (αὐτὸς δὲ ἦν ὑποχωρῶν ἐν ταῖς ἐρήμοις καὶ προσευχόμενος, "But he would often withdraw to lonely places and pray"). Jesus' withdrawal to pray is clearly presented as characteristic activity.[14] This narrative technique, the combination of the long-term build-up and immediate catalyst, is frequent in Luke. One might compare, for example, Luke 7:18–23 (Messengers from John) in which Jesus' answer concerning his healing activity has been anticipated not only by the healings performed at that very moment (7:21, ἐν ἐκείνῃ τῇ ὥρᾳ ἐθεράπευσεν πολλούς . . .),[15] but also in the healing of many in the earlier chapters (especially 5:12–16; 5:17–26; 6:6–11; 6:17–19; 7:1–10; and 7:11–17).

Likewise, the disciples' (or others') foil question or comment is regularly a feature used by the narrator in Luke's Gospel to introduce teaching material.[16] And the reader has been prepared for the content of the question, "Lord, teach us to pray even as John taught his disciples" by the reference to John the Baptist's disciples' prayer in 5:33. But the narrator has prepared for the current section in a much richer way too, and a way often missed in the commentaries less sensitive to narrative-critical concerns. As Joel Green says:

---

13. Joel Green gives this section the subtitle "The Fatherhood of God," *The Gospel of Luke*, 437.

14. Joel Green, *The Gospel of Luke*, 440.

15. Contrast the parallel in Matt 11:2–6 in which there is no immediate catalyst.

16. For an introduction to foil questions and comments in Luke, see Michael Goulder, *Luke*, 90–91 and for a discussion, see Mark Goodacre, *Goulder and the Gospels*, 146–50.

Earlier, in a scene characterized as this one is by the relative seclusion of Jesus with the disciples, Jesus referred to God as his Father five times, both in prayer and instruction (10.21–22). In that cotext, he spoke of himself as the Son who was uniquely able to reveal the Father to those whom he chose. *This is precisely what he does in the current scene.*[17]

In other words, Jesus is now enacting, in 11:1–13, that commission first revealed in 10:22 Πάντα μοι παρεδόθη ὑπὸ τοῦ πατρός μου, καὶ οὐδεὶς γινώσκει τίς ἐστιν ὁ υἱὸς εἰ μὴ ὁ πατήρ, καὶ τίς ἐστιν ὁ πατὴρ εἰ μὴ ὁ υἱὸς καὶ ᾧ ἐὰν βούληται ὁ υἱὸς ἀποκαλύψαι ("All things have been committed to me by my Father. No one knows who the Son is except the Father, and no one knows who the Father is except the Son and those to whom the Son chooses to reveal him"). Jesus calls his disciples together and chooses to reveal to them what he has recently received from his Father; and he teaches them appropriately about the mutual fictive kinship, and their relationship to God in prayer.

Two more features ought to be noticed. First, the direct speech in 11:5–8 continues uninterrupted in 11:9–13. The occasional tendency to place a break between pericopae here, on account of the presence and absence of parallels, vv. 5–8 being L material[18] and vv. 9–13 double tradition, should be avoided.[19] Narrative criticism teaches the reader to take seriously the points at which the narrator signals a break, and there is no such signal here. Verses 9–13 follow seamlessly from vv. 5–8, affirming God's grace in giving his children what they ask.

Second, there is a device used here that will reappear in the next example: parable illuminated by appended exhortation based upon and adding to it. Theme, vocabulary, and imagery from the parable recur in the exhortatory material — θύρα κέκλεισται (door shut, v. 7) and τῷ κρούοντι ἀνοιγήσεται (to the one who knocks, it is opened, v. 10), father and children (vv. 7 and 11–13), giving (δίδωμι, vv. 7, 8, 9 and 13 and ἐπιδίδωμι, vv. 11–12) and the "how much more" concept beginning with εἰ (if, vv. 8 and 13). A famous example of the same thing, exhorta-

---

17. Joel Green, *The Gospel of Luke*, 438; emphasis original.

18. Some of course place the Friend at Midnight parable in Q, e.g., David Catchpole, *The Quest for Q*, Chapter 7 ("Prayer and the Kingdom"). In some ways this simply reinforces the point, that 11:5–13 makes good, coherent sense as a unit, and that damage is done to it if one element is eliminated.

19. In Kurt Aland, ed., *Synopsis Quattuor Evangeliorum,* for example, Luke 11:1–13 is divided into three separate pericopae: 185. The Lord's Prayer; 186. The Importunate Friend at Midnight; and 187. Encouragement to Pray.

tion developing out of a previous parable, is found in 16:1–13 (Unjust Steward).

Source-Critical Implications

When we turn to looking at 11:1–13 in source-critical perspective, we see an L sandwich, Q — L — Q, with both of the Q sections paralleled in different parts of the Sermon on the Mount, the Lord's Prayer in Matt 6:6–13 and the "Ask and you shall receive" material in 7:7–11. Now let us suppose that Luke, the "real author," has taken over this material from the Matthew's Sermon. The question that arises is whether or not his relocation of this material is appropriate. Is it artistically inferior to the location in Matthew? Is an appeal to Q necessary here? The answer, in the light of the brief narrative-critical analysis above, is surely not. The reader has been prepared for this material in a highly relevant co-text in 10:21–22, which introduces the Fatherhood of God; the unit develops this theme by sandwiching the double tradition material either side of the carefully crafted and appropriate Friend at Midnight.[20] The whole is introduced by a typical foil comment, the content of which has been prepared beforehand both by long-term precedent (Jesus' habit of praying) and immediate catalyst (Jesus' prayer in 11:1).

Indeed, one might even say that the setting for the "Ask and you shall receive" material (Matt 7:7–11 // Luke 11:9–13) is more and not less comprehensible in Luke than it is in Matthew. After all, Q theorists like Fitzmyer speak of the latter part of the Sermon on the Mount as "a series of loosely related sayings,"[21] something that contrasts strikingly with the sophisticated and polished narrative context provided here by Luke.

Luke 12:13–34

Narrative-critical study

Lest this example be seen as somehow unusual, let us take as our second example the next major occurrence of Sermon on the Mount material in

---

20. Cf. Michael Goulder's argument that Luke has created the parable of the Friend at Midnight on the basis of the sayings that follow on from it, *Luke*, 495–502.

21. Fitzmyer, *Luke I–IX*, 629, concerning Matt 6:19–7:27; see further on this point above, pp. 99–102.

Luke's Central Section, Luke 12:22–31, paralleled in Matthew 6:25–34, often called "On Care and Anxiety."[22]

Now, one of the things that narrative criticism teaches us is to pay due attention to "causal links"[23] between sections and there is an important one here in 12:22, Εἶπεν δὲ πρὸς τοὺς μαθητάς, Διὰ τοῦτο ("And he said to the disciples, 'Therefore...' "). Usually one will be looking for causal links in the narrator's voice, but here there is an interesting scenario in which the chief character in the story, Jesus, himself makes the link between two sections, all the more interesting because the narrator adds that a change of audience takes place.

So why does Jesus say "Therefore" and why is there a change of audience? Luke 12:13–34 is a dramatic, imaginative section that repays careful reading. Its character is that of an interlude or digression which nevertheless affects the development of the plot. Jesus is talking in Luke 12:1–12 about the eschaton and how believers should react when it comes. A member of the large crowd crassly interrupts, attempting to redirect attention to the present by asking for an arbitration from Jesus (Luke 12:13). Jesus does not, of course, accept the invitation to arbitrate, but refocuses the teaching about the eschaton now with special reference to the issue of possessions, already a theme that the reader of Luke knows to be a highly charged one. These verses that follow (Luke 12:14–21), featuring the Parable of the Rich Fool, are spoken to the crowd, members of which are still holding on to their possessions. The message for them is Ὁρᾶτε καὶ φυλάσσεσθε ἀπὸ πάσης πλεονεξίας, ὅτι οὐκ ἐν τῷ περισσεύειν τινὶ ἡ ζωὴ αὐτοῦ ἐστιν ἐκ τῶν ὑπαρχόντων αὐτῷ ("Beware of all covetousness, for a person's life does not consist in the abundance of their possessions," 12:15). The crowd is made up of those who still have possessions, who might be tempted to treasure it up for themselves (ὁ θησαυρίζων αὐτῷ, 12:21). The audience for the next section, 12:22–31, is different. The narrator makes clear that he spoke the words "to the disciples." Why the switch in audience? If we read the section with an eye on the unfolding of the narrative earlier on, we know that some of the disciples have "left everything and followed him" (5:11, Peter, James and John, ἀφέντες πάντα ἠκολούθησαν αὐτῷ; 5:28,

---

22. Cf. also the shorter unit on light at Matthew 5:15 // Luke 11:33 and Matthew 6:22–23 // Luke 11:34–36.

23. Mark Alan Powell, "Narrative Criticism," 245: "In making sense of narrative readers are especially attentive to links that are established between the events that are related. Typical links include explicit or implicit indications that one event causes another to happen or at least makes the occurrence of the subsequent event possible or likely."

Levi, καὶ καταλιπὼν πάντα ἀναστὰς ἠκολούθει αὐτῷ; later confirmed in 18:28, Ἰδοὺ ἡμεῖς ἀφέντες τὰ ἴδια ἠκολουθήσαμέν σοι. To this group, the parable of the Rich Fool would be partly meaningless — they have no riches that they might lay up to themselves; there is no "abundance of possessions" for them. Indeed as far as this Gospel is concerned, discipleship is largely constituted by the abandonment of possessions. This becomes clearer still in Luke 14:33:

οὕτως οὖν πᾶς ἐξ ὑμῶν ὃς οὐκ ἀποτάσσεται πᾶσιν τοῖς ἑαυτοῦ ὑπάρχουσιν οὐ δύναται εἶναί μου μαθητής

In the same way, therefore, any of you who does not give up everything you have is not able to be my disciple.

But there is a temptation for such disciples who have left everything — there is the possibility that they might have anxiety about their life, what they shall eat, their body, what they should put on (12:22). And this teaching unfolds out of the parable of the Rich Fool, utilizing some of the same language and imagery. The Rich Fool builds ever bigger storehouses (ἀποθήκη, v. 18) whereas the ravens do not have storehouse or barn (ταμεῖον οὐδὲ ἀποθήκη, v. 24); the Rich Fool's life (ψυχή, v. 20) is required of him, but the disciple should not be anxious concerning life (ψυχή, v. 22); the Rich Fool decides in vain to "eat, drink, and be merry" (ἀναπαύου, φάγε, πίε, v. 19) whereas the disciple is not to be anxious about what s/he should eat (. . . τί φάγητε, v. 22). And throughout, the message of richness toward God is underlined. Thus by seamlessly juxtaposing these two sections, the author has created a unit about the right attitude to life, riches, and anxiety. Yet the eye always remains on the eschaton. In spite of the interruption by the man in the multitude (12:13), the teaching will return to the parousia in 12:32 and following, now incorporating also these reflections on attitudes to possessions.

Source-Critical Implications

It is again necessary to ask whether, in the light of these narrative-critical reflections on one passage, there is any difficulty in imagining the breaking up of the Sermon on the Mount by Luke. The answer is that it is surely not difficult to imagine the very thing that is said to be so unlikely. In both Matthew and Luke (12:22–31), Jesus' speech begins with διὰ τοῦτο ("therefore," Matt 6:25 // Luke 12:22). In Matthew this

makes good sense: the passage follows on from the saying about God
and mammon (Matt 6:24) and develops this by exhortation not to be
anxious about material things (mammon), seeking rather the kingdom
of God and his righteousness (6:33; and then the "other things" will
be added too). In Luke one has a different but equally suitable flow of
thought. His "therefore" follows on from an L parable, the Rich Fool
(Luke 12:13–21), in which a man stores up for himself treasures on
earth, only to have God intervene: "Fool! this night your life is required
of you" (Luke 12:20). The parable ends with the warning: "So it is for
those who lay up treasure for themselves, but are not rich toward God."
It is difficult to imagine a more suitable lead-in to the teaching Luke
takes over from Matthew:[24] "Therefore I tell you, do not be anxious
about your life, what you shall eat . . . " (12:22) — even if one has plenty,
like the Rich Fool, this "life is more than food" (12:23); the ravens do
not have "storehouse or barn" (12:24), unlike the Rich Fool who built
ever bigger and better ones (12:18). He invested in this life and lost even
what he had; the disciple is exhorted to seek first the kingdom, and then
one has the material things added too (12:31). Further, by directing this
section at a different audience (disciples instead of crowd), the author
shows his sensitivity to the differences in nuance that the change in audience can create. It is not, in source-critical terms, that Luke has made a
hamfisted, loose connection across two only distantly related pericopae
by means of catchword connection. Rather, he seems to have shown skill
and literary artistry in his crafting of the section, something we had not
been led to expect on the standard rhetoric of the case against Luke's
use of Matthew.

·

The question that this analysis naturally raises is why it is that something
as straightforward as this is not generally seen by those Lukan scholars
who take Q for granted. What is it that has stopped narrative-critical
sensitivity from compromising the Q theory? The answer, I think, has to
do with the continuing hegemony of a redaction-critical approach to the
Gospels that depends on and yet reinforces the source-critical status quo.
For while redaction criticism has undoubtedly been a massive asset to
sound exegesis of the Gospels, it is vulnerable at precisely the point that

---

24. See further Goulder, *Luke*, 103 and 534–39, who claims that the Parable is so appropriate in this context that it must have been composed by Luke himself; but see also my critique
in *Goulder and the Gospels*, 345–47.

is of interest to us here. Since redaction criticism of Matthew and Luke generally presupposes the Q hypothesis,[25] it is incapable of testing it. It is true that some scholars have used the success of redaction criticism as a means of arguing in favor of the existence of Q,[26] but this will always tend toward circularity, particularly given the hypothetical nature of Q which itself is reconstructed by means of redaction criticism.

Redaction-critical arguments can only take us so far when we are attempting to test our source-critical conclusions. Usually the two-source theory is assumed before the work of redaction criticism begins. It is an in-house method, devised by biblical scholars, assuming certain source-critical matters.[27] But narrative criticism is different. It is a tool that has emerged outside the confines of the small world of New Testament scholarship.[28] It is, essentially, an import, something that makes it valuable as a tool for the testing of hypotheses, like Q, that were developed within biblical scholarship.

One of the advantages of the Farrer theory is that it effectively encourages the interpreter to a more careful consideration of the literary artistry of Luke. It is not, of course, that those who accept Q have no appreciation of Luke's literary ability; many a fine study has proceeded on the assumption not only of Luke's use of Mark but also on the basis of his alleged use of Q.[29] The point is that adherents of the Farrer theory, in denying themselves the expedient of the Q hypothesis for accounting for every peculiarity in Luke's order, are inevitably more inclined to look to Luke's literary skill as a means of explaining the narrative development of his Gospel. It is simply that the admittedly large scale reworking of Matthew that is demanded by the Farrer theory places Luke's literary creativity and narrative agenda into sharper relief. Indeed Austin Farrer

---

25. There are, of course, exceptions. Michael Goulder is in many ways the redaction critic par excellence — see my comments in *Goulder and the Gospels,* 24. John Drury too, in *Tradition and Design in Luke* (London: Darton, Longman and Todd, 1976) and *The Parables in the Gospels: History and Allegory* (London: SPCK, 1985), exercises redaction-criticism throughout from the perspective of Markan Priority Without Q.

26. More accurately, it is usually both tenets of the two-source theory that are here being defended — see above, pp. 75–77.

27. Cf. John Drury, *Tradition and Design,* 43: "The trouble with all these methods [form, source, and redaction criticism] is that they study the gospels in some measure of isolation. . . . A closed field is being investigated by a closed shop."

28. Cf. Stephen D. Moore, *Literary Criticism and the Gospels: The Theoretical Challenge* (New Haven: Yale University Press, 1989) for reflections on the role that narrative criticism plays in New Testament scholarship.

29. Among multiple examples, see Christopher Tuckett, ed., *Luke's Literary Achievement. Collected Essays* (JSNTSup, 116; Sheffield: Sheffield Academic Press, 1995).

himself was aware of the greater need for sensitivity to the literary skill of Luke in attempting to demonstrate his knowledge of Matthew, to the extent that a recent commentator has characterized Farrer a "pioneer narrative critic."[30]

While the importance of appealing to literary-critical approaches has been an element in the writings of other Q skeptics, perhaps most notably John Drury,[31] the standard redaction-critical paradigm has marked the work of Michael Goulder on Luke's order and it is arguable that the implausibility of some of Goulder's reconstructions of Luke's motivations results, ironically, from his attachment to the old paradigm, in which order must always be determined by positing some kind of precedent, cue or expedient in the source material.[32] Goulder claims, for example, that Luke's use of Matthew can be demonstrated from parallels in reverse sequence in Matthew, explained on the grounds that Luke was here scrolling backwards through Matthew and picking up cues in that reverse order.[33] The difficulty with such theories is that they only succeed in underlining the scope of Luke's transformation of Matthew. In order for the transformation to be plausible, one requires also some account of

---

30. Jeffrey Peterson, "A Pioneer Narrative Critic and His Synoptic Hypothesis," *Society of Biblical Literature Seminar Papers 2000* (Society of Biblical Literature Seminar Paper Series, 39; Atlanta: Society of Biblical Literature, 2000), 651–72. Peterson concludes that "In the light cast on the Gospels by narrative criticism and related approaches, Farrer seems in some respects an interpreter half a century ahead of his time; Q meanwhile seems less a necessary postulate and more a reflection of the tendency that Gilbert Highet lampooned in classical studies as 'the habit of *Quellenforschung,* the search for sources, which began as a legitimate inquiry into the material used by a poet, historian, or philosopher, and was pushed to the absurd point at which it was assumed that everything in a [work]... was derived from earlier writers' " (671; the quotation is from Gilbert Highet, *The Classical Tradition: Greek and Roman Influences on Western Literature* [New York and London: Oxford University Press, 1949], 499).

31. In four works, the greatly underrated *Luke* (The J. B. Phillips' Commentaries; London and Glasgow: Collins, 1973); *Tradition and Design; Parables in the Gospels;* and "Luke" in *The Literary Guide to the Bible* (ed. Frank Kermode and Robert Alter; Cambridge, Mass.: Harvard University Press, 1987), 418–39. As one example among many, see Drury's comments on Luke's attitude to Matthew's discourses, "The result of such breaking up [of Matthew's discourses] is not a mess but a new creation: a single tract of teaching relieved by frequent and various narrative settings and enlivened by stories peculiar to Luke... which add so much vivacity, movement and body to the whole" (*Tradition and Design,* 144).

32. While much of Goulder's work is conducive to contemporary literary criticism, he has tended to avoid embracing it — cf. *Goulder and the Gospels,* 25f.

33. See Goulder, *Luke,* 581–83 (and frequently thereafter) and "The Order of a Crank," 121–30. I regard this as the most implausible element in Goulder's thesis on Luke's use of Matthew by some measure and did not treat it in *Goulder and the Gospels.* A useful and detailed critique of this element in Goulder's case was provided by Robert A. Derrenbacker, Jr., "Greco-Roman Writing Practices and Luke's Gospel: Revisiting Luke's Crank," paper read at the Synoptics Section of the Society of Biblical Literature, Nashville, November 2000. See also Robert A. Derrenbacker, Jr., *Ancient Compositional Practices and the Synoptic Problem* (Ph.D. Dissertation, University of St. Michael's College, Toronto, 2001), Chapter 5.

Luke's literary creativity not just in individual pericopae but also across the narrative as a whole.[34]

Indeed a focus on the narrative as a whole is a major concern of narrative criticism, and it will be unjust to it as a discipline to leave it without looking at the question of the entire narrative, not least given the fact that we have focused on selected portions of Luke in relation to Matthew. What sense can we make of the overall unfolding of Luke's narrative in relation to Matthew's? The key comes in comments made in Luke Johnson's fine article on Luke-Acts in the *Anchor Bible Dictionary*. Having commented on the renowned story-telling ability of Luke evidenced in individual pericopae, Johnson goes on to comment:

> Luke is, however, considerably more than a miniaturist. His most impressive accomplishment is the forging of these short stories (many of them already circulating in some form) into one long, coherent narrative, which with masterful control brings the reader from the mists of antiquity all the way to a rented apartment in the empire's capital city, and within the space of 52 chapters creates an uncanny sense of historical movement.[35]

The question that the sensitive source critic, who has an eye on narrative-critical matters like this, will inevitably ask is: could the author of Luke have achieved such an impression of historical movement and still have retained the great Matthean discourses, and the structure that goes with them? The answer is that it is very difficult to imagine this.[36] Luke Johnson says in a slightly different context:

> Instead of inserting great blocks of discourse material into the narrative, Luke more subtly interweaves deeds and sayings. The

---

34. It is one of the anomalies of Goulder's approach that he has stressed more than any other scholar Luke's creativity within individual units, but rarely discusses the same literary creativity when it comes to the overall conceptualization of the narrative in Luke-Acts as a whole.

35. Luke Johnson, "Luke-Acts, Book of," *Anchor Bible Dictionary* IV, 405. Cf. John Drury, "Luke's version of Mark's story thus has a leisurely unfolding and methodical attention to temporal sequence which are lacking in the original. It is much more like history, much more realistic, much easier to read.... The Matthean teaching material needs similar attention. It is dragged out of its ecclesiastically Christian setting into the marketplace, there to commend itself as an inspired common sense or "wisdom." Anything that does not survive the move simply disappears. These two dominant tendencies which govern Luke's use of the work of his predecessors, the love of both the strong story-line moving clearly through time and of salty and realistic teaching, come right into the open in the sections which are his alone," *Luke* (J. B. Phillips' Commentaries), 12–13.

36. Cf. p. 97, n. 47 above.

sayings of Jesus in Luke's Gospel consequently have a greater air of biographical plausibility (see esp. Luke 9–19).[37]

Presumably without realizing it, Johnson has effectively undermined one of the most important arguments for the existence of Q. Luke's narrative is made dramatically appealing and historically plausible by means of its order. Luke has achieved biographical plausibility in his narrative by paying careful attention to sequence (καθεξῆς), a sequence in which it is very difficult to imagine a wholesale adoption of Matthew's long discourses. Indeed it is difficult, granted Luke's use of Matthew, to imagine him doing anything other than reworking the major discourses.

We should not be surprised. This is precisely what Luke says he is going to do in his Preface, which is, one might say, the first piece of biblical narrative criticism. It is all too often missed that in 1:1–4 Luke does not describe his own work as a διήγησις[38] but uses this word when he is commenting on the works of his predecessors — "Since many have undertaken to set down a narrative of the events that have been fulfilled among us . . . " (1:1). Their narratives, apparently, fall short in some way; Luke, on the other hand, having investigated these things carefully from the beginning, promises Theophilus an account in order. So Luke is the first narrative critic, and unlike his modern counterparts he is not afraid to compare his own work with that of his predecessors. He encourages us to investigate the interaction between source criticism and narrative criticism, and to observe the chemical reaction that takes place when they meet. We will do well to follow his lead, and — who knows? — we might end up with no other option than to dispense with Q.

---

37. Johnson, "Luke-Acts," 406.
38. Against, for example, Joel Green, *The Gospel of Luke,* 1: "According to the Lukan preface (1:1–4), the author himself categorizes his work as a 'narrative,'" in a section headed 'the Gospel of Luke as "narrative" (διήγησις).'

Chapter Six

THE SYNOPTIC JESUS
AND THE CELLULOID CHRIST

The idea that there might be room for dialogue between the study of Jesus films and the Synoptic Problem might initially appear even less promising than the notion that narrative criticism might shed some light on the Synoptic Problem. The study of the Synoptic Problem is, after all, wedded to a traditional, historical-critical approach to the New Testament that has no concern with the way in which the biblical text might be appropriated and interpreted in twentieth-century cinema. Yet some brief critical reflection might make us more optimistic about the possibilities, for one of the reasons for the widespread antipathy towards the Synoptic Problem is the notion that the experts go over old material again and again, digging up foundations and relaying them, restating arguments and reworking tired replies to them.[1] Injection of some fresh perspectives and new approaches is long overdue.[2] But what kind of new perspective could reflection on Jesus films generate? One avenue open to us would be to observe that the cultural reception and appropriation of the biblical text is now being taken seriously by some for the first time. Leading authorities have begun to work on ways in which we might, to use Larry Kreitzer's term, "reverse the hermeneutical flow."[3] That is, film and fiction might be studied with a view to stimulating our imagination, asking fresh questions and finding new answers when we do our exegesis of the text, and thus revitalizing our biblical scholarship.

---

1. Cf. Stephen Patterson, "these discussions seem to go on *ad infinitum*." Review of Christopher Tuckett, *Q and the History of Early Christianity, JBL* 117 (1998): 744–46 (744).

2. This is all the more so given the fact that for some scholars, as Jeffrey Peterson puts it, "the Synoptic problem is a trial to be endured periodically at the hands of enthusiasts rather than a topic of genuine interest, and discussion of same more a visit to the dentist than a day at the races." See "A Pioneer Narrative Critic," 663–64, n. 29.

3. L. J. Kreitzer, *The New Testament in Fiction and Film: On Reversing the Hermeneutical Flow* (The Biblical Seminar, 17; Sheffield: JSOT Press, 1993).

Although Kreitzer does not himself discuss the Synoptic Problem, William Telford, when reflecting on Kreitzer's proposal, writes:

> Allowing for the differences between ancient texts like the Gospels and modern texts, it can help us, if we may sum up, to appreciate the various ways that sources can be used and so illuminate compositional and redactional processes and the phenomenon of intertextuality at work within the Bible itself. Such study also assists us to recognise the creative power of the literary and religious imagination, even when operating upon sources, and so helps us to make more allowance for this factor in our literary and historical studies.[4]

The potential ramifications of Telford's insight for the study of the Synoptics are huge. Recognizing "the creative power of the literary and religious imagination," for example, might help us to dispense with sole dependence on those all-too-wooden models still used by most scholars of the Synoptic Problem. One might also profitably consider the "phenomenon of intertextuality," illuminated by the Jesus films, as a way of avoiding the scissors-and-paste methods that even yet pervade the discipline.[5] What, though, of the specifics? How might paying attention to Jesus films shed fresh light on the Synoptic Problem? I would like to propose that Jesus films could be helpful in the following ways, and I will then illustrate the point by returning once more to our most important example, the treatment of the Sermon on the Mount.

1. Jesus films variously harmonize, epitomize, expand, omit, change, and manipulate their sources, the Gospels, in what one might call a creative interaction with them. The complex task of analyzing this interaction might help us to counter the obsession of some contemporary scholarship for seeing the Gospels in isolation from one another, a tendency that can make us forget that these are texts that have always had an intimate relationship with one another.

---

4. W. R. Telford, "The New Testament in Fiction and Film: A Biblical Scholar's Perspective" in *Words Remembered, Texts Renewed: Essays in Honour of John F. A. Sawyer* (ed. Jon Davies, Graham Harvey, and Wilfred Watson; JSOTSup, 195; Sheffield: Sheffield Academic Press, 1995), 360–94. Quotation from 388.

5. The contributors to *Screening Scripture: Intertextual Connections Between Scripture and Film*, edited by George Aichele and Richard Walsh (Harrisburg, Pa.: Trinity Press International, 2002) use the lens of intertextuality to read scripture and film, including the Jesus films.

2. Since several of the Jesus films provide us with examples of ways in which the Gospels might be creatively reworked, they can provide helpful analogies for the way in which certain of the Gospels might themselves have creatively reworked their source material.

3. Such engagement might stimulate us to use our imagination, something all too lacking in much Synoptic study, especially in finding a way of freshly assessing the two-source theory.

Cinematic Sermons on the Mount

A good example of the way in which we might breathe fresh air into the Synoptic Problem by watching films is provided by focusing on the Sermon on the Mount. Since practically all of the Jesus films,[6] including even the seminal parody *Monty Python's Life of Brian,* find a place for the Sermon on the Mount in their narrative, and since the question of the relationship between Matthew and Luke here is pivotal to the study of the Synoptic Problem, there will be no better place to begin than this. As we have seen on several occasions, many critics believe it is well nigh impossible that Luke could have "destroyed" Matthew's Sermon on the Mount and thus Matthew and Luke are likely to be independent of one another. Given that a key element in this is simply a value judgment that takes it for granted that Matthew's arrangement of material is preferable to Luke's, the question that arises is whether it is necessary for us to share this judgment. What kind of attitude have others in history taken to Matthew's Sermon? Is its integrity always to be respected, a perfect unit never to be disturbed? Attention to films in the genre *Jesus film* will help us to answer this question. The best-known of these include *King of Kings* (Nicholas Ray, 1961),[7] *The Greatest Story Ever Told* (George Stevens, 1965), *The Gospel According to St Matthew* (Pier Paolo Pasolini, 1964), *The Last Temptation of Christ* (Martin Scorsese, 1988)

---

6. There are two possible exceptions — *Jesus of Nazareth* (dir. Franco Zeffirelli, 1977) does not really depict a Sermon on the Mount, though it does have much of the Sermon material (see n. 10 below) and *The Miracle Maker* (dir. Derek W. Hayes and Stanislav Sokolov, 1999), which features only three pieces of Sermon material, and not at the same setting, Log and Speck; Ask and you shall receive; and Two Builders.

7. W. Barnes Tatum, *Jesus at the Movies: A Guide to the First Hundred Years* (Sonoma, Calif.: Polebridge, 1997) prefers to call this "Samuel Bronston's *King of Kings*" (Chapter Five) following the film's original publicity, especially as Nicholas Ray did not have the final cut (75). This is (at least) a useful reminder that the habit of calling films by their director's name is potentially misleading.

and the TV series *Jesus of Nazareth* (Franco Zeffirelli, 1977).[8] How do these films treat the Sermon?

Broadly speaking, the following four elements occur in all these films' treatment of it. In each case the way in which the Sermon is treated in the Jesus films has features in common with the way that Luke has treated the Sermon on the assumption that he had a copy of Matthew's Gospel.

1. Location in the Narrative

The Sermon on the Mount is situated early in Matthew's story of Jesus: before the Twelve have been named, before any accounts of miracles; before any sayings material; the ministry is hardly yet underway. The positioning of such a large block of teaching so early in the story is one of the most striking — and on first reading unexpected — features of Matthew's Gospel. It is hardly surprising that all of the Jesus films, without exception, hold the Sermon back for later in the ministry. *The Greatest Story Ever Told*, for example, situates the Sermon much later in its narrative, over an hour into the three-hour film, after much of the ministry in Galilee has happened, including miracles, teaching, the call of Matthew, and the arrest of John the Baptist. Indeed in the interests of narrative continuity, Matthew's eighth beatitude (on persecution) is brought forward to first place in a cut that takes us from the death of John the Baptist to this new first beatitude. Herod Antipas's instruction, which concludes the previous scene, "Now take as many men as you need and arrest the Nazarene," segues splendidly to a shot of Herod's troops followed by Max von Sydow's Jesus calling to the crowds this now appropriate and ironic beatitude, "Blessed are they which are persecuted for righteousness' sake."

King of Kings is no different in relocating the Sermon, holding it back until more has happened. In both *King of Kings* and in *Greatest Story*, the Sermon is situated in the narrative after healings, the Woman taken in Adultery and John the Baptist's Death have taken place. In *Jesus of Nazareth* the Sermon, insofar as it appears at all, is saved for even later in the narrative — halfway through the third of the four ninety-minute segments that make up the series, not only after the disciples have been

---

8. For further details of these and other Jesus films, see W. Barnes Tatum, *Jesus at the Movies*; Richard C. Stern, Clayton Jefford, and Guerric Debona, *Savior on the Silver Screen* (Mahwah, N.J.: Paulist, 1999); W. Telford, "Jesus Christ Movie Star: The Depiction of Jesus in the Cinema" in *Explorations in Theology and Film: Movies and Meaning* (ed. Clive Marsh and Gaye Ortiz; Oxford: Blackwell, 1997), 115–39; and Mark Goodacre, *The New Testament Gateway: Jesus in Film*, http://ntgateway.com/film.

sent out but also after Peter's Confession at Caesarea Philippi. In other words, it appears well over halfway through Jesus' ministry.

What, then, of Pasolini's *Gospel According to St Matthew*? Is it any more faithful to the Matthean text? It too apparently feels uncomfortable with an early Sermon and brings forward material from the end of Matthew 9 and the beginning of Matthew 10 — the "Harvest is Plentiful" saying and the naming of the Twelve. It is immediately *preceded* by the story of the Leper, which comes immediately *after* the Sermon in Matthew (8:1–4).

Does this correspond to anything in Luke's treatment of the Sermon on the assumption that he too knew Matthew? Indeed it does; Luke's Sermon on the Plain (6:20ff), like Pasolini's Sermon, takes place shortly after the naming of the twelve. Similarly, the story of the Leper has already been recounted by Luke (5:12–16). As in all the films mentioned, there has been substantial healing and some teaching ministry already in Luke by the time that the Sermon begins. Perhaps Luke, like the directors of the Jesus films, felt uneasy about a substantial body of teaching addressed to "his disciples" (Matt 5:1–2 // Luke 6:20) that takes place before most of them have even been called. When the Sermon begins in Matthew, four have been called so far (Matt 4:18–22). Luke's later Sermon on the Plain, on the other hand, addresses disciples subsequent to the calling and choosing of more than just those four (Luke 5:1–11, 5:27–31, 6:12–16).

2. Abbreviation, Omission and Redistribution

A second feature common to the adaptations of the Sermon by Jesus films is abbreviation. In each one of the above films, the Sermon is substantially shorter than its Matthean exemplar. Of course some versions are longer than others. *The Gospel According to St Matthew* has the longest of the sermons, 958 words (by my count) in total. Even this contrasts strongly with Matthew's Sermon which (by my computation) is 2,325 words of English text in the RSV. Pasolini's Sermon is less than half the length.[9]

---

9. See W. Barnes Tatum's helpful description of the way Pasolini deals with the Sermon on the Mount, *Jesus at the Movies*, 106–7. Tatum lists the five Matthean discourses and adds: "Pasolini has incorporated these discourses into his film as *discourses* very unevenly, or not at all. The initial discourse on the higher righteousness, the Sermon on the Mount (chapters 5–7), does find its way into the film as a distinct entity. The sayings Pasolini selected from the gospel for the film include such familiar teachings as the Beatitudes, the Golden Rule, and the Lord's Prayer." Note also Tatum's comment that "Although Pasolini has not carried over into the film

George Stevens's *Greatest Story Ever Told* hardly keeps even the bare bones of Matthew's Sermon. We have, as usual, the Beatitudes and the Lord's Prayer, but otherwise only the sayings on salt and light (Matt 5:13–16). The Sermon in *Jesus of Nazareth* is shorter still — it has merely the Beatitudes and the Lord's Prayer, the latter introduced simply with "In your prayers, remember your father knows what your needs are before you ask him."[10]

For all of these films, Jesus' two-thousand-plus words of *oratio recta* in Matthew are simply too much, and the Sermon is cut drastically. It reminds us, once more, of Luke's Gospel, whose Sermon is less than a third of the length of Matthew's. I count 739 words of English text in the RSV, that is, it is longer than the shortest film versions of the Sermon (*Jesus of Nazareth, Greatest Story*) and a little shorter than the longest (Pasolini). Luke, like the filmmakers, may have felt that so much direct speech all at once would be too much to keep the audience interested; it might compromise the narrative flow and weaken the literary impact of the story.

But Luke does not, of course, reject all of the material he does not use from Matthew's Sermon. On the contrary, much of it appears elsewhere at appropriate points in the narrative, Care and Anxiety (Matt 6:25–34) appropriately conjoined with the Parable of the Rich Fool, for example (Luke 12:13–34). Likewise the Jesus films. Unused parts of the Sermon crop up elsewhere in the narrative, Care and Anxiety being a special favorite, used in different spots in both *Greatest Story* and *Jesus of Nazareth*.[11]

So we have another thing common to Luke and the Jesus films, abbreviation by means of omission and redistribution.

3. Restructuring of the Sermon

The relocation of the Sermon, with the attendant omission and redistribution of material in both the Jesus films and (on the assumption of his knowledge of Matthew) Luke's Gospel necessitates some reworking

the five great discourses so literarily characteristic of the gospel of Matthew, he has retained the underlying shape of Jesus' ministry" (ibid., 107).

10. Much of the Sermon material is held over until the Temple sequence at the end of Jesus' ministry in *Jesus of Nazareth*. There is no real sermon *on the mount* in Zeffirelli's film.

11. It might be objected that the Jesus films are here influenced by Luke in their placement of some of these materials, but to stress this would be to miss the point. If the Jesus films are influenced by Luke here, then we have an artistic decision in favor of Luke's reordering of the Sermon and against the idea that that such a reordering would be the destructive work of a crank.

of the remaining material to give it coherence. Although all agree that the Sermon should begin with the Beatitudes (except *Last Temptation*), and most want to keep the Lord's Prayer, there is otherwise little consensus about which parts are essential and how these parts might be structured. For example, neither *King of Kings* nor *The Gospel According to St Matthew*, nor *Greatest Story* nor *Jesus of Nazareth* closes the Sermon with the parable of the Two Builders. One might say, if one is going to use the language of "violence" and "destruction," that the Jesus films in this respect demolish the framework of Matthew's Sermon even more blatantly than does Luke. One might prefer, however, not to use such language and to suggest instead that George Stevens, Nicholas Ray, Pier Paolo Pasolini and Franco Zeffirelli have all creatively and critically reworked Matthew's Sermon in accordance with their narrative agenda.

It is not the only respect in which the Jesus films apparently take further something that is already evident in Luke's postulated redaction of the Sermon. For Luke actually imports a saying into his Sermon from elsewhere in Matthew, Matt 15:14 // Luke 6:39 ("A blind person is not able to lead a blind person, are they?"). The same feature, importing sayings from elsewhere, is taken to extreme by *King of Kings* which features material not only from Matthew's Sermon (Love your Enemies; Log and Speck; Care and Anxiety; Ask and You Shall Receive) but also a great deal from outside of Matthew's Sermon — "the kingdom of God is within you" from Luke 17:21, "Come unto me" from Matthew 11:28–30 and the Good Shepherd from John 10.

4. Adding and Enhancing Dramatic Elements

As I have hinted, this relocation, abbreviation, redistribution, importing, and restructuring is not arbitrary but performs an important function. All is in the service of increasing the dramatic appeal of the films in which the Sermon appears in an attempt to make the story somewhat less ponderous for an audience trained on thrills, romance, and action. But how does one inject some dramatic life into a long monologue like the Sermon on the Mount? One technique, of course, would be regular cutting and imaginative use of camera angles. *The Greatest Story* attempts this with its short sermon — all is done in long shots with no close-ups of Jesus' face. The dramatic Utah landscape is the background to Jesus, who stands on a precipice surrounded by the Twelve, neatly sitting in a circle and the crowd in the foreground. The longest, most panoramic shot is used for its first beatitude (here persecution); there is a change of shot, looking up at von Sydow's Jesus from the crowd for the next seven beatitudes; and a further change of shot, moving back and farther west for "salt" and "light."[12]

But skillful changes of camera angle might not be enough to sustain the audience through a longer Sermon like that in *King of Kings*. Ray takes us through the Sermon, therefore, with the clever device of inter-locutors who put foil questions and comments before Jesus to prompt or introduce each little section. One of these is directly drawn from one of Luke's resettings of material from the Sermon, the section on prayer in Luke 11:1–13. There the disciples ask Jesus to teach them to pray. So too in *King of Kings*, the Lord's Prayer is introduced by someone who says, "Teach us to pray." Others of the foil questions and comments find par-allels in the Gospels (e.g., the Lawyer's Question in Luke 10:25ff, etc.); others are invented for the film.

The same feature is consciously taken up and developed in Scorsese's *Last Temptation of Christ*. In its short parallel to the Sermon on the Mount,[13] members of the crowd keep interrupting Jesus, sometimes off-camera, and as Jesus walks around in the crowd in an attempt to answer them, the camera follows him. As the drama intensifies, Scorsese uses a handheld camera in imitation-documentary style: the camera does not know where the next comment is coming from and it cannot always catch up with Jesus who on one occasion even walks quickly out of shot. The Beatitudes (and Woes) are dramatized, the product of Jesus' lively interaction with the crowd. It is one of the most compelling scenes in any Jesus film.

Now Luke's Sermon on the Plain only begins to hint at the need for the breaking up of the direct speech, which is so important a feature of *King of Kings* and *The Last Temptation*. For, whereas in Matthew there is no break in 138 verses and over 2,000 words, in Luke the narrator

---

12. Cf. W. Barnes Tatum's description of the Sermon in *The Gospel According to St Matthew*, "In the film, the sermon represents a *tour de force*. The sermon is shot as a series of a dozen or more close-ups of Jesus' face with a cut to a different pose between each of the spoken segments of the sermon. For example, the viewer sees Jesus with his head uncovered when he declares the Beatitudes but, immediately thereafter, with his head covered for his pronouncement of the Golden Rule. Throughout the Sermon, therefore, Jesus appears as 'a talking head' " (*Jesus at the Movies*, 106–7).

13. The "Sermon" in *Last Temptation* actually begins with a version of the parable of the Sower and one might therefore comment that this is not, strictly speaking, a version of the Sermon on the Mount. However, careful attention to Scorsese's comments on this scene in D. Thompson and I. Christie, eds., *Scorsese on Scorsese* (Updated ed.; London: Faber & Faber, 1996) shows how far the director saw it critically interacting with the depictions of the Sermon on the Mount in *King of Kings*, *Greatest Story* and *Monty Python's Life of Brian*.

offers a brief comment halfway through his 30 verses at 6:39 ("And he told them a parable...."). There are no foil questions and comments here, but we do not have to look far to find them elsewhere in Luke, for they are a key feature in particular of the Central Section. Sayings material, including material paralleled in Matthew's Sermon, is regularly introduced by the kinds of comments used by Nicholas Ray to dramatize the Sermon in *King of Kings*. The woman in the crowd says, "Blessed is the womb that bore you and the breasts that gave you suck" (11:27–28); a man in the crowd speaks up in 12:13, "Teacher, tell my brother to divide the inheritance with me." Or before the parable of the Great Supper, someone reclining with Jesus says, "Blessed is he who eats bread in the kingdom of God" (14:15).

The feature, in short, is a prominent one in both *King of Kings* and Luke's Gospel and it is likely that the reason for its use is similar. Like Nicholas Ray, Luke is trying to produce a plausible, sequential, and dramatic narrative. Luke is quite unlike Matthew and does not appreciate the long, unbroken monologues given by Jesus. He wants to take the reader with him from one incident to another. Whereas in Matthew the discourses tend to interrupt the narrative, in Luke the sayings material complements and grows out of the narrative.

•

We looked earlier at William Telford's observations on the ways in which the study of the New Testament in film and fiction might help us, with Kreitzer, "to reverse the hermeneutical flow." In the conclusion to the same article, Telford reflects:

> There are resemblances between our canonical Gospels and the works of fiction and film that are based upon them. The Gospels used sources but also creatively embellished them by means of their literary imagination, in line with their ideology and in response to their contemporary context.[14]

The suggestion of this chapter is that Telford's insight is fundamentally on the right lines. The Jesus films provide the scholar of the Synoptics with a stimulus for rethinking the question of Gospel sources and interrelationships. Specifically, critical reflection on the way that the Jesus films depict the Sermon on the Mount gives us a means of testing one of

---

14. W. R. Telford, "The New Testament in Fiction and Film," 388.

the standard criticisms of Luke's postulated treatment of the same material. One of the very things that many have claimed to be implausible about the Farrer theory's Luke is one of the very things he shares with Jesus films, the desire to do something radical with Matthew's Sermon on the Mount, to abbreviate, to relocate, to redistribute, to restructure but most importantly to add some dramatic, biographical plausibility to the substance of it. If we were fond of the language of trajectory and tendency, we might say that Luke is on a trajectory, at the culmination of which are the Jesus films, the tendency of which is creatively and critically to rework the Sermon on the Mount.[15]

However, the parallels provided by the Jesus films are, of course, only partial and failure to appreciate the shortcomings of the analogy will inevitably deprive this discussion of force. The two millennia separating Luke from the Jesus films is accentuated by the manifest difference in genre between the ancient Gospel and the modern film. Further, we should not ignore the possibility that some of the Jesus films are influenced by the very reworkings by Luke that we have been discussing. On these occasions, Luke does not so much parallel the Jesus films as provide a source for them.

Yet to place undue stress on these facts in this context would be to miss the point. Of course, on occasion, the Jesus films are themselves influenced directly by Luke, but where this happens we have what amounts to a decision in favor of the Lukan narrative arrangement over against the Matthean arrangement, itself a factor that draws attention to, and so undermines, the value judgment concerning the supposed superiority of Matthew's order. Further, in Pasolini's film we see all of the key features (relocation, abbreviation, redistribution, restructuring, and the enhancing of dramatic elements) at work even in a film describing itself as *The Gospel according to St Matthew*, which is using solely the Matthean text.[16]

Moreover, the manifest difference in genre between the ancient Gospel and the modern film actually aids one in reflecting critically on standard

---

15. In using the language of trajectory, it is worth adding that the film *Jesus* (John Krish and Peter Sykes, 1979), which is based solely on Luke's Gospel, moves further along the same trajectory by setting Luke's Sermon in a marketplace and having Jesus walking around, delivering individual lines to specific people, also shortening the whole while appropriately maintaining Luke's location in the narrative.

16. The wording of the film's text is surprisingly little influenced by Luke — there are (at best) only a handful of minor agreements with Luke against Matthew, most of which might straightforwardly be assigned to independent redaction.

approaches to the Synoptic Problem since it draws attention to the fact
that here, in the Jesus films, we have the views not of contemporary
scholars but of contemporary artists about what constitutes a discrimi-
nating, creative reworking of the Sermon on the Mount. The Jesus films
thus provide us with a unanimous witness against the standard claims
about the impossibility of Luke's having reordered Matthew's Sermon.

To see the point clearly, we need to remember that the standard view
is based simply on a subjective statement of preference in favor of Matthew's order over Luke's. Fitzmyer assumes that "so literary an artist as
Luke" would not have desired "to destroy the Matthean masterpiece of
the Sermon on the Mount"[17] and there is no further discussion of the
matter. Fitzmyer is here, like many others, repeating a pronouncement
against the likelihood of a critical reworking of the Sermon by Luke
on the assumption that Matthew's version is a "masterpiece" and that
Luke's, by implication, is not. Subjective claims like this are the most
difficult elements in discussions of the Synoptic Problem for they are the
least critical, least testable elements within the discipline. They acquire
their force simply by frequent repetition and repeated assumption, leading ultimately to an uncritical reentrenching of the paradigm. But what
the Jesus films provide is a genuine means of testing such subjective
claims, of seeing whether others — not least those outside of the narrow
confines of the guild, those uninfluenced by the repeated assumptions
that have become part of the standard two-source paradigm — share
our claims. And the manifest evidence is that in this case they do not.

The intention of this chapter is not simply to provide an interlude
in the discussion of that most brow-furrowing of issues, the Synoptic
Problem, but to attempt to stimulate the reader's imagination, suggesting
one way in which we might revive interest in the Synoptic Problem and
at the same time promote a rapprochement between historical-critical
methods and contemporary approaches. More than anything else, the
films we have been discussing provide rich analogies for the study of the
Synoptics. The difficulty, after all, with much Synoptic study is that it
has become so self-referential, rooted in the repetition of arguments that
have long since ceased to be persuasive but which nevertheless continue
to be used for lack of adequate alternatives.

Let us therefore indulge ourselves with one final analogy. One of the
shortcomings of the Q hypothesis is the restraint it puts on commentators

---

17. See above, p. 110, n. 12.

of Luke. Where we might have seen Luke's literary ability at work in a creative and critical interaction with Matthew as well as Mark, we have all too often turned to Q to explain the quirks of Luke's Gospel. But perhaps Luke is like Martin Scorsese and the third Gospel like *The Last Temptation of Christ*. Anyone watching the latter will be struck by the extent to which it is both derivative and subversive, influenced by and yet critical of those Jesus films that came before it. The Sermon is in Scorsese's film a development of the *King of Kings* Sermon, taking further the idea of crowd interaction but replacing the beautiful, unchangeable, picture book Jesus with a neurotic, uncertain, three-dimensional figure. What Scorsese does is to interact with his sources. They influence him yet he is critical of them.[18] This is quite like Luke's approach to Matthew, best seen as an interaction that involves Luke in both embracing and rejecting Matthew, superseding it by rewriting it. Is this the profile of a crank or of a literary artist at work? Perhaps the study of the Jesus film will help us, at last, to give Luke the benefit of the doubt.

---

18. For some fascinating insights into Scorsese's ambiguous relationship with the Jesus films that were produced before *Last Temptation*, see D. Thompson and I. Christie, eds., *Scorsese on Scorsese*.

Chapter Seven

HOW BLESSED ARE THE POOR?
Source-Critical Reflections on the First Beatitude in Matthew, Luke, Thomas and Q

Consensus positions in synoptic criticism, especially on questions concerning individual units of tradition, are not easy to come by. But one such consensus view is strong, the question of the most original form of the first beatitude. It is almost universally held[1] that the first beatitude in Q should be reconstructed in line with the Lukan version, "Blessed are the poor" (6:20), and, in addition, that this beatitude originates with Jesus — perhaps also witnessed independently in the identical beatitude in Thomas 54, which also has "Blessed are the poor." The last two words in Matthew's version, then, "Blessed are the poor *in spirit*" (Matt 5:3), are a "spiritualizing gloss" on the Q version better preserved by Luke.[2]

---

1. For a discussion of the standard view as "misleading," see Hans Dieter Betz, *The Sermon on the Mount*, 111–19, especially 115.

2. The only group of scholars standing outside of the consensus tend to be adherents of the view that Luke knew Matthew's Gospel. See, for example, Austin Farrer, "On Dispensing," 64; Michael Goulder, *Luke*, 348–51; Eric Franklin, *Luke*, 319–21; and John Drury, *Tradition and Design*, 134–35, especially the comment "The Matthean beatitudes which Luke keeps are all to do with deprivation (poverty, hunger, weeping, persecution). The four which he omits are all to do with positive qualities (meekness, mercy, purity of heart, peace-making). He has no quarrel with the latter category, but a major aspect of his theology requires his own arrangement" (135). Adherents of the Griesbach hypothesis also see Luke's version as secondary — cf. Allan J. McNicol et al., eds., *Beyond the Q Impasse*, 104–5. However, in an extraordinary chapter in *The Gospel of Jesus*, W. R. Farmer contends that the Griesbach hypothesis is more conducive to the thesis of "God's Special Commitment to the Poor" (Chapter 8), including in his exposition some comments on Matt 5:3 // Luke 6:20. Notice in particular the comment, "Unless we conclude that Luke has preserved the more original form of the Beatitudes as they stood in the hypothetical Q document, we are left in doubt whether Q contained a beatitude concerning 'the poor.' The Matthean form of the Beatitudes may well have originated with Jesus" (103). But it is consensus among Q scholars that Luke 6:20 is the more original form in Q and, as it happens, it is also regularly claimed that it goes back to the historical Jesus (though one should be wary of the implication that Q theorists see a necessary conjunction between Q and the historical Jesus). Farmer claims that "reconstructions of Jesus' message based on Markan priority and the existence of Q have not given God's preferential love for the poor an important role in understanding Jesus," citing John Dominic Crossan's *The Historical Jesus* and Burton L.

One good sign of a consensus position is that the matter is thought to be so clear, so well sustained that it does not even require argument.[3] The bare statement of the presumed facts, the assertion that this is how the matter stands, is thought to be quite enough. Helmut Koester, for example, simply refers in passing to "the typical Matthean interpolation 'in spirit' (τῷ πνεύματι)."[4] Or one sees the simple appeal to what "most would agree" to be the case as when Christopher Tuckett writes:

> In the first beatitude, most would agree that the object of the beatitude in Q is the "poor," and that Matthew's "poor in spirit" is due to his redactional change, "spiritualizing" the beatitude in the same way as he has modified the "hungry" of Matt 5:6 to refer to those who "hunger and thirst for righteousness."[5]

Yet in spite of the overwhelming nature of the consensus, the position is problematic. It can be argued that good, strong evidence pointing in a different direction is repeatedly overlooked. If this proves to be the case, it will be most inconvenient since consensus positions are so difficult to come by. But the desire to avoid inconvenience has never been an adequate criterion for not considering the evidence, so let us analyze the data afresh and see in which direction it seems to be pointing. There is every reason to see Luke's version of the first beatitude as secondary to Matthew's and thus that the Q theory's argument from greater Lukan primitivity, for this beatitude at least, is unnecessary.

Mack's *The Lost Gospel* (ibid., 103–4 and 214, n. 2). Such a claim is particularly odd given the stress in both works on the beatitude "Blessed are the poor" in Q 6:20. Cf. John S. Kloppenborg Verbin, *Excavating Q*, 269, n. 3.

3. Cf. Richard Bauckham, ed., *The Gospels for All Christians*, 11–12.

4. Helmut Koester, *Ancient Christian Gospels*, 74; cf. 72. Note that the words in Matthew are τῷ πνεύματι and not, as they are sometimes represented, ἐν πνεύματι, e.g., by David Catchpole, *The Quest for Q*, 81; Stephen J. Patterson, *The Gospel of Thomas and Jesus*, 42–43; Robert A. Derrenbacker, Jr., and John S. Kloppenborg Verbin, "Self-Contradiction," 59.

5. Christopher M. Tuckett, *Q and the History of Early Christianity*, 223. See further Christopher M. Tuckett and Michael D. Goulder, "The Beatitudes: A Source-Critical Study," *NovT* 25 (1983): 193–216. For the originality of the Lukan version see further Hans-Joachim Degenhardt, *Lukas: Evangelist der Armen* (Stuttgart: Katholisches Bibelwerk, 1965), 45–53 and Schürmann, *Lukasevangelium*, 339–41; Schulz, *Q. Die Spruchquelle der Evangelisten* (Zürich: Theologischer Verlag, 1972), 77. Many other examples could be given. For thorough treatments of the Beatitudes, there are two indispensable sources, J. Dupont, *Les Béatitudes* (Paris: Gabalda, I–II 1969; III 1973) and Hans Dieter Betz, *The Sermon on the Mount*. See too Davies and Allison, *Matthew*, 1:429–69. The issue is only complicated within Q scholarship by those proposing that Matthew and Luke were dependent on different versions of Q, a Q^Matt and a Q^Luke, e.g., Ulrich Luz, *Matthew 1–7*, 227–29.

The Lukan Preference for "the Poor"

One of the fundamentals in the reconstruction of Q is the attempt, in the first instance, to analyze whether the given wording of a Matthean or Lukan version of a Q pericope contains language clearly belonging to the conceptual framework of one of those evangelists.[6] If the wording of one of the two is less blatantly characteristic of its evangelist than the wording in the other of the two, scholarship tends to give the unanimous opinion in favor, quite naturally, of the one with the less characteristic wording. So here, which of the evangelists has wording more blatantly characteristic of his writing? Given the unanimity of the opinion concerning Matthew's secondariness, the answer is, surprisingly but quite clearly, Luke. The unqualified term πτωχοί ("poor") occurs on several other occasions in Luke (for example 4:18 L (LXX), 14:13 L, 14:21 QD),[7] whereas the qualification τῷ πνεύματι ('in spirit') is never found outside of this context in Matthew, let alone the term οἱ πτωχοὶ τῷ πνεύματι ("the poor in spirit").[8] But such linguistic observations can be, as is all too rarely acknowledged, at best not very telling and at worst misleading;[9] I do not think that a great deal of stress can be put on this but, for what it is worth, the evidence tells in favor of Lukan secondariness.

More important is a fact known by everyone who has read the most basic of introductions to Luke's Gospel, that this is the Gospel of the underdog, the outcast, the poor, the downtrodden, the marginalized. From the Magnificat at one end of the Gospel to the Widow's Mite at the other, Luke's is the Gospel that consistently seems to maintain what these days might be called a "preferential option for the poor."[10]

---

6. Cf. the introduction to each volume of *Documenta Q*, v, which speaks of occasions when the evangelists can be seen to be "furnishing it [a Q saying] with a framework that belongs to the conceptual interests of that Evangelist." On the reconstruction of Q, see further above, pp. 62–63.

7. πτωχός has figures of 5/5/10/4; it occurs at Matt 5:3 // Luke 6:20; Matt 11:5 // Luke 7:22; Matt 19:21 // Mark 10:21; Matt 26:9 // Mark 14:5 and Matt 26:11 // Mark 14:7; Mark 12:42; Mark 12:43 // Luke 21:3; Luke 4:18; Luke 14:13; Luke 14:21; Luke 16:20; Luke 16:22; Luke 18:22; Luke 19:8.

8. Catchpole draws attention to Matt 27:50 diff. Mark 15:37 "for another redactional reference to the human spirit," *The Quest for Q*, 84. The fact that this, "Jesus ... gave up his spirit" (ἀφῆκεν τὸ πνεῦμα), is the best evidence that can be found elsewhere in Matthew for the alleged redactional addition of τῷ πνεύματι in 5:3 illustrates the weakness of the case from linguistic evidence.

9. For some reservations on the over-application of simple linguistic counts, see *Goulder and the Gospels*, 88.

10. This does not mean, of course, that the theme is not present in the other Gospels, e.g., the Widow's Mite pericope is shared with Mark (12:41–44).

Under such circumstances, we are not in the least surprised to find the Lukan Jesus standing up and uttering his first blessing on "the poor." It is difficult to imagine "poor in spirit" fitting as clearly into that agenda.

This observation is nuanced and further reinforced by the fact that the Sermon on the Plain is not, for Luke, Jesus' inaugural sermon. Jesus' in-augural sermon in Luke is in Nazara (4:16–30) where, in striking parallel to the opening line of the second Sermon, Jesus pronounces a blessing on the poor, Πνεῦμα κυρίου ἐπ᾽ ἐμέ, οὗ εἴνεκεν ἔχρισέν με εὐαγγελίσασθαι πτωχοῖς, "The spirit of the Lord is upon me, for he has anointed me to proclaim good news to the poor" (4:18). This passage needs to be taken seriously, coming as it does at the agenda-setting outset of Jesus' public ministry. Luke seems to be using the text to define for the reader Jesus' identity, inspiration, and gospel as the one anointed (ἔχρισέν) by the Spirit, whose mission is to evangelize the poor. Little is surprising, then, when in the next great sermon, the first thing that Jesus does is to pronounce good news, the promise of the kingdom and so special blessing, on the poor. Isaiah 61 is clearly a hugely important text to Luke; one might almost say that it is in his bloodstream. The further "scripturizing" or, if one prefers, "septuagintalizing" of Matthew 5:3, which already has intertextual echoes of the same chapter,[11] comes ap-propriately and naturally to the third evangelist.[12] It is a fine example of the way that the third evangelist works, interacting with his sources, influenced even by his sources' sources, seeing their allusions, combin-ing them with his own agenda and creatively drawing out his favorite themes and stamping them with a distinctive Lukan Christology.

Eschatological Reversal

The Lukan nature of this beatitude is strengthened further by another key Lukan theme, one that is illustrated as clearly here at the outset of the Sermon on the Plain as it is anywhere in Luke's Gospel: the theme

---

11. Matthew's use of Isaiah 61 in the Beatitudes is widely recognized; for a useful treatment, see Davies and Allison, *Matthew,* 1:436–39.

12. In spite of his support for the consensus view on the origin of this beatitude (see above), Christopher Tuckett comes close to this when he speaks of the "actualization of the prophecy of Isa. 61:1" here (Q, 223). Tuckett thinks, however, that the earlier passage, Luke 4:16ff has its origins in Q and so one can trace the Isaiah 61 reference to the poor through from Q 4:18 to Q 6:20 to Q 7:22.

of eschatological reversal.[13] Once again, the Magnificat sets up this key element in Luke's agenda:[14]

> He has scattered those who are proud in their inmost thoughts.
> He has brought down rulers from their thrones but has lifted up the humble.
> He has filled the hungry with good things but has sent the rich away empty. (Luke 1:52–53)

Luke's blessing on the poor is one that carries with it the inevitable woe or curse on the rich. Thus, just as we see "the poor" prioritized in Jesus' evangelization in Luke, so too we consistently find the Magnificat echoed: the rich are sent away empty. They go to their death with nothing.[15] The rich man in Luke 12:15–21 is a "fool" for this very reason, that he has stored up things that he loses at the point of his death: "Then who will get what you have prepared for yourself?" (12:20). The Rich Man in 16:19–31 is addressed in a similar way: "Son, remember that in your lifetime you received your good things . . . " (Luke 16:25).

It is not surprising, then, that the Lukan beatitude on the poor carries with it a corresponding woe on the rich stressing that they have received their reward, Πλὴν οὐαὶ ὑμῖν τοῖς πλουσίοις, ὅτι ἀπέχετε τὴν παράκλησιν ὑμῶν, "But woe to the rich! For you have received your consolation" (6:24).[16] The same theme pervades Luke, punctuating the Gospel at key moments, expressed in the same terminology. Each time (1:46–55: Magnificat, 6:20–26: Blessing and Woe; 12:15–21: Rich Fool; 16:19–31: Dives and Lazarus) there is a reversal in which rich people are held already to have received their reward on earth, the poor receiving their reward in the kingdom of heaven; and this is illustrated each time

---

13. For a fine monograph dealing with this theme, see John O. York, *The Last Shall Be First: The Rhetoric of Reversal in Luke* (JSNTSup, 46; Sheffield: JSOT Press, 1991). For a recent comment on this from a source-critical perspective, see Allan J. McNicol et al., eds., *Beyond the Q Impasse*, 40.

14. Cf. Luke T. Johnson, *The Writings of the New Testament* (London: SCM, 1986), 215: "Mary's canticle established a pattern of divine reversal. The rich are sent away empty and the powerful brought low, while the poor are lifted up. Luke's blessing of the poor fits within this pattern of messianic reversal. He does not prescribe a 'spiritual attitude' for his followers but announces that God is upsetting the measure of the world."

15. Cf. John Drury, *Tradition and Design*, 135.

16. There is no consensus in Q scholarship as to whether the Woes originate with Luke or not. The relevant volume of *Documenta Q*, not yet published, will be the best place to see the contrasting views on the subject. In the mean time, see John Kloppenborg, *Q Parallels*, ad loc. The International Q Project decided against inclusion (see *The Critical Edition of Q*, ad loc.).

in a context of hunger and feasting.[17] In the Magnificat, the hungry are "filled with good things" (πεινῶντας ἐνέπλησεν ἀγαθῶν, 1:53) and the "rich sent away empty" (καὶ πλουτοῦντας ἐξαπέστειλεν κενούς, 1:53); in the Rich Fool, his goal is to "Take life easy, eat, drink, and be merry" (ἀναπαύου, φάγε, πίε, εὐφραίνου, 12:19) and Dives feasts sumptuously every day (εὐφραινόμενος καθ᾽ ἡμέραν λαμπρῶς, 16:19) while Lazarus hungers (16:20–21). Indeed, one might say that the parable of the Rich Man and Lazarus is a "narrativizing" of this the first beatitude and woe: Lazarus, described twice as πτωχός (poor, 16:20 and 16:22) is blessed — he receives "the kingdom of God," that is, he goes to Abraham's bosom (16:22). The Rich Man, ὁ πλούσιος, is cursed — he has "already received [his] consolation" (6:24, παράκλησις; cf. 16:25 παρακαλεῖται).

And the key point for the question over the more original form of the first beatitude is this. Once one has seen how far eschatological reversal, especially reversal involving "poor" and "rich," is a theme in Luke, it becomes difficult to imagine how Luke would or could have phrased a woe corresponding to a beatitude on the "poor in spirit." Woe to the rich in spirit? Woe to the rich in flesh? Woe to those who are not poor in spirit?[18] Such a thing would be a literary nightmare and a contradiction to Luke's practice elsewhere. No, where there is a blessing on the poor in spirit, the reader should not be at all surprised to see Luke rephrasing with his favorite "poor," characteristically drawing them into a Lukan eschatological reversal scenario, in which the poor are rewarded and the rich condemned.

Narrative-Critical Reading

But there is yet another reason that we should not be surprised about the Lukan reference here to "the poor," the fact that it makes such good

---

17. Cf. L. Schottroff and W. Stegemann, *Jesus von Nazareth — Hoffnung der Armen* (3d ed.; Stuttgart: Kohlhammer, 1990), 38–46, who treat the Woes, the Magnificat and Dives together, but regard them all as pre-Lukan.

18. Cf. Austin Farrer, "Dispensing," 64: "Even the apparently plain cases [of alleged greater Lukan primitivity] turn out to be not plain at all. We all agree at first sight that Christ is more likely to have blessed the poor, than the poor in spirit. "In spirit" looks like an editorial safeguard against misunderstanding: to be in lack of money is not enough. St. Luke's phrase, then, is the more primitive. But on the other hand St. Luke's eight beatitudes-and-woes with their carefully paired antitheses are not a more primitive affair than St. Matthew's eight beatitudes, but very much the reverse. And the phrase "in spirit" cannot stand in St. Luke's beatitudes-and-woes without overthrowing the logic of the paragraph. The poor are opposed to the rich. The poor in spirit would challenge comparison with the rich in flesh, but that does not mean anything. Thus St. Luke may well have read "in spirit" in St. Matthew, and dropped it in obedience to the logic of his own thought."

narrative-critical sense in Luke. I preface my comments here with a brief comment recapitulating some of the ground covered in Chapter 5 above. Source criticism, as it is still often practiced, regularly fails to take seriously the overall narrative agendas of the texts from which the pericopae under scrutiny have been taken. Counting words, considering redactional preferences, analyzing order: all these things are of limited value unless the exegete also pays careful attention to the narrative context in which a given passage is located. If it is reasonable to hope that source critics might get less possessive about the Synopsis, and if narrative critics can begin to look outside the narrow confines of concentrating purely on one Gospel at a time, there are prospects for some genuinely profitable interaction between the two subdisciplines, enabling source critics to dispense with some of the weaker, old-fashioned elements in their analysis of the ordering of Gospel materials and helping narrative critics to enrich their studies by comparative study of intimately related texts.

Now one of the things that narrative criticism encourages the reader to do is to take seriously the audiences for sayings material. So to whom is the Sermon addressed in Luke? It is, as it is in Matthew (5:2), addressed to "the disciples" (6:20a).[19] In the words of the New American Standard translation, "And turning His gaze toward His disciples, He *began* to say, "Blessed *are* you *who are* poor, for yours is the kingdom of God." There is something important going on here in Luke's narrative, something that is all too often missed.[20]

It appears that the disciples are being addressed directly as οἱ πτωχοί, "the poor." Why is this? The narrative-critical eye will notice that the narrator has been careful to point out, in passages only shortly before this discourse, that the disciples he has called only followed him after they had "left everything," first in the case of Peter, James, and John and then in the case of Levi:

καὶ καταγαγόντες τὰ πλοῖα ἐπὶ τὴν γῆν ἀφέντες πάντα ἠκολούθησαν αὐτῷ.

And having pulled up the boats on the shore, *having left everything,* they followed him (Luke 5:11).

---

19. Luke is careful also to generalize the audience so that the Sermon can have wider applicability — 7:1, . . . εἰς τὰς ἀκοὰς τοῦ λαοῦ ("in the hearing of the people"), cf. Matt 7:28–29.

20. Though see Robert C. Tannehill, *The Narrative Unity of Luke-Acts. A Literary Interpretation: 1. The Gospel according to Luke* (Philadelphia: Fortress, 1991), 206–10, and Michael Goulder, *Luke*, 348–50, though without observing the specific connection with 5:11, 5:28, etc. Joel Green, *The Gospel of Luke*, is not, however, convinced of the link.

καὶ <u>καταλιπὼν πάντα</u> ἀναστὰς ἠκολούθει αὐτῷ

And *having left everything*, having got up, he followed him.
(Luke 5:28).

In other words, the Sermon on the Plain is apparently addressed not
simply to "the poor" in general,[21] but it also has, at the same time, a
targeted, specific message to the community of disciples who, as one of
the major elements in their decision to follow Jesus, have abandoned
everything.

As we saw above in relation to Luke 12:22–34, the theme of the poverty that accompanies discipleship surfaces at key moments in Luke's
narrative. In particular, Luke 12:22–34 ("On Care and Anxieties") is
addressed to the disciples, and is all the more noticeable because of
the contrast with the material that precedes it, the Rich Fool parable
(12:13–21) that is addressed to the crowd in general. While the Rich
Fool is appropriately directed at characters like the interlocutor who had
interrupted Jesus by asking for arbitration in a property dispute (12:13–
14), characters who were still, apparently, holding on to possessions, the
teaching about care and anxiety is addressed to those, the disciples, who
did not have possessions, those who might well worry about what they
could eat and what they might wear. The context and rationale for the
voluntary poverty appears to be the disciples' mission — the Twelve take
with them no staff, no bag, no bread, no money, no extra tunic (Luke
9:3) and the Seventy likewise take no purse, no bag, no sandals (10:4),
eating and drinking what their hosts place before them (10:7–8). The disciples' voluntary poverty is thus narrated (5:11, 5:28), celebrated (6:20),
reinforced (9:1–6; 10:1–12) and the day-by-day ramifications discussed
(12:22–34). Indeed the keynote teaching on discipleship ends with the
following comment:

οὕτως οὖν πᾶς ἐξ ὑμῶν ὃς οὐκ ἀποτάσσεται πᾶσιν τοῖς ἑαυτοῦ
ὑπάρχουσιν οὐ δύναται εἶναί μου μαθητής.

So then, none of you can be My disciple who does not give up all
his own possessions (14:33).[22]

---

21. It may need to be underlined that the Lukan audience in the Sermon on the Plain is both
general and specific, the disciples in the hearing of the people (7:1, see above, n. 19). Luke's
treatment of the poor here coheres with this approach — it has both universal relevance and a
more nuanced, specific applicability to this one subgroup, the disciples. See also n. 22, below.
22. See above, pp. 114–16. The point needs to be qualified by observing that while — for
Luke — true disciples are confined to the ranks of "the poor," the converse does not of course

When narrative criticism interacts with source criticism in this way, it is difficult to avoid the conclusion that Luke would not have wanted to write "poor in spirit" here in 6:20 if indeed it stood in his source. Not only does the author depict Jesus' life as involving a messianic mission to the poor, alongside the promise of eschatological reversal in which the rich are cursed, but also it is the clear course that has been laid in both the immediate and the broader contexts in Luke. Whether one takes Luke's source as Q or Matthew, that source here featured an address to the disciples.[23]

Indeed, the narrative-critical perspective is here bolstered by the redaction-critical observation that these references to the disciples' voluntary poverty appear in redactional modifications of Mark (1:20 // Matthew 4:22 and Mark 2:14 // Matthew 9:9 respectively[24]), represented in the quotations above in the underlined words.[25] But in short, the value of a narrative-critical reading is that it takes seriously both the context in which "Blessed are the poor" occurs and the audience for the saying, noting how it coheres with the broader narrative agenda of Luke's Gospel. For the source critic, this is evidence that ought to be taken seriously, for it appears to confirm that if indeed Luke knew Matthew's Gospel, we might have expected him to have redacted it in this way.

Yet before we can be quite sure about the likelihood that it is Luke who dropped τῷ πνεύματι rather than Matthew who added it, it is necessary to ask two more questions. First, is not the claim that Matthew "spiritu-

---

follow. While the disciples are all poor, "the poor" are not all disciples. Cf. Robert Tannehill, *Luke* (Abingdon New Testament Commentaries; Nashville: Abingdon, 1996), 115, "Statements elsewhere do not limit concern for the poor to those who have already become disciples (cf. 1:52–53; 7:22; 14:21). In 16:19–25 poor Lazarus is not comforted because he is a follower of Jesus. Jesus, however, would like to believe in God's kingdom for them, which may mean living as disciples." It should also be added that there is evidence within Luke for disciples with wealth, but in each case it is to be used in service of the kingdom of God, 8:1–3 and 16:9. On the latter, see especially Robert Tannehill, *Luke*, 248–49. See also Eric Franklin, *Luke*, 319–20. And see n. 25 below.

23. For the two-source theory, Q also directed the Sermon to the disciples — Q 6:20b, καὶ [[ἐπάρ]]ας το[[ὺς ὀφθαλμοὺς]] αὐτοῦ [[εἰς τοὺς]] {μαθητὰ}[[ς]] {αὐτοῦ} [] λεγ [<>]...(James M. Robinson et al., eds., *The Critical Edition of Q*, 46–47).

24. In Mark 1:20 the disciples leave Zebedee in the boat with the hired servants; in Mark 2:14 there is no comment about leaving anything. See too the minor redactional modification of Mark 10:21 (ὅσα ἔχεις πώλησον καὶ δὸς τοῖς πτωχοῖς) in Luke 18:22 (πάντα ὅσα ἔχεις πώλησον καὶ διάδος πτωχοῖς).

25. Also relevant is Luke 19:1–9 in which Zacchaeus gives half his possessions to the poor, perhaps in order that he has some remaining to pay back four times those he has defrauded (cf. Luke 3:13). The theme looks forward to the early chapters of Acts, especially 2:44–45 and 4:32–36.

alized" the Q beatitude somehow self-evident? Is this not a clear element in his overall agenda? Second, what of the evidence from the Gospel of Thomas in which this beatitude also appears: does it not provide an independent witness to the primitivity of the Lukan version?

Does Matthew "Spiritualize" the Beatitude?

The claim that Matthew has "spiritualized" the Q beatitude, transforming "poor" to "poor in spirit" rests, of course, on the notion that Luke better preserves the Q wording, a notion that is open to challenge from the sheer pervasiveness and distinctiveness of the Lukan version of the beatitude and its associated woe. But is it based on anything other than that? There are further elements. First, there is the analogy of Q 7:22[26] in which the evangelizing of "the poor" is again mentioned; this, some scholars believe, witnesses to concern for "the poor" as a major concern in Q. In Matthew 11:5 // Luke 7:22, the list of Jesus' deeds, drawn from Isaiah 35 and 61, concludes with the pronouncement that "the poor are evangelized," πτωχοὶ εὐαγγελίζονται,[27] and Catchpole speaks of the tension between Matt 11:5, which lists activities that have been reported variously in Matt 8–9, and Matt 5:3 "where," he says, "contrary to Matthew's normal implication that poverty really is poverty (cf. 19:21; 26:9, 11), we are faced with something different, 'poverty in spirit.' "[28] The argument is not compelling. Even if one accepts that the simple variation between "poor in spirit" in one context and "poor" in another constitutes a major tension, it is clear that the direct allusion to the LXX of Isaiah 61 (εὐαγγελίσασθαι πτωχοῖς, "to evangelize poor people") will

---

26. This means the Q text allegedly underlying Matthew 11:5 // Luke 7:22, see above, pp. 7–8.

27. Isaiah 61:1 LXX . . . εὐαγγελίσασθαι πτωχοῖς. The recently published (1992) Qumran fragment 4Q521 provides a fascinating parallel to Matthew 11:5 // Luke 7:22. Recent discussions include James D. Tabor and Michael O. Wise, "4Q521 'On Resurrection' and the Synoptic Gospel Tradition: a Preliminary Study," in *Qumran Questions* (ed. James H. Charlesworth; The Biblical Seminar, 36; Sheffield: Sheffield Academic Press, 1995), 151–63; Edward P. Meadors, "The 'Messianic' Implications of the Q Material," *JBL* 118 (1999): 253–77; André Caquot, "Deux textes messianiques de Qumrân," *Revue d'histoire et de philosophie religieuses* 79/2 (1999): 155–71; Michael Becker, "4Q521 und die Gesalbten," *Revue de Qumran* 18 (1997): 73–76; and Hans Kvalbein, "Die Wunder der Endzeit. Beobachtungen zu 4Q521 und Matth 11,5p." *ZNW* 88 (1997): 111–25. See further literature cited in these articles. Although often linked with Q in these discussions, it needs to be noticed that reconstructed Q has no more in common with 4Q521 than have Matthew and Luke here. Indeed Matthew, who prefaces the material featuring the Isaianic quotations with the narrative comment that John had heard about τὰ ἔργα τοῦ Χριστοῦ (11:2), here echoes Isaiah 61:1 (πνεῦμα κυρίου ἐπ' ἐμέ, οὖ εἵνεκεν ἔχρισέν με) and 4Q521, which mentions "his Messiah."

28. *The Quest for Q*, 17.

account for the wording in Matt 11:5. Matthew is here drawn by the wording of his source in Isaiah. One can see the same thing happening with another element in Matthew 11:5, κωφοὶ ἀκούουσιν ("the deaf hear") in which the source in Isaiah 35:5 (LXX ὦτα κωφῶν ἀκούσονται, "the ears of the deaf will hear") generates wording that is not entirely consonant with the story in Matthew 9:32–34 in which ἐλάλησεν ὁ κωφός ("the dumb man *spoke*," 9:33): Any tension between Matt 11:5 and Matt 5:3 is only that which is naturally created by Matthew's attempt to point directly to the Isaianic passage in the one context, and more allusively and subtly in the other place.[29] It is unnecessary to insist on "tension" when what we have is simply subtle variation in the use of Scripture to suit different contexts.

The second matter that is brought forward in this context is that Matthew also apparently "spiritualizes" another beatitude, 5:6, μακάριοι οἱ πεινῶντες καὶ διψῶντες τὴν δικαιοσύνην, "Blessed are those who hunger *and thirst for righteousness*," contrasted with μακάριοι οἱ πεινῶντες νῦν, "Blessed are those who hunger now" in Luke 6:21. Both Catchpole and Tuckett point out that Luke is interested in righteousness as a theme and would hardly have dropped it here. Catchpole is especially forthright:

> To exert oneself in terms of righteousness or, as it might be put, to hunger and thirst for righteousness reflects the supreme religious priority as far as Luke is concerned. How extraordinary that he should remove it, not once but twice (Matt 5:6, 10)![30]

While Catchpole's stress on the importance of the general theme to Luke may be a useful corrective to Goulder's claim that "Luke elsewhere lacks Matthew's zeal for righteousness,"[31] his argument against Lukan redaction of the Matthean beatitude is inadequate for at least two reasons. First, it is important not simply to appeal to general themes but to observe the nuances in the evangelists' use of them. Not only

---

29. Once again, to be fair to Catchpole, it is important to add that his primary target here is Michael Goulder, for whom Matthew has created "Blessed are the poor in spirit" by "glossing" Isaiah 61:1, C. M. Tuckett and M. D. Goulder, "The Beatitudes: A Source-Critical Study," *NovT* 25 (1983): 193–216 (209). See *The Quest for Q*, 18. However, even here it is worth observing that Goulder distinguishes between different uses of the Hebrew Bible in the two places. In 5:3–12, Matthew is working creatively, using Isaiah 61:1 as a base text, whereas in Matt 11:5 he is engaged in what approximates to quotation. In such circumstances the "glossing" of Isaiah is appropriate in one context but inappropriate in the other.

30. *The Quest for Q*, 20. C. M. Tuckett and M. D. Goulder, "Beatitudes," 200.

31. C. M. Tuckett and M. D. Goulder, "Beatitudes," 209.

does Catchpole play down Luke's apparent reticence to use the word δικαιοσύνη ("righteousness," 7/0/1+4), which appears only once in the Gospel (1:67), but also he does not acknowledge that there are major differences in the way Matthew and Luke use the theme. While for Matthew δικαιοσύνη ("righteousness") is something after which disciples might hunger and thirst (here) or for which they might seek (6:33; contrast Luke 12:31),[32] for Luke the theme tends to be used in relation to characterizing the pious individual's life, supremely Jesus' (Luke 23:47, Ὄντως ὁ ἄνθρωπος οὗτος δίκαιος ἦν, "Certainly this man was innocent," contrast Mark 15:39) but also those like Joseph of Arimathaea, ἀνὴρ ἀγαθὸς καὶ δίκαιος, "a good and *righteous* man," Luke 23:50, contrast Mark 15:43). Indeed it may be for this reason that Luke is reticent to use the noun δικαιοσύνη ("righteousness") since the adjective δίκαιος (17/2/11+6, "righteous") is much more conducive to this nuance in Luke's thinking.

But a second issue is more important. For Catchpole's and Tuckett's point to be established, one would require Luke's formulation of the beatitude to be in some way uncharacteristic of him. And that is precisely what we do not have. Rather, as with the first beatitude, here there is a beatitude that is characteristic of Luke's Gospel, which is thoroughly consonant with Luke's literary agenda and which makes sense in its narrative context. Luke regularly works out the theme of poverty by relating it to hunger, and seldom thinks of poverty and hunger without invoking the theme of eschatological reversal. The Magnificat has the directly corresponding theme, "He has filled the hungry with good things; and the rich he has sent away empty" (1:53). Indeed it is striking that Luke often, in passages involving this kind of eschatological reversal, focuses specifically, as here, on hungering and eating. Dives's luxury lifestyle is defined by the "fine linen" he wore but most importantly by the fact that he "feasted sumptuously every day" (Luke 16:19). Likewise Lazarus's poverty is defined in terms of his "desire to be fed with what fell from the rich man's table" (16:20). So, too, the Rich Fool decides, having stored up his goods for many years, to "eat, drink, and be merry" (12:19).

As with "blessed are the poor in spirit," one has to ask here what a woe associated with "Blessed are those who hunger and thirst for

---

32. For full treatment of the subject, see Benno Przybylski, *Righteousness in Matthew and his World of Thought* (SNTSMS, 41; Cambridge: Cambridge University Press, 1980).

righteousness" might look like. For an author like Luke, for whom the kingdom of God involves the hungry being satisfied, and the rich having already received their consolation, "Blessed are those who hunger now" cannot for a moment be thought un-Lukan. Catchpole's claim that it would have been "extraordinary" for Luke to have removed Matthew's reference to righteousness here only works on a narrow redaction-critical model in which it is regarded as inevitable for the evangelists to have taken over every congenial word, phrase, or theme from their sources. But it is unnecessary to assume that the evangelists' default position was to keep their sources unchecked, and only to alter them when they found them in some way objectionable. Even if it is true that Luke would have appreciated the notion of hungering and thirsting for righteousness, this does not mean that Luke would have necessarily copied it verbatim, particularly given his own literary agenda, particularly at this point in the narrative. Redaction criticism without consideration of broader narrative context in the Gospels, and the literary agenda of the evangelists is, in the end, a blunted instrument that can only detract from our appreciation of the Gospels and their writers.

Finally, in this section, it will be worth pausing for a moment to consider the very use of the term "spiritualizing" to describe Matthew's alleged behavior, and to reflect on the meaning of the term πτωχοὶ τῷ πνεύματι, "poor in spirit."[33] The difficulty for modern scholars answering the question about the meaning of this term is that it has so often been cast in terms of the Lukan parallel. The question is thus unduly focused on the alleged addition of the term τῷ πνεύματι (" . . . in spirit") and adequate attention is not paid to the term as a whole. One of the consequences of this is that interpreters quickly assume that Matthew's Jesus is here talking about the spiritual state of the individual, a kind of poverty in [i.e., lack of] spirit, an idea immortalized by the New English Bible's painfully misleading paraphrase, "How blessed are those who know their need of God," an idea that is coherent neither in the context in Matthew nor in the contemporary literature. For when one begins to pay attention to the whole phrase, it is striking that there is a close parallel in Qumran literature, where in 1QM 14.7 there is mention of ʿaniyye ruaḥ, "the humbled/afflicted in spirit."[34] The term appears to be

---

33. The most extensive treatment of the topic remains Dupont, *Béatitudes*, III, 385–450.

34. Cf. Matthew Black, "The Aramaic Dimension in Q," *JSNT* 40 (1990): 33–41 (40, n. 13): "It seems to me more than probable that it is this (Aramaic) expression which lies behind the Matthean translation-Greek πτωχοὶ τῷ πνεύματι; Luke simplifies by eliminating the

used, perhaps with conscious allusion to Isaiah 66:2, as a metaphor to
describe the redeemed community, "the perfect of way," "the remnant,"
who are contrasted with "the hard of heart." It is a descriptor that might
successfully be applied to the way in which the faithful are represented
in Matthew's Gospel, those who follow Jesus to be discipled in the kingdom of heaven, and who resist the hypocrisy, as Matthew sees it, of the
Pharisees and Scribes, and so it is an entirely appropriate term for use
at the beginning of Matthew's most important set piece in which the
redeemed community is addressed on a mountain by this new Moses.[35]

In relation to this, it seems that the term "spiritualizing" is not a particularly helpful one. Not only does it beg the question by assuming that
the tradition inevitably developed along a "spiritualizing" and "ethiciz-
ing" trajectory,[36] but one suspects that it ultimately tells us more about
our own secularizing agenda than it does about the first century. Marcus
Borg, for example, writes:

> Jesus spoke harshly about wealth. In our discomfort with these say-
> ings, we have often metaphorized them, as if they refer to spiritual
> poverty and spiritual wealth, a process that can be traced back at
> least to Matthew's Gospel. But initially they referred to real wealth
> and real poverty.... The sayings against wealth are thus part of
> Jesus' criticism of the domination system.[37]

But while the critique of our discomfort with Jesus' harsh comments
about wealth is undoubtedly well-placed, the attempt to project this "discomfort" onto a spiritualizing, metaphorizing trajectory already present
in the way Matthew interprets the Jesus tradition goes far beyond the
evidence. If one wanted to engage in this kind of speculation on scholarly
anxiety over sayings attributed to Jesus in the Gospels, then one might
equally point to discomfort with a beatitude often seen to be about de-

---

Semitism but lays himself open to the charge of 'ebionitism.' If this is correct, the interpretation
of Matt 5:3 proposed seems to rule out altogether or to relegate the 'religious' or 'spiritual'
understanding of the First Beatitude to a subsidiary role; and it links Matt 5:3 (and 4) with
Isa. 61:1–2."

35. For the Moses typology, see Dale Allison, *The New Moses: A Matthaean Typology*
(Edinburgh: T & T Clark, 1993).

36. For the assumption that there was such a "spiritualizing trajectory," cf. James M. Robinson, "The Jesus of Q as Liberation Theologian," in *The Gospels behind the Gospels*, 259–74
(263–64).

37. N. T. Wright and Marcus Borg, *The Meaning of Jesus: Two Visions* (London: SPCK,
1999), 73. Cf. John Dominic Crossan's comment that "It is hard to imagine a saying more
initially radical than 43 *Blessed the Poor* [1/3] and thereafter more safely relegated to the
confines of normalcy if not banality," *The Historical Jesus*, 270.

pendence on God. Perhaps we are all too eager to discover a message more palatable in a secularized society, in which "spiritualizing" represents a secondary, negative development of material originally more conducive to a social gospel.[38]

The Saying in Thomas

There is, however, one more important piece of evidence to be considered. Some scholarship, especially recently, has claimed that the Gospel of Thomas, independently of Matthew and Luke, witnesses to the greater primitivity of the Lukan form "Blessed are the poor."[39] The difficulty with this question is that it is inevitably affected by prior decisions, usually on the basis of other evidence, concerning whether or not Thomas is independent of the Synoptic Gospels. There is, unfortunately, no time to debate the question here[40] except insofar as the argument impinges on our discussion of this beatitude. One of the most forthright arguments in favor of complete Thomasine independence at this point is made by John Dominic Crossan, for whom the independence of Thomas — and, for that matter, the existence of Q — are major assumptions in his work.

When attempting to illustrate the independence of Thomas from the Synoptics, Crossan chooses this beatitude as his prime example. His argument therefore needs to be taken seriously. Crossan says:

> One example may again suffice. The first beatitude in Luke 6.20b has "Blessed are you poor, for yours is the kingdom of God," but in Matt 5.3, "Blessed are the poor in spirit, for theirs is the kingdom of heaven." Scholars had long considered that "in spirit" was a personal, redactional addition by Matthew himself. Now in Gos. Thom. 54 we have, "Blessed are the poor, for yours is the kingdom of heaven." Precisely what is missing is the proposed editorial addition of Matthew. But what if one objects that Thomas has simply copied Luke here? That will not work. One would have at least

---

38. For reflections on a related tendency in historical Jesus research, see Dale Allison, "The Secularizing of the Historical Jesus," forthcoming in *Perspectives in Religious Studies* and also available on Allison's home page (*http://www.pts.edu/allisond.html*, accessed 2001).

39. No scholars are (to my knowledge) suggesting a direct literary link between Thomas and Q. The point is that if Thomas is independent of the Synoptics, Thomas 54 might witness to the currency of the Lukan form of the beatitude in primitive tradition. For a discussion from this perspective, see Stephen J. Patterson, *Gospel of Thomas and Jesus,* 42–44.

40. For the case for Thomasine dependence on the Synoptics, see Christopher Tuckett, "Thomas and the Synoptics," *NovT* 30 (1988): 132–57; for a recent discussion see Risto Uro, "*Thomas* and the Oral Gospel Tradition."

to argue that Thomas (a) took the third person "the poor" from
Matthew, then (b) the second person "yours" from Luke, and (c) re-
turned to Matthew for the final "Kingdom of Heaven." It might be
simpler to suggest that Thomas was mentally unstable.[41]

The argument, especially insofar as it is based on Crossan's (a) and
(b), is fallacious, as a careful look at a Synopsis, shown on the following
page, will make clear. It is clear from the Synopsis that there is verbatim
agreement between Matthew and Luke over the key phrase, μακάριοι οἱ
πτωχοί, "Blessed are the poor." If Thomas is dependent on the Synoptics
at this point, it is incorrect to insist that Thomas would have needed to
have taken "the third person 'the poor' from Matthew." Dependence
on Luke would suffice. The reason for the common translation of Luke
6:20b "Blessed are (you) poor" is the second clause, a clause that Luke
and Thomas share, both addressing the audience in the second person,
"yours (ὑμετέρα / ⲦⲰⲦⲚ̄) is the kingdom of God / heaven."[42]

Indeed the only thing that differs between the Thomasine version and
the Lukan version is "heaven" (ⲠⲎⲨⲈ) against "God" (θεός), Crossan's
(c) above. But there is nothing surprising about this, and dependence
on the last clause of the Matthean beatitude is not a necessary thesis.
We will not expect to see "kingdom of God" (ἡ βασιλεία τοῦ θεοῦ) in
Coptic Thomas for the phrase is entirely absent in the Gospel, in which
we always find just "kingdom" (ⲘⲚ̄ⲦⲈⲢⲞ) or "kingdom of the heavens"
(ⲦⲘⲚ̄ⲦⲈⲢⲞ ⲚⲘ̄ⲠⲎⲨⲈ) or "kingdom of the father" (ⲦⲘⲚ̄ⲦⲈⲢⲞ Ⲙ̄ⲚⲈⲒⲰⲦ).[43]

---

41. John Dominic Crossan, *Four Other Gospels: Shadows on the Contours of Canon* (Minneapolis: Seabury, 1985), 37. In *The Birth of Christianity,* Crossan again mentions this beatitude
in the context of the question of Thomasine independence of the Synoptics: "What if one raises
the possibility that the author of *Thomas* created a collection of sayings after having heard
or read the synoptic gospels in the distant past?... Why did the author choose *those* sayings
rather than all the others available for inclusion? Why, to give a specific example, did the author manage to hear or read that *set* of beatitudes in Matthew and Luke and remember them
as the discrete ones given in the *Gospel of Thomas* 54 (poor), 68–69:1 (persecuted), and 69:2
(hungry)?" (118). However, he does not allude to his earlier argument from the content and
wording of this beatitude in Matthew, Luke and Thomas. Cf. also p. 322 for a brief discussion
of the "in spirit" clause.
42. W. Schrage, *Das Verhältnis des Thomas-Evangeliums zur synoptischen Tradition und
zu den koptischen Evangelienübersetzungen. Zugleich ein Beitrag zur gnostischen Synoptikerdeutung* (BZNW, 29; Berlin: Töpelmann, 1964), 118–19 also speaks of Thomas 54 as
representing a mixed text, though he uses the claim in exactly the opposite way to Crossan,
claiming that this is a sign of Thomasine conflation of Matthew and Luke.
43. Cf. Dieter Muller, "Kingdom of Heaven or Kingdom of God?" *Vigiliae Christianae* 27
(1973): 266–76: "Wherever the Kingdom is mentioned, the Coptic displays a marked preference for the absolute of this term (log. 3, 22, 27, 46, 49, 82, 107, 109, 113), but occasionally
substitutes either 'Kingdom of the Father' (log. 57, 76, 96–98, 113) or 'Kingdom of Heaven'
(log. 20, 54, 114)" (272).

Matthew 5:2–3	Luke 6:20	Thomas 54
καὶ ἀνοίξας	καὶ αὐτὸς ἐπάρας	ⲡⲉⲭⲉ ⲓⲥ ⲭⲉ
τὸ στόμα	τοὺς ὀφθαλμοὺς	
αὐτοῦ ἐδίδασκεν	αὐτοῦ εἰς	
αὐτοὺς	τοὺς μαθητὰς αὐτοῦ	
λέγων·	ἔλεγεν·	
μακάριοι οἱ πτωχοὶ	μακάριοι οἱ πτωχοί	ϩⲛ̄ⲙⲁⲕⲁⲣⲓⲟⲥ ⲛⲉ ⲛ̄ϩⲏⲕⲉ
τῷ πνεύματι, ὅτι	ὅτι	ⲭⲉ
αὐτῶν ἐστιν	ὑμετέρα ἐστὶν	ⲧⲱⲧⲛ̄ ⲧⲉ
ἡ βασιλεία τῶν	ἡ βασιλεία τοῦ θεοῦ.	ⲧⲙⲛ̄ⲧⲉⲣⲟ ⲛ̄ⲙ̄ⲡⲏⲩⲉ
οὐρανῶν.		

And having opened his mouth, he taught them, saying, "Blessed are the poor in spirit, for theirs is the kingdom of the heavens."	And having raised his eyes to his disciples, he said, "Blessed are the poor for yours is the kingdom of God."	Jesus says this, "Blessed are the poor for yours is the kingdom of the heavens."

"Kingdom of heaven" is simply a standard Thomasine term: he does not write "kingdom of God" anywhere else, so we do not expect him to write it here either.[44]

Yet even if all this were not the case, it might be said that the process parodied by Crossan is not as implausible as he attempts to make it. Does not our earliest evidence consist precisely of mixed quotations of this kind, when Justin Martyr, for example, apparently remembers elements from different parts of parallel texts? But the overwhelming problem here is simply that Crossan is using conflicting English translations, one of Luke that translates "Blessed are you poor" (so many translations[45]) and one of Thomas (Thomas Lambdin's) that translates "Blessed are the poor"[46]

---

44. Cf. Stephen J. Patterson, *The Gospel of Thomas and Jesus,* 43. The point needs to be qualified by observing that the Oxyrhynchus fragments do feature the term "kingdom of God" (ἡ βασιλεία τοῦ θεοῦ) once certainly (Logion 27) and once possibly (Logion 3). In the latter case, notice the argument by Dieter Muller for restoring "kingdom of heaven" here (P Oxy 654, line 11): Muller, "Kingdom of Heaven," see previous note. If anything, the fact that "kingdom of God" might have lain behind some of the instances of "kingdom," "kingdom of heaven" and "kingdom of my Father" strengthens the case for disregarding the stress placed on "kingdom of heaven" by Crossan.

45. "Blessed are you (ye) poor" is found in the King James, the Revised Standard Version, the New American Standard Bible, the New International Version and the New Revised Standard Version, among many others.

46. Thomas O. Lambdin, "The Coptic Gospel According to Thomas" in *Nag Hammadi Codex II, 2–7,* 2 vols. (ed. Bentley Layton; NHS 20–21, The Coptic Gnostic Library; Leiden: Brill, 1989), 1:52–93.

and this is not an adequate basis for sustaining the desired argument, much less for pronouncing on the state of Thomas's mental health.[47]

Conclusion

Anyone who has seen *Monty Python's Life of Brian* (dir. Terry Jones, 1979), the opening scene of which is devoted to comical attempts to decipher the precise wording of Jesus' beatitudes among those standing at a distance, may view the pages here devoted to the wording of one of them with at least a hint of amusement. In defense of spending this amount of time on the first beatitude, I would draw attention to the sheer prevalence of the view that Luke's "Blessed are the poor" is more original than Matthew's "Blessed are the poor in spirit," and its place as a textbook example of the argument that sometimes Matthew, sometimes Luke will have had the more original form of a Q saying, one of the pillars of the standard case for Q. While there are problems with the underlying assumptions and general logic of that argument,[48] this chapter has focused on the attempt to demonstrate that in this one famous case, Luke's dependence on Matthew is plausible, and that it is at least as strong as the notion that they independently edited Q. The standard view, that Matthew "spiritualized" a Q beatitude better represented in the Lukan version, does not pay adequate attention to any of the following points:

1. A blessing on the poor coheres with one of Luke's most insistent themes, a theme standing at the agenda-setting outset of Jesus' public ministry, when he announces the fulfillment of Isaiah 61 in his sermon in Nazara (4:16–30). The theme resonates throughout Luke's Gospel, which, as every introduction tells us, is the Gospel of the underdog.

---

47. The difficulty is compounded in R. W. Funk and R. W. Hoover, eds., *The Five Gospels,* which presents a synopsis of this beatitude using arbitrarily conflicting translations, "Congratulations to the poor" for Thomas and "Congratulations, you poor" for Luke (292), creating the impression of difference between the two where there is none. Stephen Patterson's more nuanced treatment of this saying, *The Gospel of Thomas and Jesus,* 42–44, is focused on the attempt to demonstrate that the saying is not derived from Luke. He rightly draws attention to the possibility of independent derivation of "kingdom of heaven" in Matthew and Thomas and adds, "As for the agreements with Luke, they may well stem from a primitive version of the beatitude shared by both; they do not necessarily suggest any literary dependence of Thomas on Luke" (43). This judgment depends largely on the prior assumption that "the Matthean phrase ἐν πνεύματι [*sic*] (in spirit) . . . is widely recognized as secondary" (ibid.), and the notion that Luke's version better represents Q, the very matters under discussion in this chapter.

48. See above, pp. 61–66.

2. The beatitude in Luke has a related woe (6:23) that forms a typical example of Lukan eschatological reversal in which the poor are blessed and the rich condemned, a theme introduced in the Magnificat (1:46–55) and repeated often, most notably in the parable of Dives and Lazarus (16:19–31), which might be described as a kind of narrative version of Luke's first two beatitudes and woes, contrasting hunger and satisfaction, now and in the kingdom of God.

3. The narrative critic will be sensitive to both the audience and the narrative context of this beatitude in Luke, which is addressed to "disciples," who, in Luke, have "left everything" (Luke 5:11, 5:28) to follow Jesus. Since in Luke poverty appears to be a prerequisite for discipleship (14:33), we will hardly be surprised to see the disciples blessed as "the poor."

4. Arguments for Matthean posteriority, based on alleged tensions between Matthew 5:3 ("poor in spirit") and 11:5 (" ... evangelize the poor"), and on the analogy of "hungering *and thirsting for righteousness*," are unconvincing. Further, the idea that Matthew is "spiritualizing" his source does not take seriously the evidence for the meaning of the term both in Qumran literature and in its context in Matthew.

5. The argument that the Gospel of Thomas 54 provides an independent witness to the primitivity of "Blessed are the poor" is weak.

Since consensus positions in biblical exegesis are difficult to come by, it is indeed an inconvenience to have a question mark placed over one usually thought to be so solid, not least on a topic conducive to a desire to reconstruct a primitive Christian tradition in which the poor are congratulated and the complacency of the rich is challenged. In such circumstances, one can only say that if it is right to challenge injustice and to fight against poverty, then it is right to do so regardless of any attempt to derive extra legitimacy from the dubious reconstruction of the precise wording of a saying in a hypothetical document.[49]

---

49. At a late stage in the writing of this manuscript, I received a copy of H. Benedict Green, *Matthew: Poet of the Beatitudes* (JSNTSup, 203; Sheffield; Sheffield Academic Press, 2001), a major new study of the literary history of the Beatitudes from the perspective of the Farrer theory. See especially Chapter 9, "Sources or Influences," for the material dealt with here.

Chapter Eight

MAJOR AND MINOR AGREEMENTS

For some time now, Q skeptics have been drawing attention to some of the minor agreements between Matthew and Luke against Mark as the Achilles heel of the two-source theory.[1] It is a mark of the success of this strategy that Q theorists regularly accept that these minor agreements do indeed constitute a problem for their theory. The admission is often tempered, however, with the claim that this is the only major problem faced by the two-source theory, and that it can be overcome by appealing to a variety of mitigating factors, chief among which are the possibility of independent redaction by Matthew and Luke, the influence of Q, text-critical uncertainty and the influence of oral tradition. But the minor agreements should not be underestimated. Not only should the difficulties they pose for the Q theory be taken seriously, but also it is important to recognize that they represent only one element in a spectrum of evidence that is uncongenial to Q, a spectrum that is all too easily missed if one insists too strongly on the term "minor."

Let us begin by reviewing the problems that the minor agreements cause for the two-source theory. The situation is straightforward. If Matthew and Luke redacted Mark independently of one another, which is the essential premise of the Q theory, then we should not expect to see the number and quality of minor agreements between Matthew and Luke against Mark that in fact we do see. The number of minor agreements itself tends to surprise those who have not spent much time with the Synopsis. Although different counts vary widely,[2] it is worth drawing

---

1. The most important recent publication on the minor agreements is G. Strecker, ed., *Minor Agreements: Symposium Göttingen 1991* (Göttingen: Vandenhoeck & Ruprecht, 1993). For a good introduction to the problem the minor agreements pose for the two-source theory, see E. P. Sanders and M. Davies, *Studying the Synoptic Gospels*, 67–83. For the role they play in the Farrer theory and especially in Michael Goulder's work, see further my *Goulder and the Gospels*, Chapter 3 and the literature cited there, though now see also A. Ennulat, *Die "Minor Agreements": Untersuchung zu einer offenen Frage des synoptischen Problems* (WUNT 2/62; Tübingen: J. C. B. Mohr [Paul Siebeck], 1994) and literature cited elsewhere in the current chapter.

2. It is difficult to judge the precise number of minor agreements, or to assess the significance

attention to Sanders and Davies's point that there is hardly a pericope in the triple tradition that does not feature minor agreements.[3] And there are pericopae like the Paralytic (Matt 9:1–8 // Mark 2:1–12 // Luke 5:17–26) or the Five Thousand (Matt 14:13–21 // Mark 6:30–44 // Luke 9:10–17) that feature multiple minor agreements, many of which are not straightforwardly explained as the result of coincidental independent redaction.

Nevertheless, it remains difficult to assess the significance of the number of minor agreements. How many is too many?[4] How much force can a cumulative case have?[5] The difficulty is that so many of the minor agreements are explicable in terms of common sense and the standard redactional practices of Matthew and Luke, δέ for καί, the elimination of historical presents and so on. Under such circumstances it is not easy to judge how significant the overall number may be. The problem is compounded by the impression created by the seminal studies of the

---

of the number. It depends, among other things, on whether and how one counts agreements in omission as well as more positive agreements; and there are many minor agreements that are disputed on text-critical and contextual grounds. Michael Goulder speaks on one occasion of "more than 750 minor agreements" ("On Putting Q to the Test," 218) and on another of "some thousand" (*Luke*, 47; cf. 48). The most liberal count is Richard B. Vinson, *The Significance of the Minor Agreements as An Argument Against the Two-Document Hypothesis* (Duke University Ph.D. thesis, 1984), who has a figure of 2,354 (420, n. 5). But cf. Timothy A. Friedrichsen, "The Minor Agreements of Matthew and Luke Against Mark: Critical Observations on R. B. Vinson's Statistical Analysis," *ETL* 65 (1989): 395–408, especially 401. The key tool for studying the minor agreements remains Frans Neirynck, *The Minor Agreements of Matthew and Luke Against Mark, with a Cumulative List* (BETL, 37; Leuven: Leuven University Press, 1974).

3. See E. P. Sanders and M. Davies, *Studying the Synoptic Gospels*, 67.

4. The most sustained attempt to evaluate the significance of the number of minor agreements is Richard B. Vinson's dissertation (see n. 2, above). He studies the minor agreements and finds a 21.2 percent rate of minor agreements (expressed as a percentage of the total words in Mark). This contrasts massively with two analogous cases set up by Vinson, ten graduate students independently editing the same text (2.1 percent rate) and early Christian apologists quoting the Greek classical writers (3.3 percent). Timothy A. Friedrichsen (see n. 2, above) criticizes both choices of analogy, the contemporary experiment because it is too far removed in time, language, and so on from the Synoptics, and the early Christian apologists because they are quoting and not rewriting texts (see especially pp. 407–8). He does not, however, address the fact that the experimental data produced such strikingly similar figures in contrast with the synoptic minor agreements. Further, Friedrichsen's appeal to mitigating factors like the influence of Q and textual corruption are unhelpful. The minor agreements Vinson discusses do not include those normally attributed to Mark-Q overlap, so the point about Q is irrelevant. On the issue of textual corruption, see further below.

5. See Goulder's interesting argument concerning clusters of "not very Lukan" words in certain minor agreements, taking Matt 16:21 // Mark 8:31 // Luke 9:21 as a test case. See, however, F. Neirynck and T. A. Friedrichsen, "Note on Luke 9:22, A Response to M. D. Goulder," *ETL* 65 (1989): 390–94; also in F. Neirynck, *L'Evangile de Luc — The Gospel of Luke* (BETL, 32; Leuven: Leuven University Press, 1991), 393–98 and *Evangelica II. 1982–91: Collected Essays* (ed. F. Van Segbroeck; BETL, 99; Leuven: Leuven University Press, 1991), 43–48. For an evaluation, see *Goulder and the Gospels*, 96–98.

minor agreements from the two-source perspective, by B. H. Streeter in
English-speaking scholarship and Josef Schmid in German.[6] As Goulder
points out, the many insignificant minor agreements can all too quickly
swamp the really important ones, not least given the fact that significant
minor agreements are often given the same kind of summary treatment
that is provided for those that are less striking.[7] Thus Michael Goulder's
approach, in a series of studies from 1978 onwards,[8] has been to draw
special attention to several of the really remarkable minor agreements in
an attempt to place two-source theorists on the back foot.

The Minor Agreements: Three Examples

It will be worth drawing attention to several examples of minor agreements between Matthew and Luke against Mark to illustrate the case.
The first is taken from the Sadducees' Question About the Resurrection
(Matt 22:23–33 // Mark 12:18–27 // Luke 20:27–40). This is a good
example of a minor agreement that looks ordinary at first[9] but which on
closer inspection is more striking:

Matt 22:27	*Mark 12:22*	*Luke 20:32*
ὕστερον δὲ πάντων ἀπέθανεν ἡ γυνή.	ἔσχατον πάντων καὶ ἡ γυνή ἀπέθανεν	ὕστερον καὶ ἡ γυνὴ ἀπέθανεν
Later than all, the woman died.	Last of all also the woman died.	*Later* also the woman died.

The word ὕστερον ("later") is a particular favorite of Matthew's and
occurs seven times in his Gospel in total. In Matt 21:37 (Wicked Hus-
bandmen) the same substitution, ὕστερον ("later") for ἔσχατον ("last,"

6. B. H. Streeter, *The Four Gospels;* see especially 293–331. J. Schmid, *Matthäus und Lukas: Eine Untersuchung des Verhältnisses ihrer Evangelien* (Freiburg: Herder, 1930), 31–80.
    7. "Much the predominance of the thousand MAs [=minor agreements] arises from weak-
nesses in Markan style which Luke might have wished to change anyhow; only a small
proportion, perhaps forty or fifty, represent substantial problems to the paradigm. The reader
thus gains the sense of being swept along by wave after wave of obviously sensible, well-based
explanations, and his critical faculties are lulled when a more genuine difficulty is being met"
(*Luke,* 48).
    8. "On Putting Q to the Test," *NTS* 24 (1978): 218–24; "Luke's Knowledge of Matthew,"
in G. Strecker, ed., *Minor Agreements,* 143–60; *Luke,* 47–50 and *passim.* For full treatment of
the different arguments used by Goulder, and the scholarly reactions to them (especially those
by C. M. Tuckett and F. Neirynck), see my *Goulder and the Gospels,* Chapter 3.
    9. J. C. Hawkins, for example, puts this in the category of minor agreements that "consist
of words so ordinary and colourless and so nearly synonymous with Mark's that the use of
them may be merely accidental," *Horae Synopticae: Contributions to the Study of the Synoptic
Problem* (2d ed.; Oxford: Clarendon, 1909), 209.

Mark 12:6), occurs in a similar context — ὕστερον ("later") is the word Matthew uses for representing the last in a series and it means something like "finally."[10] The word is a bit unusual; outside of Matthew's seven usages and this one parallel in Luke, it occurs only twice elsewhere in the whole of the New Testament.[11] It seems far more plausible that Luke has taken over an idiosyncratic Matthean word usage here than that both Matthew and Luke have independently coincided in substituting the same word.

This example formed one of six "striking" minor agreements featuring language that is both positively Matthean and at the same time un-Lukan which I produced in *Goulder and the Gospels*.[12] Frans Neirynck[13] engages in a characteristically thorough analysis of each of my examples and while hinting that they are less striking than I had claimed, he has particular difficulty with the case from independent redaction in this example, admitting that the figures of 7/0/1+0 for ὕστερον ("later") "are impressive" but adding the following comments:

> Yet Mt's phrase ὕστερον πάντων remains close to Mk's ἔσχατον πάντων (last of all) and is unique in Mt (and in the NT). The adverbial ἔσχατον (Mk) is little used (only once in the New Testament, 1 Cor 15:8: the same phrase ἔσχατον πάντων) and the coincidence of an identical substitute in Mt and Lk cannot be excluded. That Luke writes ὕστερον (and not ὕστερον πάντων like Mt) may indicate independent redaction.[14]

Neirynck thus concedes that the usage is Matthean and does not deny that it is un-Lukan. The fact that they differ over πάντων does not alter this and may only show that Luke was sensitive to the oddity of Matthew's phrase. Of course, as Neirynck says, "the coincidence of an identical substitute in Mt and Lk cannot be excluded," but while all things are possible, not all things are equally probable. Surely the point of the case from independent redaction is that it rests on the plausibility and not simply the possibility of both Matthew and Luke making the identical changes to Mark independently of one another.

---

10. The New International Version, the Revised Standard Version and the New American Standard Bible all translate the term as "finally" in both Matthew and Luke here.

11. John 13:26 and Hebrews 12:11. The figures for the Gospels are thus 7/0/1+0.

12. Mark Goodacre, *Goulder and the Gospels*, Chapter 3. I also found one — or possibly two — minor agreements satisfying the reverse conditions, positively Lukan and un-Matthean.

13. Frans Neirynck, "Goulder and the Minor Agreements," *ETL* 73 (1997): 84–93.

14. Ibid., 89.

For a second example, let us have a closer look at a minor agreement that has often been thought to be unproblematic for the theory of Matthew's and Luke's independence, from the story of the Paralytic:

Matt 9:2	*Mark 2:3–5*	*Luke 5:18–20*
καὶ ἰδοὺ προσέφερον αὐτῷ παραλυτικὸν ἐπὶ κλίνης βεβλημένον.	καὶ ἔρχονται φέροντες πρὸς αὐτὸν παραλυτικὸν αἰρόμενον ὑπὸ τεσσάρων.	καὶ ἰδοὺ ἄνδρες δέροντες ἐπὶ κλίνης ἄνθρωπον ὃς ἦν παραλελυμένος, καὶ ἐζήτουν αὐτὸν εἰσενεγκεῖν καὶ θεῖναι ἐνώπιον αὐτοῦ. καὶ
	καὶ μὴ δυνάμενοι προσενέγκαι αὐτῷ διὰ	μὴ εὑρόντες ποίας εἰσενέγκωσιν αὐτόν διὰ
τόν ὄχλον,	τὸν ὄχλον, ἀπεστέγασαν τὴν στέγην ὅπου ἦν, καὶ ἐξορύξαντες χαλῶσι τὸν κράβαττον ὅπου ὁ παραλυτικὸς κατέκειτο.	τὸν ὄχλον, ἀναβάντες ἐπὶ τὸ δῶμα διὰ τῶν κεράμων καθῆκαν αὐτὸν σὺν τῷ κλινιδίῳ εἰς τὸ μέσον ἔμπροσθεν τοῦ Ἰησοῦ.
καὶ ἰδὼν ὁ Ἰησοῦς τὴν πίστιν αὐτῶν εἶπεν τῷ παραλυτικῷ....	καὶ ἰδὼν ὁ Ἰησοῦς τὴν πίστιν αὐτῶν λέγει τῷ παραλυτικῷ....	καὶ ἰδὼν τὴν πίστιν αὐτῶν εἶπεν... ...
And <u>behold,</u> they brought to him a paralytic, lying <u>upon a bed,</u>	And they come to him bringing a paralytic carried by four.	And <u>behold,</u> men bringing <u>upon a bed</u> a person who was paralyzed, and they were seeking to bring him in and lay him before him.
	And not being able to bring him because of the crowd, they uncovered the roof where he was, and having dug through, they lowered the pallet on which the paralytic was lying.	And when they had not found a way to bring him in because of the crowd, having ascended upon the roof, they lowered him through the tiles into the middle before Jesus.
And when Jesus had seen their faith, he said to the paralytic....	And when Jesus had seen their faith, he says to the paralytic....	And when he had seen their faith, he said....

Most scholars believe that Matthew and Luke both independently replace Mark's κράβαττος (pallet) because it is a "vulgar word."[15] But as Michael Goulder points out,[16] Luke appears to be happy to use the word elsewhere, and in similar contexts. In Acts 5:15 people bring the sick onto the streets and lay them ἐπὶ κλιναρίων καὶ κραβάττων (upon mattresses and pallets) and in Acts 9:33 Aeneas (who, like the man here in Luke 5:18, is paralyzed, παραλελυμένος) has been lying on a κράβαττος (pallet) for eight years.[17] It seems unlikely, therefore, that Luke has altered Mark because he finds this word "vulgar" and the oddity of the change is exacerbated by the fact that for Luke a κλινή (bed) never elsewhere appears in this kind of context. Rather, Luke seems to think of a κλινή (bed) as something raised off the ground because in 8:16, "No one lights a lamp and . . . puts it under a bed" (ὑποκάτω κλίνης, cf. Mark 4:21, ὑπὸ τὴν κλίνην).[18] And in his only other use of the word (Luke 17:34), it is a household fixture occupied by two people. The word κλινή (bed) is clearly more grandiose for Luke than is κράβαττος (pallet), and his use of it here in a minor agreement with Matthew is striking. One might say that it is particularly stark given the context here in Luke, in which this κλινή (bed) is being lowered through the roof of a house (contrast Matthew).[19]

For a third example of an interesting minor agreement (shown on the following page), let us turn to the best-known one of all, the minor agreement that has caused more trouble to two-source theorists than any other.

This is a particularly remarkable minor agreement; Matthew and Luke agree in inserting the same sequence of five words in the identical place in the narrative. Moreover, one of those words, παίω (to strike), is a rare

---

15. B. H. Streeter, *The Four Gospels*, 299, and frequently thereafter.

16. Michael Goulder, "On Putting Q to the Test," 222–23; *Luke,* 331 and "Luke's Knowledge of Matthew," in G. Strecker, ed., *Minor Agreements,* 143–60 (150).

17. C. M. Tuckett in his response to Goulder's "On Putting Q to the Test" concedes this point: "Certainly the use of κράβαττος in Ac. 5.15 must cast doubts on theories that Luke changed κράβαττος in Mk. 2.4 because he disliked Mark's vulgar word," "On the Relationship Between Matthew and Luke," *NTS* 30 (1984): 130–42 (133).

18. κράβαττος occurs eleven times in the New Testament, Mark 2:4, 9, 11, 12; and 6:55; and in a similar context in John 5:8, 9, 10, 11; Acts 5:15 and 9:33. κλινή occurs eight times, Matt 9:2, 6; Mark 4:21; 7:4 (though here only a hesitant reading); Luke 5:18; 8:16; 17:34; and Rev 2:22.

19. Tuckett says that Goulder overstates the evidence, claiming that "it is by no means certain that κλινή in Biblical Greek means a four-poster" ("On the Relationship Between Matthew and Luke," 133). However, it is Luke's usage that is all-important here and Tuckett does not answer the point about Luke 8:16, ὑποκάτω κλίνης, and misses the other key Lukan usage of κράβαττος in Acts 9:33.

Matt 26:67–68	Mark 14:65	Luke 22:64
τότε	Καὶ ἤρξαντό τινες	καὶ
ἐνέπτυσαν εἰς τὸ	ἐμπτύειν αὐτῷ καὶ	
πρόσωπον αὐτοῦ καὶ	περικαλύπτειν αὐτοῦ	περικαλύψαντες αὐτὸν
ἐκολάφισαν αὐτόν, οἱ	τὸ πρόσωπον καὶ	
δὲ ἐράπισαν	κολαφίζειν αὐτὸν καὶ	ἐπηρώτων
λέγοντες,	λέγειν αὐτῷ,	λέγοντες,
Προφήτευσον ἡμῖν,	Προφήτευσον	Προφήτευσον,
Χριστέ, <u>τίς ἐστιν ὁ</u>		<u>τίς ἐστιν ὁ</u>
<u>παίσας σε;</u>		<u>παίσας σε;</u>
	καὶ οἱ ὑπηρέται	
	ῥαπίσμασιν αὐτὸν.	
	ἔλαβον.	

Then they spat	And some began to spit	
into his	on him, and to cover his	
face, and struck him; and	face, and to strike him,	and having blindfolded him,
some slapped him,	saying to him,	they asked him,
saying, "Prophesy to us,	"Prophesy!"	saying "Prophesy!
you Christ! <u>Who is it that</u>		<u>Who is it that</u>
<u>struck you?</u>"		<u>struck you?</u>"
	And the guards received	
	him with blows.	

word in the Gospels; it occurs only here in Matthew and only here in Luke.[20] This is the kind of evidence that normally inclines one strongly in favor of direct literary dependence.[21]

The standard defense from the two-source perspective appeals to a conjectural emendation of the text of Matthew. For those unfamiliar with it, conjectural emendation might be defined as "the act of ignoring all manuscripts and providing our own alternative,"[22] something that is practiced for internal reasons when it is very difficult to make sense of the text as it stands, and usually only when a text's main witnesses are few and late. In the case under discussion, the thesis is that the words τίς ἐστιν ὁ παίσας σε; ("Who is it who struck you?") origi-nally appeared only in Luke, but at a later stage texts of Matthew were

20. Otherwise, παίω occurs in the New Testament only at Mark 14:47 and (the parallel) John 18:10; also at Rev 9:5.

21. Michael Goulder dwells on this minor agreement in *Luke*, 6–11 in an attempt to drive home the difficulties it poses for the two-source theory. For a discussion of the role it plays for Goulder, see my *Goulder and the Gospels*, 102–7 and the literature cited there.

22. David Parker, *The Living Text of the Gospels* (Cambridge: Cambridge University Press, 1997), 113. For his discussion of this minor agreement, see pp. 112–17. Parker's conclusion is that "we defend the right to offer conjectural emendation, but consider it unnecessary here" (117).

assimilated to those of Luke. Since there is no extant manuscript or pa-tristic citation in which the words are absent from Matthew, the case for emendation has to rely solely on internal factors. For Neirynck, the necessary internal evidence is found in the fact that the blindfolding of Jesus is absent in Matthew and this, he claims, makes the question "Who is it who struck you?" incoherent. This contrasts with Luke, who has the blindfolding as well as the question.[23] But the case for making a conjectural emendation here is weak. The text of Matthew has many witnesses, a good number close in time to the autograph, and in the end it is difficult to avoid the conclusion that the use of conjectural emen-dation here simply constitutes a desperate response to data that do not fit the two-source theory.[24] The suggested grounds for the emendation are not strong. There are plenty of other examples of incoherence in the Synoptics where scholars rightly avoid conjecturally emending the text. The very principle of *lectio difficilior* in any case rebels against it. Furthermore, the text in Matthew can easily be understood without the emendation, whether one appeals to Goulder's claim that minor over-sights are a widespread feature of Matthew's redaction[25] or whether one takes seriously the statement that "they spat into his face" (ἐνέπτυσαν εἰς τὸ πρόσωπον αὐτοῦ).[26]

The case from conjectural emendation crumbles still further when one notices that Matthew's general approach here is quite characteristic of his writing in general. Mark has here a typically dark, ironic scene, in which Jesus is taunted "Prophesy!" while his tormentors are in the very

---

23. F. Neirynck, "ΤΙΣ ΕΣΤΙΝ Ο ΠΑΙΣΑΣ ΣΕ, Matt 26:68 / Luke 22:64 (diff. Mark 14:65)," *ETL* 63 (1987): 5–47; reprinted in *Evangelica II*, 95–138 (subsequent page references are to the latter edition). For a general discussion of textual criticism and its relationship to the minor agreements, with special reference to conjectural emendation in this passage, see Christopher Tuckett, "The Minor Agreements and Textual Criticism" in G. Strecker, ed., *Minor Agreements*, 119–41.

24. Goulder speaks here of "the end of rational discussion," "Luke's Use of Matthew," 155. The key point is Goulder's comment that "We cannot exclude the *possibility* of errors in all our witnesses, but we are justified in positing such only when we cannot make sense of our texts without them. This is by no means the case here (154–55)."

25. Goulder, *Luke*, 9; "Luke's Use of Matthew," 153–55; Goodacre, *Goulder and the Gospels*, 104.

26. It is worth noticing that the Gospel of Peter parallel to this passage says that they "spat in his eyes" (ἐνέπτυον αὐτοῦ ταῖς ὄψεσι, 3:9); cf. Matthew's comment that "they spat *into* his face" (ἐνέπτυσαν εἰς τὸ πρόσωπον αὐτοῦ, Matt 26:67). Cf. W. R. Farmer, *The Synoptic Problem*, 149: "The question, 'who struck you' (in Matthew) heightens the emphatic quality of the scene, for it pictured Jesus with other men's spittle running down his face and buffeted by their blows, being so distracted by this abuse he could only with difficulty have identified those who had struck him."

act of fulfilling Jesus' own prophecies (10:34, "they will mock him, and spit upon him, and flog him, and kill him") and, furthermore, as this action is going on, Peter is in the act of fulfilling Jesus' own prophecy of 14:30 ("this day, this very night, before the cock crows twice").[27] This kind of dark, dramatic irony runs through the whole of Mark's Passion Narrative, but is systematically explicated and clarified in Matthew's much more straightforward account.[28] The addition of τίς ἐστιν ὁ παίσας σε, downplaying and explicating the darker Markan scene by making it now purely a question of second sight, is the kind of thing we might expect from Matthew.

All in all it is difficult to find the case for conjecturally emending the text of Matthew here convincing, and it seems to be done solely in order to save the thesis of Matthew's and Luke's independence from one another. As Goulder has rightly stressed, this minor agreement is indeed one that tests the two-source theory and finds it wanting.[29]

---

27. Donald H. Juel, *The Gospel of Mark* (Interpreting Biblical Texts; Nashville: Abingdon, 1999), 27, uses the latter element as an example of the type of thing missed by those trained as source critics: "One of Jesus' prophecies is being fulfilled to the letter — at the moment Jesus is being mocked as a prophet inside the house. Readers are expected to appreciate the irony in a way no one in the story can. The relationship between the mockery and Peter's denial seems obvious — but not a single commentator preoccupied with Mark's sources ever noted it." Cf. Morna D. Hooker, *A Commentary on the Gospel According to St Mark* (London: A & C Black, 1991), 363, who also comments on the connection. However, I am not aware of any commentator who comments on the link between the Passion Predictions like 10:34 and this passage.

28. Notice, for example, the contrast over the so-called Centurion's confession. In Mark 15:39 the Centurion says, presumably sarcastically, "Truly this is a son of God" when he observes "how Jesus thus breathed his last" (ὅτι οὕτως ἐξέπνευσεν) while the reader is given privileged information to which the Centurion does not have access — the rending of the curtain in the temple (15:38). In Matthew, by contrast, there are others with the Centurion and their confession is a natural response to the earthquake that now attends Jesus' death (Matt 27:54).

29. Other attempts to deal with this minor agreement include the claim that it is due to shared oral tradition, e.g., Marion L. Soards, *The Passion According to Luke: The Special Material of Luke 22* (JSNTSup, 14; Sheffield: JSOT Press, 1987). Cf. F. Bovon, *Das Evangelium nach Lukas 1. Teilband: Lk 1,1–9,50* (EKKNT 3/1; Zürich: Benzinger; Neukirchen-Vluyn: Neukirchener Verlag, 1989) and to some extent J. Fitzmyer, *The Gospel According to Luke*, who go for forms of the oral tradition theory to explain some of the minor agreements. Cf. also Raymond E. Brown, *The Death of the Messiah: From Gethsemane to the Grave. A Commentary on the Passion Narratives of the Four Gospels* (2 vols.; The Anchor Bible Reference Library; New York: Doubleday, 1994), 44–45, 784, and 857. J. Dominic Crossan, *Birth of Christianity*, 54, comments on Brown's suggestion: "This presumes that oral versions of an event (if such existed) were so syntactically fixed that they could override the syntactically fixed written versions. It presumes, in other words, that those oral versions were so verbally precise that they could add a five-word verbatim sequence at one point in a scribally copied version without otherwise disturbing its original content." One might add for other minor agreements that so often the links are of a peculiarly literary kind, the preference of κλινή over κράβαττος, or the spelling of Ναζαρά (Matt 4:13 // Luke 4:16).

Minor Agreements, Texts, and Recensions

The third example discussed above, the minor agreement at Mark 14:65, is particularly outstanding because it is a case where even the most convinced advocates of the thesis of coincidental independent redaction resort to a form of text-critical argument. But even if it is difficult to be persuaded by the case for conjectural emendation in Matthew 26:68, what about the more general case from the uncertainty of our textual and recensional evidence?[30] In one of the most recent statements on the problem the minor agreements pose for the two-source theory, John S. Kloppenborg Verbin makes the case for taking text-critical and recensional problems seriously:

> The lack of a consensus [among two-source theorists] regarding the minor agreements derives from two factors: (1) it is impossible to reconstruct with absolute precision the Greek text of any of the gospels; and (2) the transmissional processes by which one gospel came to be used by another evangelist are not known at all. In this situation, critics assume a range of transmissional and editorial models or working hypotheses, each with its own implicit canons of plausibility. To proceed on the twin assumptions that the Nestle-Aland (27th) text closely approximates that of the final form of the gospels and that Matthew and Luke knew Mark in the *same* form that we have, implies that the solution to the minor agreements must lie in coincidental editorial modification or the occasional influence of non-Markan tradition. If, however, one assumes a less controlled transmission of texts, either "between" the gospels or in the earliest stages of scribal transmission (or both), the minor agreements might more plausibly be addressed as a recensional or text-critical problem.[31]

On one level Kloppenborg is making an important point, offering a sober reminder to scholars of the Synoptic Problem that Nestle-Aland[27]

---

30. On the question of text criticism and the minor agreements, see further Christopher Tuckett, "The Minor Agreements and Textual Criticism"; E. Burrows, "The Use of Textual Theories to Explain the Agreements of Matthew and Luke Against Mark" in *Studies in New Testament Language and Text* (ed. J. K. Elliott; Leiden: Brill, 1976), 87–99; and F. Wheeler, *Text Criticism and the Synoptic Problem: A Textual Commentary on the Minor Agreements of Matthew and Luke Against Mark* (Doctoral Dissertation, Baylor University, Waco, Texas, 1985).

31. John S. Kloppenborg Verbin, *Excavating Q*, 36. See also Kloppenborg's helpful diagrams on 37.

offers at best only an approximation to the original texts of the Gospels.[32] The sophistication of the critical text can all too easily seduce scholars into imagining that they are dealing with something far more concrete and stable than is in fact possible.[33] But the relationship of our text-critical uncertainties to the question of the minor agreements by no means inevitably resolves itself in favor of the two-source theory. There is a difficulty here that is rarely, if ever, recognized in the literature:[34] that while textual corruption may indeed have generated minor agreements, it may also have eliminated minor agreements. Thus the impossibility of reconstructing "with absolute precision the Greek text of any of the gospels" and our ignorance concerning "the transmissional processes by which one gospel came to be used by another evangelist" does not necessarily argue in favor of the two-source theory. It is just as important a theoretical possibility that the transmissional processes, and the history of the manuscript tradition, might have limited the number of minor agreements we now see in our critical texts. Indeed one might say that the clear and well-known scribal tendency to harmonize Mark's text toward that of Matthew may have significantly reduced the number of significant minor agreements we now see.

It is quite right, in other words, to bear in mind our uncertainty about the early stages of Gospel transmission when reflecting on the Synoptic Problem. But to appeal to this uncertainty as a means of dealing with the minor agreements is to appeal to the unknown in an attempt to avoid a stumbling block for the two-source theory, an unknown that might just as plausibly reveal further and not fewer problems for the two-source theory. Unless there are strong grounds for thinking that the absent evidence would indeed argue in favor of the two-source theory, which there are not, the appeal to the absence cannot forward the debate.

---

32. It might be added that this is one of the values of using the Huck-Greeven Synopsis in addition to Aland, in spite of the much greater popularity of the latter. Greeven's text differs in many ways from that of NA[27].

33. Cf. David Parker, *The Living Text of the Gospels*, Chapter 7 ("Secrets and Hypotheses"), which looks at the relationship between text-criticism and the Synoptic Problem and proposes a three-dimensional diagram "in which the third dimension represents a series of contacts between texts each of which may have changed since the previous contact" (121).

34. The closest I am aware of is F. Wheeler's *Text Criticism and the Synoptic Problem*, which analyses fifty-two minor agreements that have been attributed to textual corruption by different scholars. One of the interesting things about Wheeler's study is that even among the minor agreements chosen for his study, viz. those that have been singled out by previous scholarship as potential candidates for textual corruption, the evidence goes in both directions, some minor agreements eliminated and some retained.

Are the Minor Agreements Too Minor?

A further defensive tactic used recently by adherents of the Q hypothesis involves the claim that the minor agreements are so minor that they cannot carry the weight claimed for them by scholars like Michael Goulder. This is a highly significant claim, for it aims to take some of the Q skeptics' favorite evidence and to relativize it to the extent that it becomes as problematic for them as it does for Q theorists. Christopher Tuckett makes the point with his characteristic clarity and force:

> The fact that the Minor Agreements are so minor makes it very hard to believe that Luke has been both influenced positively by Matthew's text in such (substantively) trivial ways, but also totally uninfluenced by any of Matthew's substantive additions to Mark. Undoubtedly the Minor Agreements constitute a problem for the 2ST [two-source theory], but precisely their minor nature constitutes a problem for Goulder's theory as well.[35]

Tuckett's statement illustrates a difficulty arising from the degree of emphasis that Michael Goulder has placed on the minor agreements in his case against Q.[36] In the attempt repeatedly to point to a concrete difficulty for the two-source theory, Goulder has inadvertently given the impression that the best evidence in Q skeptics' favor is only "minor." But this perspective is, I think, just a trick of the light, and on closer examination it turns out to be based on a fallacy.[37]

On the Farrer theory it is simply not the case that Luke is "totally uninfluenced by any of Matthew's substantive additions to Mark." On the contrary, Luke regularly includes Matthew's substantive additions to Mark, but these tend to get placed into a special category of their own labeled "Mark-Q overlap." The minor agreements are thus only part of a broader spectrum and we might properly speak of a sliding scale of Matthean influence on Luke, from pure triple tradition passages which feature minor agreements, to Mark-Q overlap passages which feature major agreements between Matthew and Luke against Mark,

---

35. Christopher Tuckett, *Q and the History of Early Christianity,* 28. Tuckett makes a similar point in "The Minor Agreements and Textual Criticism," 140. See further n. 39 below.

36. Cf. T. A. Friedrichsen, "The Matthew-Luke Agreements Against Mark: A Survey of Recent Studies: 1974–1989" in F. Neirynck, ed., *L'Evangile de Luc,* 335–91, "the MAs [=minor agreements] cannot bear all the weight (φορτία δυσβάστακτα!) put on them" (384).

37. This section of the chapter is a revision of my "A Monopoly on Marcan Priority," 607–12, which itself developed an observation in *Goulder and the Gospels,* 126.

to double tradition passages where Luke is dependent solely on Matthew. It is the attempt to categorize all of the data in accordance with the demands of the two-source theory, minor agreements into one class, Mark-Q overlaps into another, double tradition into another, that causes us to miss this.

Tuckett, for example, deals with the different elements of Luke's agreement with Matthew against Mark under these different headings. When writing on the minor agreements he asks the following question: "Why should Luke have allowed Matthew's text to influence him in such a minor way as to create these small agreements, but rarely in any major way?"[38] When talking about the Mark-Q overlaps, however, he rightly describes them as "major agreements" between Matthew and Luke against Mark:

> Indeed the agreements between Matthew and Luke are so extensive (and it is only because they are so extensive that one postulates a parallel, non-Markan version) that these texts are often called "major agreements." They really constitute a separate category and cause no real difficulty for the Two-Source theory provided one accepts the possibility in principle of overlapping sources.[39]

Thus, where Luke agrees with Matthew against Mark in relatively minor ways, this tends to be called "minor agreement." Where Luke agrees with Matthew against Mark in relatively major ways, this tends to be called "Mark-Q overlap."[40] The pervasive use of this nomenclature, which is derived from the two-source theory, is causing us to miss one of the most interesting features among all the synoptic data, the fact that there

---

38. *ABD* VI, 267.

39. Ibid. These observations should be qualified by drawing attention also to Tuckett's treatment of minor agreements and Mark-Q Overlaps in *The Revival of the Griesbach Hypothesis: An Analysis and Appraisal* (SNTSMS 44; Cambridge: Cambridge University Press, 1983), Chapters 7–8. He suggests that one of the conditions for seeing Mark-Q overlap is evidence of another source underlying the Matthean and Lukan version, i.e., the Matthean version will not be explicable solely as Matthean redaction of Mark. The difficulty with this perspective is that one of the key pieces of evidence in favor of another underlying source is the substantial agreement between Matthew and Luke against Mark — one can see this clearly in the *ABD* quotation above. Further, Matthew's use of Mark need not imply that Matthew had no other sources for this material. The point is that Luke is here showing literary agreement with the Matthean version of the triple tradition, regardless of Matthew's own sources in reworking Mark.

40. Cf. also John S. Kloppenborg Verbin, *Excavating Q*, 92, which speaks of "most recent reconstructions of Q" as including both double tradition and "items triply attested *where the degree of agreement against Mark is substantial* and where the agreements are not likely to be merely coincidental, that is, the result of the independent editorial improvements of Mark by Matthew and Luke" (emphasis added).

is a continuum, from pure triple tradition to pure double tradition, with varying degrees of agreement along the way, from relatively minor to quite major agreement between Matthew and Luke against Mark. The minor agreements are indeed troubling to the two-source theory but they are only troubling insofar as they constitute one element in a broader spectrum of evidence, all of which is conducive to the Farrer theory.

The Logic of the Appeal to Minor Agreements

The reason that Q skeptics have appeared to place so much stress on the minor agreements is that they have to work within the framework imposed by the two-source theory. They are drawing attention to a major anomaly for that theory[41] in the attempt to undermine its key premise, the independent use of Mark by Matthew and Luke. It is not open to Q skeptics to point to the major agreements in this context because they are generally attributed to Mark-Q overlap.[42] Yet there is a still more disconcerting problem posed by the appeal to the minor agreements, for there have been several challenges to the very logic of the argument that the minor agreements have a major role to play in the case against Q.

Christopher Tuckett, Frans Neirynck, and Timothy Friedrichsen have claimed that even if victory in the argument over the minor agreements were to be conceded to Farrer, Goulder, and others, this would still not necessarily point to the abandonment of Q. The argument has been made repeatedly and it will be worth pausing to take it seriously. In response to Goulder's 1978 article, "On Putting Q to the Test," which provided twelve minor agreements which Goulder thought to be decisive, Christopher Tuckett writes:

> If one of his examples were established, this would indicate that Luke knew Matthew, but this would not of itself prove that the whole Q hypothesis was invalid. It might be that Luke used Q for most of the "double tradition" but that he also knew Matthew's gospel and used it occasionally.[43]

---

41. Goulder speaks of it as an "aberrant factor" (*Luke*, 47), "a thorn in the side of the standard theory" (*Luke*, 50).

42. In other contexts, however, Mark-Q overlaps do pose problems for the two-source theory as E. P. Sanders and Margaret Davies have been keen to stress, E. P. Sanders, "The Overlaps of Mark and Q and the Synoptic Problem," *NTS* 12 (1972–73): 453–65; E. P. Sanders and Margaret Davies, *Studying the Synoptic Gospels*, especially 78–83.

43. C. M. Tuckett, "On the Relationship Between Matthew and Luke," 130.

Frans Neirynck reacted to Goulder's case in a similar way:

> If Lukan knowledge of Matthew would be the conclusion to be
> drawn from the MAs [=minor agreements], then Luke would have
> used Mark notwithstanding his knowledge of Matthew, and the
> inference could only be that elsewhere, where Luke is using another
> source, a similar subsidiary influence of Matthean reminiscences
> can be expected.[44]

Neirynck describes this assumption that the minor agreements necessitate the abandonment of the Q theory as "the Farrer fallacy"[45] and he elaborates on the point again in response to Michael Goulder's 1985 essay, "A House Built on Sand,"[46] in which Goulder had put special stress on the problems posed for the two-source theory by the minor agreement at Mark 14:65:

> Let us take it more simply: the reasoning from analogy can not
> go beyond the limits of the similarity. If there is any subsidiary
> dependence upon Matthew in the triple tradition, how can this
> prove that there is anything more than subsidiary dependence in
> the double tradition?[47]

Neirynck further attempts to drive the point home in response to my comments on the situation in *Goulder and the Gospels*. After a lengthy critique of Goulder's case from the minor agreements, I had commented:

> Goulder's argument works quite legitimately by attempting to demonstrate that the Minor Agreements show Lukan knowledge of
> Matthew, and that this knowledge makes the theory of primary
> Lukan dependence on Matthew in double tradition material likely.[48]

Neirynck quotes this, as well as my earlier comment on the possible inferences from the minor agreements and he concludes:

---

44. F. Neirynck, "Recent Developments," 34.

45. Neirynck appeals here to R. Morgenthaler, *Statistische Synopse*, 301–5. The latter appeals to "Die falsche Alternative: Q-Existenz *oder* Bekanntschaft Mt-Lk" (300–301). But it is not a question of opposing alternatives — of course it is *possible* to postulate dependence of Luke on both Q and Matthew but to stress this possibility begs the question; the point concerns the foundational premise of the Q hypothesis, viz. the independence of Matthew and Luke, which the minor agreements place in question.

46. "A House Built on Sand" in *Alternative Approaches to New Testament Study* (ed. A. E. Harvey; London: SPCK, 1985), 1–24. A revised version of this chapter subsequently appeared as Chapter 1 in *Luke*.

47. "ΤΙΣ ΕΣΤΙΝ," 115.

48. *Goulder and the Gospels*, 128.

I have to repeat I think: the inference from the acceptance of subsidiary Matthaean influence cannot be *"primary* Lukan dependence." This distinction between subsidiary and primary is far from irrelevant.[49]

In spite of the fact that the debate is now approaching something like an impasse, the issue is actually straightforward. The difficulty arises from the way in which Neirynck is characterizing Goulder's argument. In his 1987 comment quoted above, he begins "Let us take it more simply: the reasoning from analogy can not go beyond the limits of the similarity."[50] The problem is that *the argument is not an argument from analogy.* If it were, of course Luke's subsidiary use of Matthew in triple tradition could only demonstrate Luke's subsidiary use of Matthew in double tradition. But no, Goulder's argument — and Farrer's before him — is not an argument from analogy or inference. Rather, it is an attempt to demonstrate that the theory of Matthew's and Luke's independent use of Mark is untenable given the presence of the minor agreements. And the reason for stressing the independence of Matthew and Luke is that, usually speaking, this is the foundational premise of the Q hypothesis (see above, pp. 46–47).[51] For this reason, Timothy Friedrichsen's argument also misses the point. He states, in relation to Chapter One of Goulder's *Luke:*

> To place his treatment of the MAs [=minor agreements] in the section "The Arguments Against Q" (46–51) is logically flawed. Goulder would do his position more good if he were to rightfully place the study of the MAs in a section entitled "The Arguments Against the Independence of Matthew and Luke."[52]

If these two things, the Q hypothesis and the independence of Matthew and Luke, were unrelated, the argument would be legitimate. However, the independence of Matthew and Luke is usually taken to be the essential premise for the Q hypothesis, since if Matthew and Luke independently edited Mark in the triple tradition, the double tradition

---

49. F. Neirynck, "Goulder and the Minor Agreements," 93.
50. "ΤΙΣ ΕΣΤΙΝ," 115.
51. Neirynck's references to the handful of scholars who have posited Luke's dependence on both Q and Matthew is a red herring since their reasons for postulating Q are not based on the standard, foundational premise of the Q hypothesis that Matthew and Luke were independent of one another.
52. T. A. Friedrichsen, "Survey," 384.

necessitates the existence of a common source. It is thus entirely proper to take evidence in favor of Luke's knowledge of Matthew, evidence like the minor agreements, as evidence that compromises the Q theory. It is not that two theories have been artificially opposed; it is that the one theory, Luke's knowledge of Matthew, takes away the very reason for postulating the other theory, Q.

It may be that the confusion arises because Goulder does not state what he regards as implicit. Thus, to make it explicit, his statements might be reframed in this way: "I do not see how we are to avoid the conclusion that Luke knew Matthew: and *[given that the Q hypothesis is predicated on the assumption that Luke did not know Matthew,]* that conclusion entails the end of Q."[53] Or, similarly, "The evidence from the agreements shows that Luke knew Matthew, and *[since this runs contrary to the basic premise behind the Q hypothesis, that Matthew and Luke are independent of one another]* that Q is *therefore* no longer a valid hypothesis."[54] In other words, if it is thought to be simply a question of precision in one's choice of language, then let us attempt to reframe it in this way: the minor agreements show that Luke knew Matthew, and Lukan knowledge of Matthew compromises the premise of the Q theory, that Luke and Matthew were independent of one another.

Of course the argument does not stop there. Evidence of contact between Matthew and Luke here simply presses all the more urgently the importance of looking at the standard arguments against Lukan knowledge of Matthew elsewhere, and this is why when Farrer introduces the minor agreements in "On Dispensing with Q," he goes on in that very context to discuss the traditional difficulties alleged for Luke's knowledge of Matthew.[55] Likewise, Michael Goulder's "On Putting Q to the Test" deals with the minor agreements in a context that makes clear that "the two traditional arguments against Lukan knowledge of Matthew," viz. the arguments from order and from alternating primitivity, also need to be addressed.[56]

The minor agreements are useful because they place a question mark over the hypothesis of Luke's independence from Matthew. They constitute evidence that is anomalous for the two-source theory. Q theorists cannot be let off the hook either by appeals to textual corruption, or by

---

53. "On Putting Q to the Test," 234, with my addition in italics.
54. Ibid.
55. Farrer, "On Dispensing," 62.
56. "On Putting Q to the Test," 234.

drawing attention to their minor character, or by questioning the logic of their opponents' argument. The problem of the minor agreements is here to stay. The decision we have to face is whether to continue to live with the problem, or to prefer a theory on which they are explained plausibly as part of a broader spectrum of evidence that points in the same direction.

Chapter Nine

NARRATIVE SEQUENCE IN A SAYINGS GOSPEL?
Reflections on a Contrast between Thomas and Q

One of the most exciting things about the discovery of the Gospel of
Thomas has always been the light that it promises to shed on Q. One
of Austin Farrer's criticisms of the Q hypothesis was the claim that Q
as a document is without parallel, an anomaly in early Christianity of
such magnitude as to cast doubt on its very existence. "There is no independent evidence for anything like Q," he said. "To postulate Q is to
postulate the unevidenced and the unique."[1] But no sooner had Austin
Farrer written these words than Thomas was to make its dramatic entry
on the scene.[2] Some were quick to point out how hollow Farrer's words
sounded in the light of the grand discovery.[3]

Since then, it has often been stated that the discovery of Thomas has

---

1. Austin Farrer, "On Dispensing with Q," 58.
2. John Kloppenborg criticizes Farrer: "It is not altogether clear what Farrer meant by
'documents of the Q type.' In 1957 a sayings gospel such as the *Gospel of Thomas* was already
published and the Oxyrhynchus fragments had been available for more than half a century,"
"The Theological Stakes in the Synoptic Problem" in *The Four Gospels 1992: Festschrift Frans
Neirynck* (ed. F. Van Segbroeck et al.; BETL 100, Leuven: Leuven University Press, 1992), 1:93–
120 (115). Kloppenborg's 1957 date is the date of the first reprint of the book. It is practically
certain, however, that Farrer had not read the Gospel of Thomas before writing "On Dispensing
with Q": the editio princeps, A. Guillaumont, H.-Ch. Puech, G. Quispel, W. Till and Yassah
'Abd al Masih, eds., *The Gospel According to Thomas: Coptic Text Established and Translated*
(Leiden: Brill, 1959), appeared four years after the first publication of Farrer's article in 1955.
Farrer may have been aware of the Oxyrhynchus fragments, but scholarship of his day was
divided on the identity and genre of Gospel from which the fragments came.
3. See, for example, J. Fitzmyer, "The Oxyrhynchus Logoi of Jesus and the Coptic Gospel
According to Thomas," now reproduced in *The Semitic Background of the New Testament:
A Combined Edition of Essays on the Semitic Background of the New Testament and A
Wandering Aramean: Collected Aramaic Essays* (The Biblical Resource Series; Grand Rapids:
Eerdmans; Livonia, Mich.: Dove, 1997), 355–433 (419). From more recently, see Robert W.
Funk et al., *The Five Gospels*, 12: "The existence of Q was once challenged by some scholars on the grounds that a sayings gospel was not really a gospel. The challengers argued that
there were no ancient parallels to a gospel containing only sayings and parables and lacking
stories about Jesus, especially the story about his trial and death. The discovery of the Gospel
of Thomas changed all that. Thomas, too, is a sayings gospel that contains no account of Jesus'
exorcisms, healings, trial or death."

strengthened the Q theory. One of the most recent statements of the matter, by Richard Valantasis, provides a good example:

> The Synoptic Sayings Source Q that Matthew and Luke used was considered a collection of sayings of Jesus *without any narrative frame*. The content of this Synoptic Sayings Source Q could only be established by comparing *the sayings* common to Matthew and Luke and by then reconstructing the common text; the genre of collections of "sayings of Jesus" remained theoretical. With the discovery of the Gospel of Thomas in Coptic, scholars finally had an actual document *in the same genre as had been theorized, an existent gospel composed only of sayings of Jesus in a collection of sayings*. Although the Gospel of Thomas is not believed to be the source that Matthew and Luke used, the fact that many of the sayings from it directly paralleled sayings known from the common Synoptic Sayings Source Q added strength to the argument that such a source could have existed. The two-source hypothesis was in this way strengthened and renewed by the discovery.[4]

The statement is typical[5] and the focus is, as usual, on the identity of genre between the two texts, a genre that is described as "a collection of sayings of Jesus without any narrative frame." However, the sheer emphasis in the literature on this presumed identity is such that it is causing us to pay too little attention to clear contrasts between Q and Thomas, the most manifest of which is the existence in Q of the very thing that the genre "Sayings Gospel," as exemplified by Thomas, would appear to exclude: a narrative sequence. I will argue that the narrative sequence in Q is best explained not on genre-critical grounds but on source-critical grounds, as providing strong evidence for Luke's use of Matthew as well as Mark.

---

4. Richard Valantasis, *The Gospel of Thomas* (New Testament Readings; London and New York: Routledge, 1997), 2–3; emphasis added.

5. Other recent examples include Lawrence M. Wills, *The Quest of the Historical Gospel: Mark, John and the Origins of the Gospel Genre* (London and New York: Routledge, 1997), "Just as the discovery of a complete text of the *Gospel of Thomas* strengthened the arguments for the existence of Q . . . " (51); Mark Allan Powell, *The Jesus Debate* (Oxford: Lion Publishing, 1999), 50: "The *Gospel of Thomas* is a collection of sayings attributed to Jesus, similar in form to what is assumed for the Q document"; ibid., 78, " . . . the *Gospel of Thomas,* which is similar to Q in form, that is, a collection of sayings rather than a narrative account of Jesus' life." Among many older relevant comments, see Claus-Hunno Hünzinger, "Aussersynoptisches Traditionsgut im Thomas-Evangelium," *Theologische Literaturzeitung* 85 (1960): col. 843–44, "The existence of the sayings-collection genre is now proved" (col. 834).

To begin with, I would like to take the Q hypothesis for granted and
to claim that there is clear evidence of a narrative sequence, especially
in its first third. This is a controversial claim and it naturally requires
illustration and defense. My point is not simply to stress the well-known
fact that there are narrative elements within individual units in Q. Every
reconstruction of Q includes the Temptation narrative (Q 4:1–13), the
Centurion's Servant (Q 7:1–10) and the Messengers from John (Q 7:18–
35), as well as sometimes the brief exorcism at the introduction of the
Beelzebub controversy (Q 11:14). There is no doubt that these elements
are present in Q: we have close verbatim agreement between Matthew
in Luke in pure double tradition material (Q 7:1–10 and 7:18–35) and
in Mark-Q overlap material (Q 4:1–13, cf. 11:14), the kind of agreement that necessitates reading these texts in Q.[6] While such elements do
witness to some contrast between Q and Thomas, since the latter rarely
has narrative elements within individual units,[7] they do not constitute
as major an anomaly for the Q-Thomas comparison as another, related
factor. There is a narrative sequence across the consecutive units that
make up especially the early part of Q, a narrative sequence of the kind
that is conspicuously absent in Thomas.

The Narrative Sequence in Q 3–7

In Q 3:2, John is introduced.[8] Subsequently he is located in "all
the region of the Jordan" (πᾶσα . . . η . . . περίχωρο . . . τοῦ Ἰορδάνου,

---

6. For a recent dissenting voice, see James D. G. Dunn, "Jesus in Oral Memory: The Initial
Stages of the Jesus Tradition," *Society of Biblical Literature Seminar Papers 2000* (Society of
Biblical Literature Seminar Paper Series 39; Atlanta: Society of Biblical Literature, 2000), 287–
326, who is concerned by the narrative format of this pericope and suggests that like some other
double tradition material, it should be attributed to independent retelling of a story received by
Matthew and Luke orally (298–300). The difficulty with this viewpoint is not only that there
is substantial verbatim agreement between Matt 8:8–10 // Luke 7:6b–9, but also that there is
agreement in order (only the Leper, Matt 8:1–4, which Luke has already recounted in 5:12–
16 // Mark 1:40–45 intervenes between the Sermon on the Mount // Plain and this pericope);
there is even a narrative segue parallel in Matthew 7:28 // Luke 7:1a, on which see further
below. These are just the kinds of things that usually incline one towards literary contact of
some kind.

7. Cf. Thomas 20, 22, 60, 61, 72, and 79 as sayings for which settings are provided. These
do not, however, provide examples of narrative in the way that we find in the Q pericopae
mentioned. In these cases in Thomas it is always setting + saying without any developed direct
narrative sequence or causality.

8. I will be working throughout solely on the basis of the International Q Project's Critical
Text of Q now published in *The Critical Edition of Q* (see above, pp. 6–9). The reasons for

Q 3:3)[9] where, apparently, he baptizes with a baptism that is in some way specially characteristic of him (Q 3:7, βάπτισ[[μα]] αὐτοῦ, "*his* baptism," to which people, probably "crowds,"[10] are said to have come (Q 3:7, ε[[ἰπ]]εν τοῖς ἐ[[ρχ]]ομένο<ι>ς [[ὄχλοις]] [[ἐπὶ τὸ]] βάπτισ[[μα]] αὐτοῦ), and to whom John speaks about their presumption in coming to him for baptism (Q 3:7b–8), warning them to "bear fruit worthy of repentance" (Q 3.8).

The next section in Q (3:16–17) continues the baptism theme but now builds on it. As before, there is a juxtaposition of baptism with direct address (Q 3:16, ἐγὼ μὲν ὑμᾶς βαπτίζω [[ἐν]] ὕδατι ...), but with the introduction of a new theme, the prophecy of "the coming one" (ὁ ἐρχόμενος) who will baptize with holy spirit and fire, to whom John subordinates himself. This section, Q 3:16–17, thus provides a fine segue into the next section, Q 3:21–22, in which Jesus is introduced.[11] While the precise wording of Q 3:21–22 is unrecoverable, it seems likely that it contained some mention of the "spirit" descending "upon" Jesus (ἐπ᾽ αὐτόν, Matt 3:16 // Luke 3:22) along with some indication that he was God's "son."[12]

---

this should be obvious: the IQP's work is held in high esteem internationally and represents a massive advance on any previous attempt to reconstruct Q. It is important, too, that I do not appear to be manipulating Q to make it fit my theory. If given wording is not in the Critical Text of Q, it is not discussed in this chapter. James Robinson comments that *The Critical Edition of Q* will be "equally usable for scholars of all opinions" (lxvi), adding that "those who deny the existence of Q as a whole will not of course be satisfied" (lxvii, n. 156). I do not think that even this is the case. The great advantage to Q skeptics of the *Critical Edition* is that it provides them with a concrete text that is available for testing. One thus avoids the inevitable slipperiness of some source criticism. Please note that this chapter was prepared in accordance with the Critical Text of Q given in *JBL* from 1990 to 1997 (see above, p. 7, n. 27), which was all that was available at the time; the text here reflects the text given there. At some points this contrasts in minor ways with the text subsequently published in *Critical Edition,* which became available only at a late stage in the production of this manuscript.

9. For a recent comment on the importance of this setting in Q, see John S. Kloppenborg Verbin, *Excavating Q,* 118–21. Kloppenborg claims that the phrase, which "occurs in the Tanak principally in connection with the story of Lot," witnesses to Q's redactional interest in the Lot story also found elsewhere in Q.

10. ὄχλοις is one of those words that has a "probability of only {on a descending scale of {A} to {D}. But that John addresses people "coming" to his baptism is clear here.

11. It is a famous difficulty whether or not one should include 3:21–22 in Q. James Robinson is in favor of this — see nn. 14 and 15, below, but Kloppenborg is against it, *The Formation of Q,* 84f., *Excavating Q,* 93. Here I maintain the policy in this chapter of following the IQP Critical Text in considering this as part of Q, *Critical Edition of Q,* 18–20, though note that Q 3:21–22 is placed in double pointed brackets, which indicate "a whole verse ascribed to Q [that] is unreconstructable," e.g., *JBL* 112 (1993): 500–506 (501).

12. The International Q Project gives the gist of thought in English translation as follows: <<John baptized Jesus and heaven opened...the spirit...upon him....Son....">> The difficulty with this verse is that it is a major agreement between Matthew and Luke against Mark (normally called "Mark-Q overlap") and there are several triple agreements.

But precise reconstruction is not necessary for us to see how the gist of the baptism pericope clearly sets the scene for the very next section in Q, the Temptation narrative, Q 4:1–13, which takes for granted both Jesus' sonship and his now special relationship with the spirit.[13] Just as 3:16–17 segued without difficulty into 3:21–22, so now 3:21–22 seamlessly links to 4:1–13. First, it is the keynote of the Temptation narrative that Jesus is tested as God's son, twice emphasizing *if you are the son of God*, εἰ υἱὸς εἶ τοῦ θεοῦ . . . (4:3, 9).[14] Second, the scene is set with the notice that it was *the spirit* who led Jesus into this new location in Q, the wilderness (Q 4:1, [[ὁ]] Ἰησοῦς δὲ [[]]ἡ . . . [[ὑπὸ]] τ[[οῦ]] πνεύματ[[ος]] ε . . . τη . . . ἐρημ . . .).[15]

At this point we reach Q 4:16. All we know here is that Q certainly contained reference to Ναζαρά, which we know from other sources to have been Jesus' home.[16] Did Q at this point, like Matthew and Luke, record Jesus' departure from Nazara to live in Capernaum where we later find him (Q 7:1)? Perhaps, but all we can say with confidence here

---

13. H. Schürmann, *Das Lukasevangelium* (HTKNT 3/1; Freiburg: Herder & Herder, 1969), 197 and 218 and I. H. Marshall, *The Gospel of Luke: A Commentary on the Greek Text* (Exeter: Paternoster, 1978), 150, both note that the Son of God Christology presupposed by the temptations suggests the existence of a preceding baptismal account containing this motif. Cf. too Migaku Sato, *Q und Prophetie: Studien zur Gattungs- und Traditionsgeschichte der Quelle Q* (WUNT 2/29; Tübingen: J. C. B. Mohr [Paul Siebeck], 1988), 25.

14. Cf. James M. Robinson, "The Sayings Gospel Q" in *The Four Gospels 1992: Festschrift Frans Neirynck,* vol. 1 (ed. F. Van Segbroeck et al.; BETL 100, Leuven: Leuven University Press, 1992), 361–88. Robinson observes that if there is no baptism in Q, "Why then are we at the Temptation launched, without any preparation, into a discussion of the validity of Jesus being the Son of God, if he has not even been so designated? The inclusion of Jesus being designated God's Son by the heavenly voice, or some equivalent, is needed in the narrative preface to Q for it to cohere" (384).

15. Ibid., 385: "The Baptism of Jesus is also presupposed in another trait of the Temptation.... This reference to the Spirit, like the title Son of God, is something for which one would hardly be prepared, if one were to eliminate the immediately preceding verses (Q 3:22), the baptismal report that the Spirit had descended on him."

16. It is arguable that the appearance of Ναζαρά in Matt 4:13 // Luke 4:16 causes insurmountable problems for the Q theory, especially if one does not read the verse in Q here. For literature on the issue, see my *Goulder and the Gospels,* 101–2 and now Frans Neirynck, "NAZARA in Q: Pro and Con," in *From Quest to Q. Festschrift James M. Robinson* (ed. Jon Ma. Asgeirsson, Kristin de Troyer, and Marvin W. Meyer; BETL, 146; Leuven: Leuven University Press, 2000), 159–69. It is not the purpose of the current chapter to look into these, however. Suffice it to say that it is far less problematic to read Ναζαρά in Q than it is to exclude it. For good, full documentation on the question of reading it in Q, see Shawn Carruth and James M. Robinson; volume editor: Christoph Heil, *Q 4:1–13, 16. The Temptations of Jesus — Nazara* (Leuven: Peeters, 1996), 392–462. Note that the earlier decision to print the verse [[. . .]] [[]] [[Ναζαρά . . .]], *JBL* 110 (1991): 494–98 (495), reflected also in James M. Robinson, "The Sayings Gospel Q," 374, n. 15, i.e., indicating that the reconstructed text "has a probability of only {C} on a descending scale of {A} to {D}," is adjusted in *Q 4:1–13, 16,* 463, in which no doubt is recorded in the Critical Text. The change is overlooked in the critical apparatus of *Q 4:1–13, 16* but is featured in *The Critical Edition of Q,* ad loc.

is that it is another example of apparent geographical progression in Q, from the region around the Jordan (Q 3:2), to the wilderness (4:1) to Nazara (Q 4:16).

The next text in Q, 6:20–49, the Inaugural Discourse, is framed by an introduction in which Jesus lifts up his eyes to address his disciples and a conclusion in which it is stated that "he completed [these] sayings," which itself serves as a transitionary formula for the story immediately following, the Centurion, since the latter is located in Capharnaum (Capernaum), the fourth place now mentioned in Q's itinerary (Q 7:1: ... ἐ[[πλήρω]]σεν [[τοὺς λόγους τούτους]] εἰσῆλθεν εἰς Καφαρναούμ).

This narrative section is then followed by another, the Messengers from John the Baptist (Q 7:18–35), which not only has an interesting narrative unity in its own right but which also has a clear continuity with most of the preceding narrative in Q. Most clearly, John reemerges here, and the section presupposes what has happened earlier, viz. that John has prophesied ὁ ἐρχόμενος, now asking whether Jesus is indeed this "coming one" or whether they should expect another. The fulfillment of John's prophecy is here made explicit by the miracles Jesus has performed, one of which has taken place in the immediately preceding Q pericope. When Jesus speaks to the crowds about John, just after his disciples have left to take their message to him, we observe again that the earlier Q narrative, in which people went out to hear and see John, is presupposed.

It seems, then, that in the material that makes up the first major part of Q, there is not only a generous helping of narrative pericopae, but there are also clear indications that the material as a whole has narrative properties. These properties can be summarized in four categories:

1. There are transitionary editorial formulas of the kind that introduce but also juxtapose successive units (3:2, 3:21–22, 4:1, ?4:16, 7:1, 7:18ff), one of the clearest examples of which is "Jesus completed these sayings ... he went to Capernaum" (7:1), linking the Inaugural Discourses with the Healing of the Centurion's Boy which follows it.

2. There is some logical narrative progression in successive units, as when we move in sequence from John's preaching about the repentance attending his own baptism (Q 3:7f), to his preaching about the coming one's baptism (Q 3:16f), to the baptism of that coming one, Jesus, by John (Q 3:21–22); or when Jesus' baptism by John

apparently prepares the way for the "spirit" to lead Jesus to the wilderness where he is tested as a "son."

3. There are signals that point forward to developments that will happen later on in the narrative, as when the prophecy of "the coming one" is taken up again by John in 7:18–35, or when in the same pericope Jesus addresses people about the prophet they went to see.[17]

4. There are signs of some kind of itinerary, or geographical progression. Q begins in the region around the Jordan (3:3), proceeds to the wilderness (4:1), thence to Nazara (4:16) and later to Capharnaum (7:1; cf. 10:15). Later still there are references to Chorazin and Bethsaida (10:14) and Jerusalem (13:34).

Thomas and Q in Contrast

In short, Q shows clear signs of narrative properties. When we turn to Thomas, however, there is nothing like this. For this is a Gospel with no narrative, no time-line and no hint of grounding in the geography of first century Palestine. There is a striking absence of anything corresponding to the features we have been observing in Q.[18] Whereas Q features a variety of references to place, in Thomas the nearest one has to a geographical reference is "the field" (ⲥⲱϣⲉ, Thom. 78). Whereas in Q there are clear transitionary formulas between one section and the next, in Thomas one has discrete, individual sayings without formal links to adjacent sayings. Whereas in Q there are clear narrative progressions from one pericope to the next, in Thomas there is nothing like this. Whereas in Q there are elements that signal developments later in the narrative, and pointers backwards to moments earlier in the narrative, in Thomas such narrative characteristics are absent. In short, Thomas is utterly indifferent to story-time.[19]

---

17. Cf. John S. Kloppenborg Verbin, *Excavating Q*, 122–24, which deals with Q's "argumentative progressions," especially in Q 3–7, utilizing some of the same evidence dealt with in this chapter, for example, "Even without Q having a narrative framework, the arrangement of elements that are distributed across a large portion of Q contributes to a logical progression in which expectations about a Coming One are raised and then resolved" (122).

18. Cf. Richard Burridge, *What Are The Gospels? A Comparison With Graeco-Roman Biography* (SNTSMS, 70; Cambridge: Cambridge University Press, 1993), 250, who observes that Thomas lacks key elements that normally constitute the *bios* like narrative, chronological markers and geographical settings.

19. This has rightly been emphasized by both Helmut Koester, "One Jesus and Four Primitive Gospels" in J. M. Robinson and H. Koester, *Trajectories Through Early Christianity* (Phila-

Furthermore, the absence of such features in Thomas does not seem accidental or in any way arbitrary but integral to the very program of the gospel. As far as we can tell, Thomas's genre, rightly perceived to be "Sayings Gospel," is a function of the document's Christology, or, one should say, its view of Jesus. For these are the words of the living Jesus and "historicizing" of the kind apparently found in Q would be quite out of place.[20] In Thomas, by contrast with Q, the question of whether this Jesus is the earthly Jesus or the resurrected Jesus is irrelevant. For Thomas, the living Jesus is made present in his word and in the interpretation of his word. If there is a key theme in Thomas, this is it: the importance of hearing Jesus' words, a theme that appears in several different forms:

> If you become My disciples and listen to My words, these stones will minister to you. (Logion 19)

> Many times have you desired to hear these words which I am saying to you, and you have no one else to hear them from. (Logion 38)

And it is surely for this reason that Thomas repeats the mantra, "Whoever has ears to hear, let them hear!" no less than six times (sayings 8, 21, 24, 63, 65, 96).

In other words, Thomas is appropriately described as a "Sayings Gospel" for here is a document in which the gospel of Jesus is specifically constituted by hearing and interpreting his sayings and his sayings alone, as the very first logion emphasizes: "Whoever finds the interpretation of these sayings will not experience death." Within such a gospel there is indeed no need for a "historicizing" recitation of elements in Jesus' ministry, linked together in some kind of narrative sequence. The very nature of the document's outlook, itself a consequence of the document's Christology, precludes it.[21]

---

delphia: Fortress, 1971), 158–204 (esp. 167–68) and James Robinson, "Jesus from Easter to Valentinus (or to the Apostles' Creed)," *JBL* 101 (1982): 5–37 (23). Yet one still finds references to the Jesus of Thomas as the "resurrected" Jesus in contradistinction to the pre-Easter Jesus, e.g., John Painter, *Just James: The Brother of Jesus in History and Tradition* (Studies on Personalities of the New Testament; Columbia: University of South Carolina Press, 1998), 160–62, which does not seem to take seriously Koester and Robinson's genre-related point.

20. Cf. H. Koester, who rightly observes that the fundamental theological tendency of the Gospel of Thomas is "the view that the Jesus who spoke these words was and is the Living One, and thus gives life through his words" ("ΓΝΩΜΑΙ ΔΙΑΦΟΡΟΙ: The Origin and Nature of Diversification in the History of Early Christianity," *HTR* 58 (1965): 279–318, reprinted in James M. Robinson and Helmut Koester, *Trajectories,* 114–57, this quotation 139.

21. H. Koester, *Ancient Christian Gospels,* 86, comments: "Both documents presuppose that

But if this is indeed the case, it makes the contrast between Q and Thomas more striking still. We are not, apparently, dealing with an arbitrary or accidental difference between two similar documents, but something that is fundamental to the way in which one of those documents, Thomas, apparently conceives of itself. In short, we find ourselves hesitating over characterizing Q as a "Sayings Gospel" if by "Sayings Gospel" we mean something like Thomas. At the very least, we will want to know what it is about this particular sayings collection, Q, that causes it to throw up such a clear narrative sequence? Why is it that Q apparently departs so fundamentally from the form as it is exemplified in Thomas?

On the assumption of Q's existence, our first instinct will be to suggest that the contrast between Q and Thomas is natural given the diachronic change within the history of the genre. Perhaps Q is simply at a different point on the trajectory of Sayings Gospels from Thomas. Q is beginning a journey towards a biographical and narrative character, a journey on which Thomas refused to embark.[22] Several studies have pointed in this direction, not least John Kloppenborg's *The Formation of Q*, which suggests in particular that the introduction of the Temptation Story, "probably the latest addition to Q,"[23] confirms a suggestion earlier made by James Robinson that "Q was moving *toward* a narrative or biographical cast."[24] "The addition of the temptation narrative to Q," Kloppenborg claims, "is probably not enough to allow us to claim a biographical genre for Q; however its addition is one step in that direction."[25] The key point, in such circumstances, will be to avoid over-

---

Jesus' significance lay in his words, and in his words alone." I think that this is exactly right for Thomas but manifestly not the case for Q, a good example of the way in which the comparison with Thomas has a distorting effect on the interpretation of Q.

22. Cf. John Kloppenborg, *Formation*, 322: "While the *Gos. Thom.* seems to have developed the contemporizing side of the generic dialectic, Q moved in another direction...."

23. John Kloppenborg, ibid., 325.

24. Ibid., 262, emphasis original; cf. 325–27. Cf. also James Robinson, "The Sayings Gospel Q," 375.

25. John Kloppenborg, *Formation*, 326. If anything, Kloppenborg has become more forthright on this point since the publication of *Formation*. See, for example, his comments in "The Theological Stakes in the Synoptic Problem," 117: "Q itself, by its inclusion of the predictions of John (3:[2–4?], 7–9, 16–17) and the Temptation account (4:1–13) appears to have opted for a proto-biographical presentation of Jesus' sayings, and in doing so paralleled other collections which began with a testing story (Ankhsheshonq, Ahikar, the *Sentences of Secundus*)." For a thoroughgoing attempt to place Q in the *bios* category, see F. Gerald Downing, "A Genre for Q and a Socio-Cultural Context for Q: Comparing Sets of Similarities With Sets of Differences," *JSNT* 55 (1994): 3–26, reproduced in F. Gerald Downing, *Doing Things With Words*, Chapter 5, though without concentration on the kind of narrative sequence witnessed here. For a good introduction to questions of genre in relation to Q, see C. M. Tuckett, *Q*

emphasizing the significance of any contrast between, say, Thomas and Q. As Kloppenborg has rightly stressed, following Koester and Robinson, we should not see genre as a "static grid" but "a set of dynamisms which influence the hermeneutic of the contents of the collection, and which account in some measure for diachronic change within the history of a given genre."[26]

But does this option, however appealing it seems at first sight, have the potential to provide a full account of both the scope and the nature of the narrative sequence in Q? This is, after all, no mere narrative prologue, serving to set the scene for the sayings of the sage, Jesus, that follow on from it. It appears to be something much more fundamental to the way in which Q constitutes itself, a narrative sequence which runs from the introduction of John in Chapter 3 to his sending of messengers to Jesus much later on in Chapter 7, incorporating material in between that is all arranged in logical narrative sequence and framing the entirety of Q's inaugural discourse in 6:20–49.[27] This is the whole of the first third of Q and not simply a narrative preface or prologue.

But equally a matter of concern is the point at which the narrative dissipates, at Q 7:35. What we will want to know is why it is that Q seems so careful to arrange its material in narrative sequence up to this point, only to abandon it thereafter. Is it that fatigue set in, or should we look for another explanation?

We will be relieved to discover that another explanation is available, one that will take us to the heart of Q's character, and which will explain each of the quirks of Q that we have been witnessing. It is an explanation that has the additional advantage of being consonant with the case against Q, and which can be approached by returning to this chapter's starting point, Austin Farrer's comments in "On Dispensing with Q." For if we read on in Farrer's article past the rhetorical flourish about the lack

---

and the History of Early Christianity, 103–6; and the detailed survey in John S. Kloppenborg Verbin, *Excavating Q,* Chapter 3, and the literature cited in both places.

26. John Kloppenborg, *Formation,* 33.

27. The pattern is beginning to be noticed more broadly, for example Dale Allison, *The Jesus Tradition in Q,* 42: "But Q3 takes us a step towards what we may call biography. Not only are there lengthier stories about Jesus (Q 4:1–13; 7:1–10), but there is also a sense of chronology. Material is less connected by catchword or ordered by topic than it is put in chronological sequence. John, who looks forward to the coming one, speaks first. Then the temptation narrative, which shows Jesus overcoming temptation and acting as he himself will demand that others act, legitimizes him. After overcoming trial he then delivers a sermon, after which he heals someone, after which he addresses the disciples of John the Baptist, after which he speaks to the crowds."

of literary parallels for Q, we will see that his theory about Gospel origins will be expected to produce precisely the features that we have been observing in Q. For if Farrer is right to maintain Markan Priority but reject the idea that Matthew and Luke were independent of one another, then we can begin to build up a plausible picture of Luke's procedure. The third evangelist works from a base in Mark, following the latter's core narrative but then he turns to Matthew to supplement the Markan core, primarily by filling it out with the new Matthean sayings, but introducing elements along the way of Matthew's (non-Markan) narrative sequence.

Could it be that this provides the explanation that we are looking for? Well, one key advantage is something that it shares with any good hypothesis: it has predictive and explanatory power. For if Farrer is right, we will not be surprised to see "an exordium so full of dogmatic weight and historical destiny," to use his words, "peter[ing] out in miscellaneous oracles."[28] In other words, his theory will make good sense of the strongly marked narrative sequence in the first section of Q which is absent from the rest.

The key is found in some simple source-critical observations. On the Farrer theory, Q's narrative sequence is thrown up by the convergence of certain Matthean and Lukan redactional decisions concerning the way in which they restructure the Markan narrative. First, we need to pay attention to a well-known feature of Matthew, that there is a difference between its two halves, Matthew 3–11 and Matthew 12–28. Broadly speaking, Matthew 3–11 constitutes a radically restructured Mark, in which fresh material appears as part of a narrative partly in conflict with Mark, whereas in Matthew 12–28 the existing Markan framework is largely retained, the Markan narrative sequence simply getting supplemented by fresh material. The importance of this observation for our purposes is that the narrative sequence that we can see in the Q material all occurs in Matthew's first half, in the section in which Matthew is apparently restructuring his Markan source. Among other things, Matthew has Jesus leave Nazara in 4:13, has Jesus moving to Capernaum to heal the Centurion's Boy in 8:5–13 not long after finishing his sayings in the Sermon on the Mount in 5–7. And the narrative sequence dissipates at the end of the story of the Messengers from John the Baptist, which

---

28. "On Dispensing with Q," 60. For a critique of Farrer on this point, see Kloppenborg, "Theological Stakes," 118, n. 90.

occurs in Matthew 11:2–19, very close to the point where Matthew begins his faithful, sequential use of Mark, at the end of Matthew 11 and the beginning of Matthew 12.

Also well known is that almost all of Luke's Q material occurs in three blocks, broadly: Luke 3:1–4:16, Luke 6:20–7:35 and Luke 9:51–18. Now the narrative sequence that we have been observing all occurs in the material found in the first two of these blocks, Luke 3:1–4:16 and 6:20–7:35, and the Q material in these two sections is all paralleled in Matthew 3–11, where (to recapitulate the point) we see Matthew's restructured version of Mark, and none of it in Matthew 12–25, in which Matthew is following Mark. Perhaps, then, the narrative sequence in the Q material is simply the result of Luke's decision to focus on Matthew 3–11 for the first two of his non-Markan blocks, taking over some of the non-Markan Matthean narrative framework found there, like the move to Nazara (Matt 4:13 // Luke 4:16) and the Capernaum Centurion following shortly after the Sermon (Matt 7:28–29, 8:5–13 // Luke 7:1–10). Given Luke's redactional procedure on the assumption that he knows Matthew, we will not be surprised to see elements of the non-Markan narrative sequence finding their way into Luke 3–7, but dissipating thereafter. While Matthew settles into the Markan sequence for the second half of his Gospel from Chapter 12, so Luke does the opposite and departs from Mark altogether. On the Farrer theory, the presence of a narrative sequence for some Q material at the beginning of the Gospel, and the absence of a narrative sequence in the Q material throughout the rest of the Gospel, is simply a source-critical inevitability.

To some, though, this analysis will no doubt seem to beg the question. Perhaps Matthew and Luke converge in this way not because Luke knows Matthew but because they are both adopting the Q narrative. Could it be that they have both independently conflated Mark and Q, leaving us traces of Q's narrative sequence? I think that this is unlikely for two reasons. First, one of the clearest elements in the Q narrative bears the unmistakable mark of Matthew's redactional hand, Q 7:1, "he completed [these] sayings," ἐ[[πλήρω]]σεν [[τοὺς λόγους τούτους]]. The precise wording is difficult to reconstruct, but its Matthean flavor is unmistakable: it is, as every introductory book on Matthew's Gospel tells us, the way in which the narrator marks off each of Jesus' five major discourses, as here, at the end of the Sermon on the Mount/Plain. We could hardly ask for a clearer indication of the way the wind is blowing, as Michael Goulder has attempted to point out on several occasions.[29]

But there is something more decisive still. For if the Farrer theory is right, the Q narrative sequence is something that is artificially created by the extrapolation of Luke's agreement with non-Markan material in Matthew. In other words, it did not originally have a separate existence outside of Matthew's Gospel. Under such circumstances, we will expect the Q narrative to presuppose elements outside of that narrative, elements that are present in the surrounding material in Matthew in which it was originally embedded. If, on the other hand, the Q theory is right, then this material constitutes a discrete source, something separate from the Synoptic Gospels, and Q's much vaunted distinctiveness will not lead us to expect to see such features.

Well, there are several elements presupposed but not narrated in the Q material we have been discussing and I will focus on five of the most striking ones: (1) that John's baptism is a baptism of repentance (Q 3:8); (2) that John's activity was located in the wilderness (Q 7:24); (3) that John was arrested at some point (Q 7:18); (4) that Jesus performed many miracles (Q 7:18–23); (5) that Jesus is known to consort with tax collectors and sinners (Q 7:34). Each one of these features is explained without difficulty on the Farrer theory, for they are all specifically narrated in the triple tradition outside of the Q material that presupposes it. Let us take each point in turn.

1. Q 3:8 warns people who were "coming to his baptism" to "bear fruits worthy of repentance." The strong connection here presupposed between John's baptism and repentance is actually narrated in Mark, Matthew, and Luke. Indeed, it seems to be a matter of special interest to Matthew, who frames John the Baptist's speech on one side with the redactional addition Matt 3:2, in which John issues the same warning that Jesus is to issue in 4:17, μετανοεῖτε· ἤγγικεν γὰρ ἡ βασιλεία τῶν οὐρανῶν ("Repent, for the kingdom of heaven is at hand"), and on the other side with 3:11, in which Matthew adds that John's baptism was εἰς μετάνοιαν ("for repentance"). Could this be a sign that Matthew himself crafted the

29. *Luke: A New Paradigm*, 12, 376, 380; "Is Q a Juggernaut?" 671–72; "Self-Contradiction in the IQP," 515. See too from the Griesbachian perspective Allan J. McNicol et al., eds., *Beyond the Q Impasse*, 22–23, 103.

Baptist's words, characteristically expanding his Markan source in line with his distinctive interests and using typical Matthean language?[30]

2. Jesus' question in Q 7:24, "What then did you go out to the wilderness to see?" presupposes another element that is not narrated in Q: the wilderness location for John's activity. Once again, this is something directly recounted in all three synoptics but not, as far as we can tell, in Q. Perhaps this saying too was constructed by someone like Matthew who was familiar with that Markan narrative.

3. In Q 7:18–19, John sends disciples to ask a question of Jesus, and subsequently Jesus places his activity very much in the past, "What *did you* go out to see?" (7:24 and 7:26). It appears to be the case that John has been arrested; it is presupposed that his active ministry is over and he is unable to go and ask these questions of Jesus himself.[31] What Q appears to presuppose is once more made clear in the triple tradition material: that John was arrested at a point after his preaching but prior to this incident (Mark 1:14 // Matt 4:12 // Luke 3:20). Perhaps, again, this material was composed by an evangelist like Matthew in the light of the earlier development of his own narrative.

4. In Q 7:18–23, Jesus' having performed several miracles is presupposed. While Luke has a general round-up of healings in front of John's disciples (Luke 7:21), in Matthew an example of each kind of miracle mentioned has already been narrated in Matthew 8–9: *the blind see* (Two Blind Men, 9:27–31), *the lame walk* (8:5–13 and 9:2–8), *lepers are cleansed* (8:1–4), *the deaf hear* (9:32–34), *the*

---

30. The point is seen clearly in relation also to the audience for this material by William Arnal, "Redactional Fabrication and Group Legitimation: The Baptist's Preaching in Q 3:7–9, 16–17" in John S. Kloppenborg, ed., *Conflict and Invention: Literary, Rhetorical and Social Studies on the Sayings Gospel Q* (Valley Forge, Pa.: Trinity Press International, 1995), 165–80, who says (concerning Q 3:7–9) that "Its narrative setting, presupposed by the Synoptic evangelists, is inseparable from its content.... The erstwhile narrative framework does not simply provide the occasion for the saying but here provides the entire *rationale* and *motive* for it" (170).

31. That John's messengers come from prison is made explicit in the scene set by Matthew 11:2, ὁ δὲ Ἰωάννης ἀκούσας ἐν τῷ δεσμωτηρίῳ τὰ ἔργα τοῦ Χριστοῦ πέμψας διὰ τῶν μαθητῶν αὐτοῦ.... It is worth adding also that John's disciples have been introduced earlier in the narrative, at 9:14 // Mark 2:18 // Luke 5:33.

dead are raised (9:18–26).[32] Once again, the element presupposed in Q is directly related in earlier material in Matthew.

5. In Q 7:24, it is taken for granted that Jesus is known to "eat and drink" and to consort with "tax collectors and sinners." This element, again not narrated in Q, is narrated earlier in the triple tradition; indeed it is a marked element of Jesus' ministry in all three Synoptics. Here then, as in the other four cases, we have narrative material presupposed in Q that is directly recounted outside of Q, in the triple tradition material. The Q material that we find in Matthew and Luke seems to fit so well into its triple tradition contexts that we begin to wonder whether perhaps it was crafted specially to fit those contexts. In short, the hypothesis that this material in some way originates with Matthew, forged by the first evangelist as he interacts with the Markan narrative, and that the same material is subsequently taken over by Luke, seems a very attractive hypothesis.

Conclusion

When we place Thomas and Q alongside each other, one of the things that most strikes us is the presence in the hypothetical document of something conspicuous by its absence in the rediscovered document, a narrative sequence. Our surprise at seeing this in such sharp relief is compounded by two rather striking features that seem to go with the narrative sequence: (1) the intensity of the feature in the first third of Q followed by the relative lack of the feature in the latter two-thirds and (2) presuppositions made but not directly related in the narrative. Both of these properties of the Q narrative make good sense on the Farrer theory, for which the Q material is constituted by that which Luke took over from Matthew's non-Markan material. The Farrer theory therefore predicts that we will find precisely what we do in fact find, narrative

---

32. Cf. Dale Allison, *Jesus Tradition*, 46: "Also instructive is Q 7:18–23. Here Jesus says that through his ministry the blind see, the lame walk, lepers are cleansed, the deaf hear, and the dead are raised. Yet Q (unlike Mark) contains no account of such things. *Surely we should imagine that Q presupposes knowledge of miracle stories that it does not recount.* Otherwise Q 7:18–23 would do nothing but raise questions" (my emphasis). This is, I think, exactly right except that it is important to note that the miracle stories presupposed in Q 7:18–23 are largely narrated in Matthew 8–9. The only element that has not been directly "fulfilled" is κωφοὶ ἀκούουσιν, "the deaf hear," since ὁ κωφός (the deaf/dumb man) spoke (ἐλάλησεν) in Matt 9:32–33.

sequence in the double tradition material for as long as Matthew is apparently restructuring the Markan narrative, in Matthew 3–11, and an absence of narrative sequence in the double tradition from the time that Matthew begins closely following the Markan narrative, in Matthew 12–25. Under such circumstances, the narrative element in Q is no more than a source-critical inevitability emerging from quirks in the structuring of the Synoptic Gospels.

And this is apparently confirmed by the fact that throughout the narrative of Q 3–7 we have material taken for granted that is actually narrated outside of Q in triple tradition material. Once again, the predictive power of the Farrer theory is striking. If Q is constituted by what Luke took over from the non-Markan parts of Matthew, we will expect to find elements in Q that presuppose material only narrated outside of Q. If, on the other hand, the Q theory is right, we will be surprised to see the obtrusive presence of these elements in a document the existence of which is usually held to be plausible because of its distinctiveness from the Synoptic Gospels.

As I mentioned at the beginning of this chapter, one of the exciting things about the discovery of Thomas was the light it appeared to shed on Q. I think that the initial excitement was right; Thomas does indeed shed light on Q, but not in the way that many first thought. Rather than corroborating the existence of the document by providing another, better example of a text in the same genre, it shows us by means of a clear contrast with itself precisely what Q is and always has been. For while Thomas's genre is appropriately described as *Sayings Gospel,* that is a work in which eternal life is constituted solely by listening to and correctly interpreting the *words* of the living Jesus, with no interest in history, geography, or narrative, Q is something quite different. Its similarity to Thomas is the relatively superficial one that it is largely constituted by sayings material; it is its difference from Thomas that provides us with the clue about Q's true nature, that what we have here is no more and no less than the material extrapolated from comparison between the non-Markan elements common to Matthew and Luke.

EPILOGUE

It is all too easy to become absorbed in discussions of the Synoptic Problem without asking key questions concerning the relevance of one's conclusions to broader issues in studies of the New Testament and Christian origins. The problem is sharply focused for a study like this which involves the loss of an entity well-loved by New Testament scholars, the Q hypothesis, a hypothesis that had appeared to establish its utility by shedding light on the composition of the Gospels, on the literary and tradition-history behind them, and, ultimately, on the historical Jesus. On one level, it is of course a real disappointment to lose something apparently so useful, not least given recent advances in Q scholarship in which the document is becoming ever more tangible. Our familiarity with Q, our affection for it is going to make taking our leave of it a difficult thing to do. And yet, as when many relationships end, there are compensations, compensations which, in time, will make the break-up seem worthwhile. I would like to offer some reflections, finally, on what a world without Q might look like, and why there might be advantages in living in such a place.

First, to pick up an element from our final chapter, dispensing with Q has implications for the study of the Gospel of Thomas, encouraging us to take seriously the essential difference between the worldview of the Gospel of Thomas and the worldview of others in the early Christian movement. Perhaps it will allow the Gospel of Thomas to speak more eloquently about what a Sayings Gospel and a Sayings-based Christology really looks like, without undue influence from Q. After all, the double tradition material, from which Q is reconstructed, has many points of contact with other elements within the Synoptic tradition: its positive attitude to Jesus' miracle-working, for example, or its attitude to tax-collectors and sinners, or its view of the relationship between Jesus and John, none of which are at all at home in Thomas, the Sayings Gospel par excellence.

Second, acceptance of the priority of Mark alongside Luke's knowledge of Matthew fundamentally alters the way in which we might view the growth and development of the Gospel genre (or sub-genre). The Farrer theory suggests a genetic relationship among the Synoptics in which each Gospel's predecessor provides not only source material but also the catalyst for writing. Thus while Mark plausibly remains at the genesis of the Gospel genre, the first to forge together disparate traditions concerning the life of Jesus into a story culminating with the Passion and Resurrection, Matthew embraces Mark at the same time as being critical of it, using Mark, restructuring Mark, changing Mark. And Luke is then inspired by Matthew to produce his own fresh version of Mark, restructuring it in many of the same ways. Like Matthew, he adds a Birth Narrative, but improves on it; like Matthew he adds a resurrection account, but improves on it; and like Matthew he adds a lot of useful sayings material, some of which he takes directly from Matthew and some of which he gleans from elsewhere. Just as Matthew creatively but critically interacted with Mark, so now Luke creatively but critically interacts with them both. While one of the advantages of the Farrer theory is the dynamic way in which it is able to explain the historical growth and development of the Synoptic Gospels, so too this genetic relationship has the potential to provide stimulating theological reflection on the way in which these key canonical documents creatively and critically interact with one another.

Third, dispensing with Q can challenge us to rethink the role played by oral tradition in the composition of the Synoptic Gospels. One of the potential difficulties with the Q hypothesis, and something endemic to the discussion of "alternating primitivity," is the routine confusion between literary priority and the relative age of traditions. For a long time scholars have accepted that Matthew and Luke might witness to different, sometimes more primitive versions of material they share with Mark. It is an obvious extension of this principle to see Luke sometimes witnessing to more primitive versions of material he nevertheless shares with Matthew. The reduction of the variety and richness of oral tradition to the level of the reconstruction of the precise wording of a hypothetical document is one of the more unfortunate consequences of the Q theory, in which consideration of the double tradition is inevitably forced into purely literary terms. The recognition that Luke was literarily dependent on Matthew, as well as Mark, challenges the exegete to take seriously those places where he apparently witnesses to a different, perhaps more primitive tradition, leading to a reassessment of — and perhaps ultimately a more nuanced role for — oral tradition in Synoptic relationships.

Fourth, dispensing with Q reopens the question of Matthew's non-Markan sources. If the Q material was effectively generated by Luke's reworking of Matthew's non-Markan material, the question of Matthew's sources is refocused as a question about both "Q" and "M," a distinction which for Matthew becomes irrelevant, and which has interesting ramifications for the study of sayings material in early Christianity. Perhaps it will be seen to be significant that other early Christian documents like the Epistle of James or the Gospel of Thomas apparently interact extensively with Q and M but less so with L. Just as acceptance of the two-source theory generates interesting questions about the sources of Mark and Q (and, for that matter, M and L), so too acceptance of the Farrer theory generates interesting questions about the sources of Mark and the non-Markan material in Matthew (and, for that matter, L).

Fifth, to take seriously the notion that Luke used Matthew as well as Mark has consequences for our perception of Luke's literary ability. Because the scope of Luke's transformations of Matthew's non-Markan material is so great, we are encouraged repeatedly to ask questions about why he has done what he has done, and why given material is placed where it is. While the Q theory allows one to abstain from considering Luke's arrangements of material by projecting them onto the hypothetical order of Q, and Luke's conservative policy in relation to them, Q skeptics are forced to take seriously the literary rationale for the decisions Luke has apparently made, considerations that begin to look most plausible when we ask for help from hitherto underutilized friends like narrative criticism. Perhaps, in the end, dispensing with Q will mark the moment at which we finally find ourselves able to dispense also with scissors-and-paste.

But the Q hypothesis has served us well, and it is with a lump in our throats that we bid it adieu. Q stands as a monument that reminds us of many of the advances made in biblical scholarship over the last 150 years. In an age less amenable than ours to the literary creativity of the evangelists, Q helped to establish the reality of Markan Priority and played a key role in helping us to forge the tool of redaction criticism, the tool which in the end, ironically, plays a part in dispensing with it. If it is now time to take our leave of Q, it is with the hope that new insights will bring new challenges, and fresh sets of questions will provide renewed ways of firing our imagination.

BIBLIOGRAPHY

Aichele, George, and Richard Walsh, eds. *Screening Scripture: Intertextual Connec-tions Between Scripture and Film.* Harrisburg, Pa.: Trinity Press International, 2002.

Aland, Kurt, ed. *Synopsis Quattuor Evangeliorum: Locis parallelis evangeliorum apocryphorum et patrum adhibitis edidit.* Editio quindecima revisa; Deutsche Bibelgesellschaft, 1996.

Allen, Charlotte. "The Search for a No-Frills Jesus," *Atlantic Monthly* 278, 6 (December 1996): 51–68.

Allison, Dale. *The New Moses: A Matthaean Typology.* Edinburgh: T & T Clark, 1993.

————. *The Jesus Tradition in Q.* Harrisburg, Pa.: Trinity Press International, 1997.

————. Review of Hans Dieter Betz, *The Sermon on the Mount. JBL* 117 (1998): 136–38.

————. "The Secularizing of the Historical Jesus." Forthcoming in *Perspectives in Religious Studies.* Also available on Allison's home page (*http://www.pts.edu/ allisond.html*).

Argyle, A. W. "Evidence for the View that St Luke Used St Matthew's Gospel." *JBL* 53 (1964): 390–96.

Arnal, William E. *Jesus and the Village Scribes: Galilean Conflicts and the Setting of Q.* Minneapolis: Fortress, 2001.

————. "Redactional Fabrication and Group Legitimation: The Baptist's Preaching in Q 3.7–9, 16–17." In *Conflict and Invention: Literary, Rhetorical and Social Studies on the Sayings Gospel Q.* Edited by John S. Kloppenborg. Valley Forge, Pa.: Trinity Press International, 1995, 165–80.

Bauckham, Richard, ed. *The Gospels for All Christians: Rethinking the Gospel Audiences.* Grand Rapids: Eerdmans; Edinburgh: T & T Clark, 1998.

Becker, Michael. "4Q521 und die Gesalbten." *Revue de Qumran* 18 (1997): 73–76.

Bellinzoni, A. J., J. B. Tyson, and W. O. Walker, eds. *The Two Source Hypothesis: A Critical Appraisal* (Macon, Ga.: Mercer University Press, 1985).

Best, Ernest. "Mark's Readers: A Profile." In *The Four Gospels 1992. Festschrift Frans Neirynck, Volume II.* Edited by F. Van Segbroeck et al. BETL, 100; Leuven: Leuven University Press, 1992, 839–58.

Betz, Hans Dieter. *The Sermon on the Mount: A Commentary on the Sermon on the Mount including the Sermon on the Plain.* Hermeneia; Minneapolis: Fortress, 1995.

Black, Matthew. "The Aramaic Dimension in Q." *JSNT* 40 (1990): 33–41.

Blomberg, Craig L. *Jesus and the Gospels: An Introduction and Survey.* Leicester: Apollos, 1997.

Boer, M. C. de. "Narrative Criticism, Historical Criticism, and the Gospel of John," *JSNT* 45 (1992): 35–48; reproduced in John Ashton, ed., *The Interpretation of John.* 2d ed. Studies in New Testament Interpretation. Edinburgh: T & T Clark, 1997, 301–14.

Boer M. C. de, ed. *From Jesus to John: Essays on Jesus and New Testament Christology in Honour of Marinus de Jonge.* JSNTSup, 84. Sheffield: Sheffield Academic Press, 1993.

Boismard, M.-E. "The Two-Source Theory at an Impasse." *NTS* 26 (1979–80): 1–17.

———. "Introduction au premier récit de la multiplication des pains" (Mt. 14.13–14; Mc 6.30–44; Lc 9.10–11). In *The Interrelations of the Gospels: A Symposium Led by M.-E. Boismard, W. R. Farmer, F. Neirynck, Jerusalem, 1984.* Edited by David L. Dungan. BETL, 95; Leuven: Leuven University Press, 1990, 244–53.

Borg, Marcus J., and Mark Powelson, eds. *The Lost Gospel Q: The Original Sayings of Jesus.* Translated by Ray Riegert. Introduction by Thomas Moore. Berkeley, Calif.: Ulysses Press, 1996.

Borg, Marcus, ed. *The Lost Gospel Q: The Original Sayings of Jesus.* Narrated by Jacob Needleman. Introduction by Thomas Moore. Ten Speed Press. Audio, 1998.

Bovon, F. *Das Evangelium nach Lukas 1. Teilband: Lk 1,1–9,50.* EKKNT 3/1; Zürich: Benzinger; Neukirchen-Vluyn: Neukirchener Verlag, 1989.

Brown, Raymond E. *The Birth of the Messiah: A Commentary on the Infancy Narratives in Matthew and Luke.* Rev. ed. London: Chapman, 1993.

———. *The Death of the Messiah: From Gethsemane to the Grave. A Commentary on the Passion Narratives of the Four Gospels.* 2 vols. The Anchor Bible Reference Library. New York: Doubleday, 1994.

———. *Introduction to the New Testament.* ABRL; Garden City, N.Y.: Doubleday, 1997.

Bultmann, Rudolf. *History of the Synoptic Tradition.* 2d ed., English Trans., Oxford: Blackwell, 1968.

Burridge, Richard. *What Are The Gospels? A Comparison With Graeco-Roman Biography.* SNTSMS, 70. Cambridge: Cambridge University Press, 1993.

Burrows, E. "The Use of Textual Theories to Explain the Agreements of Matthew and Luke Against Mark." In *Studies in New Testament Language and Text.* Edited by J. K. Elliott. Leiden: Brill (1976): 87–99.

Butler, B. C. *The Originality of St Matthew: A Critique of the Two-Document Hypothesis.* Cambridge: Cambridge University Press, 1951.

Cadbury, H. J. *The Style and Literary Method of Luke.* Cambridge, Mass.: Harvard University Press, 1920.

————. *The Making of Luke-Acts*. London: SPCK, 1958.

————. "Four Features of Lucan Style." In *Studies in Luke-Acts*. Edited by L. E. Keck and J. L. Martyn. London: SPCK (1968): 87–102.

Caird, G. B. *Saint Luke*. Pelican Gospel Commentaries; Harmondsworth: Penguin, 1963.

Caquot, André. "Deux textes messianiques de Qumrân." *Revue d'histoire et de philosophie religieuses*. 79/2 (1999): 155–71.

Carlson, Stephen C. "Clement of Alexandria on the 'Order' of the Gospels." *NTS* 47 (2001): 118–25.

Carruth, Shawn, and Albrecht Garsky. Volume editor: Stanley D. Anderson. *Q 11.2b–4*. In *Documenta Q: Reconstructions of Q Through Two Centuries of Gospel Research Excerpted, Sorted and Evaluated*. Leuven: Peeters, 1996.

Carruth, Shawn, and James M. Robinson. Volume editor: Christoph Heil. *Q 4:1–13, 16. The Temptations of Jesus — Nazara*. In *Documenta Q: Reconstructions of Q Through Two Centuries of Gospel Research Excerpted, Sorted and Evaluated*. Leuven: Peeters, 1996.

Catchpole, David. *The Quest for Q*. Edinburgh: T & T Clark, 1993.

————. "The Anointed One in Nazareth." In *From Jesus to John: Essays on Jesus and New Testament Christology in Honour of Marinus de Jonge*. Edited by M. C. de Boer. JSNTSup, 84. Sheffield: Sheffield Academic Press (1993): 231–51.

Chapman, John. *Matthew, Mark and Luke: A Study in the Order and Interrelation of the Synoptic Gospels*. London: Longmans, Green, 1937.

Conzelmann, Hans. *Die Mitte der Zeit: Studien zur Theologie des Lukas*. BhT 17; Tübingen: Mohr, 1954; English Trans., *The Theology of St Luke*. London: Faber, 1960.

Conzelmann, Hans, and Andreas Lindemann. *Arbeitsbuch zum Neuen Testament*. Uni-Taschenbücher 52; Tübingen: Mohr Siebeck, 1998.

Cope, Lamar. "The Argument Revolves: The Pivotal Evidence for Marcan Priority is Reversing Itself." In *New Synoptic Studies: The Cambridge Gospel Conference and Beyond*. Edited by William R. Farmer. Macon, Ga.: Mercer University Press (1983): 143–59.

Creed, J. M. *The Gospel According to St Luke: The Greek Text With Introduction, Notes and Indices*. London: Macmillan, 1930.

Crook, Zeba Antonin. "The Synoptic Parables of the Mustard Seed and the Leaven: A Test-Case for the Two-Document, Two-Gospel, and Farrer-Goulder hypotheses." *JSNT* 78 (2000): 23–48.

Crossan, John Dominic. *Four Other Gospels: Shadows on the Contours of Canon*. Minneapolis: Seabury, 1985.

————. *The Historical Jesus: The Life of a Mediterranean Jewish Peasant*. Edinburgh: T & T Clark, 1991.

————. *The Birth of Christianity: Discovering What Happened in the Years Immediately After the Execution of Jesus*. Edinburgh: T & T Clark, 1999.

Davies, W. D. *The Setting of the Sermon on the Mount.* Cambridge: Cambridge University Press, 1963.

Davies, W. D., and Dale C. Allison. *A Critical and Exegetical Commentary on the Gospel According to Saint Matthew.* 3 vols. The International Critical Commentary on the Holy Scriptures of the Old and New Testaments; Edinburgh: T & T Clark, 1988–97.

Degenhardt, Hans-Joachim. *Lukas: Evangelist der Armen.* Stuttgart: Katholisches Bibelwerk, 1965.

Delobel, J. "La rédaction de Lc., IV, 14–16a et le <<Bericht von Amfang>>. In *L'Evangile de Luc — The Gospel of Luke.* Edited by F. Neirynck. BETL, 32; Leuven: Leuven University Press, 1989, 202–23.

Delobel, J., ed. *Logia: Les Paroles de Jésus — The Sayings of Jesus.* BETL, 59; Leuven: Leuven University Press, 1982.

Derrenbacker, Jr., Robert A. *Ancient Compositional Practices and the Synoptic Problem.* Ph.D. Dissertation, University of St. Michael's College, Toronto, 2001.

———. "The Relationship of the Gospels Reconsidered." *Toronto Journal of Theology* 14 (1998): 83–88.

Derrenbacker, Jr., Robert A., and John S. Kloppenborg Verbin. "Self-Contradiction in the IQP: A Reply to Michael Goulder." *JBL* 120 (2001): 57–76.

Dodd, C. H. *The Parables of the Kingdom.* Rev. ed. London: Nesbet & Co., 1961.

Downing, F. Gerald. *Doing Things With Words in the First Christian Century.* JSNTSup, 200. Sheffield: Sheffield Academic Press, 2000.

———. "Towards the Rehabilitation of Q." *NTS* 11 (1964): 169–81. Reproduced in *The Two Source Hypothesis: A Critical Appraisal.* Edited by A. J. Bellinzoni, Jr. Macon, Ga.: Mercer University Press, 1985, 269–86.

———. "Redaction Criticism: Josephus' *Antiquities* and the Synoptic Gospels." I, *JSNT* 8 (1980): 46–65; II, *JSNT* 9 (1980): 29–48.

———. "Compositional Conventions and the Synoptic Problem." *JBL* 107 (1988): 69–85. Reproduced in *Doing Things With Words in the First Christian Century.* JSNTSup, 200. Sheffield: Sheffield Academic Press, 2000.

———. "A Paradigm Perplex: Luke, Matthew and Mark." *NTS* 38 (1992): 15–36. Reproduced in F. Gerald Downing, *Doing Things With Words in the First Christian Century.* JSNTSup, 200. Sheffield: Sheffield Academic Press (2000): Chapter 9.

———. "A Genre for Q and a Socio-Cultural Context for Q: Comparing Sets of Similarities With Sets of Differences." *JSNT* 55 (1994): 3–26. Reproduced in F. Gerald Downing, *Doing Things With Words in the First Christian Century.* JSNTSup, 200. Sheffield: Sheffield Academic Press (2000): Chapter 5.

Drury, John. *Luke.* The J. B. Phillips' Commentaries, London and Glasgow: Collins, 1973.

———. *Tradition and Design in Luke's Gospel.* London: Darton, Longman and Todd, 1976.

———. *The Parables in the Gospels: History and Allegory.* London: SPCK, 1985.

———. "Luke." In *The Literary Guide to the Bible.* Edited by Frank Kermode and Robert Alter. Cambridge, Mass.: Harvard University Press, 1987, 418–39.

———. "Luke, Gospel of." In *DBI,* ad loc.

Dungan, David L. *A History of the Synoptic Problem: The Canon, the Text, the Composition and the Interpretation of the Gospels.* ABRL. New York: Doubleday, 1999.

Dungan, David L., ed. *The Interrelations of the Gospels: A Symposium Led by M.-E. Boismard, W. R. Farmer, F. Neirynck, Jerusalem, 1984.* BETL, 95; Leuven: Leuven University Press, 1990.

Dunn, James D. G. *Unity and Diversity in the New Testament: An Enquiry into the Character of Earliest Christianity.* London: SCM, 1977.

———. "Jesus in Oral Memory: The Initial Stages of the Jesus Tradition." *Society of Biblical Literature Seminar Papers 2000.* Society of Biblical Literature Seminar Paper Series 39. Atlanta: Society of Biblical Literature, 2000, 287–326.

Dupont, J. *Les Béatitudes.* Paris: Gabalda, I–II 1969; III 1973.

Ehrman, Bart. *The Orthodox Corruption of Scripture: The Effect of Early Christological Controversies on the Text of the New Testament.* Oxford: Oxford University Press, 1993.

———. *The New Testament: A Historical Introduction to the Early Christian Writings.* 2d ed. New York; Oxford: Oxford University Press, 2000.

Elliott, J. K., ed. *Studies in New Testament Language and Text.* Leiden: Brill, 1976.

Ennulat, A. *Die "Minor Agreements": Untersuchung zu einer offenen Frage des synoptischen Problems.* WUNT 2/62; Tübingen: J. C. B. Mohr (Paul Siebeck), 1994.

Enslin, Morton Scott. *Christian Beginnings.* New York: Harper and Brothers, 1938; reprinted, Harper Torchbooks; New York: Harper and Brothers, 1956.

Evans, C. F. *Saint Luke.* TPI New Testament Commentaries; London: SCM, 1990.

———. "Goulder and the Gospels." *Theology* 82 (1979): 425–32.

Farmer, William R. *Synopticon: The Verbal Agreements Between the Greek Texts of Matthew, Mark and Luke Contextually Exhibited.* Cambridge: Cambridge University Press, 1969.

———. *The Synoptic Problem: A Critical Review of the Problem of Literary Relationships Between Matthew, Mark and Luke.* New York: Macmillan, 1964; 2d ed. Dillsboro, N.C.: Western North Carolina Press, 1976.

———. *The Gospel of Jesus: The Pastoral Relevance of the Synoptic Problem.* Louisville: Westminster John Knox, 1994.

———. "Certain Results Reached by Sir John C. Hawkins and C. F. Burney Which Make More Sense If Luke Knew Matthew, and Mark Knew Matthew and Luke." In *Synoptic Studies: The Ampleforth Conferences of 1982 and 1983.* Edited by C. M. Tuckett. JSNTSup, 7. Sheffield: JSOT Press (1984): 75–98.

———. "Reply to Michael Goulder." In *Synoptic Studies: The Ampleforth Conferences of 1982 and 1983.* Edited by C. M. Tuckett. JSNTSup, 7. Sheffield: JSOT Press (1984): 105–9.

————. "The Current State of the Synoptic Problem." *Literary Studies in Luke-Acts: Essays in Honor of Joseph B. Tyson.* Macon, Ga.: Mercer University Press, 1998, 11–36.

Farmer, William R., ed. *New Synoptic Studies: The Cambridge Gospel Conference and Beyond.* Macon, Ga.: Mercer University Press, 1983.

Farrer, Austin. *A Study in St Mark.* Westminster: Dacre, 1951.

————. *St Matthew and St Mark.* The Edward Cadbury Lectures 1953–54; Westminster: Dacre, 1954.

————. "On Dispensing with Q." In *Studies in the Gospels: Essays in Memory of R. H. Lightfoot.* Edited by D. E. Nineham. Oxford: Blackwell (1955): 55–88. Reproduced on *The Case Against Q* web site, *http://ntgateway.com/Q.*

Fenton, John. *Saint Matthew.* Pelican Gospel Commentaries; Harmondsworth: Penguin, 1963.

Fitzmyer, Joseph A. *The Gospel According to Luke: Introduction, Translation and Notes. 1: I–IX.* Anchor Bible 28. New York: Doubleday, 1981.

————. *The Gospel According to Luke: Introduction, Translation and Notes. 2: X–XXIV.* Anchor Bible 28A. New York: Doubleday, 1985.

————. "The Priority of Mark and the Q Source in Luke." In *Jesus and Man's Hope.* Edited by David A. Buttrick. *Perspective* 2/1 (1970): 131–70.

————. "The Oxyrhynchus Logoi of Jesus and the Coptic Gospel According to Thomas." In *The Semitic Background of the New Testament: A Combined Edition of Essays on the Semitic Background of the New Testament and A Wandering Aramean: Collected Aramaic Essays.* The Biblical Resource Series. Grand Rapids: Eerdmans, 1997, 355–433.

France, R. T. *Matthew: Evangelist and Teacher.* Exeter: Paternoster, 1989.

France, R. T., and D. Wenham, eds. *Gospel Perspectives II: Studies of History and Tradition in the Four Gospels.* Sheffield: JSOT Press, 1981.

————. *Gospel Perspectives III: Studies in Midrash and Historiography.* Sheffield: JSOT Press, 1983.

Franklin, Eric. *Luke: Interpreter of Paul, Critic of Matthew.* JSNTSup, 92. Sheffield: Sheffield Academic Press, 1994.

————. "A Passion Narrative for Q?" In *Understanding, Studying and Reading. New Testament Essays in Honour of John Ashton.* Edited by Christopher Rowland and Crispin H. T. Fletcher-Louis. JSNTSup, 153. Sheffield: Sheffield Academic Press (1998): 30–47.

Friedrichsen, Timothy A. "The Minor Agreements of Matthew and Luke Against Mark: Critical Observations on R. B. Vinson's Statistical Analysis." *ETL* 65 (1989): 395–408.

————. "The Matthew-Luke Agreements Against Mark: A Survey of Recent Studies: 1974–1989." In *L'Evangile de Luc — The Gospel of Luke,* Edited by F. Neirynck. BETL, 32; Leuven: Leuven University Press, 1989, 335–91.

————. "New Dissertations on the Minor Agreements." *ETL* 67 (1991): 373–94.

———. " 'Minor' and 'Major' Matthew-Luke Agreements against Mk 4,30–32." In *The Four Gospels 1992. Festschrift Frans Neirynck,* Volume 1. Edited by F. Van Segbroeck et al. BETL, 100; Leuven: Leuven University Press, 1992, 649–76.

Frye, Roland Mushat. "Literary Criticism and Gospel Criticism." *Theology Today* 36 (1979): 207–19.

Fuchs, Albert. *Sprachliche Untersuchungen zu Matthäus und Lukas: Ein Beitrag zur Quellenkritik.* AnBib, 49. Rome: Biblical Institute Press, 1971.

———. "Die agreements der Perikope von der Taufe Jesu Mk 1,9–11 par Mt 3,13–17 par Lk 3,21–22." In *Studien zum Neuen Testament und seiner Umwelt. Serie A* 24 (1999): 5–34.

———. "Zweiquellentheorie oder Deuteromarkus?" *Bibel und Kirche* 54 (1999): 63–69.

———. "Exegese im elfenbeinernen Turm. Das quellenkritische Problem von Mk 1,2–8 par Mt 3,1–12 par Lk 3,1–17 in der Sicht der Zweiquellentheorie und von Deuteromarkus." In *Studien zum Neuen Testament und seiner Umwelt. Serie A* 20 (1995): 23–149.

Fuller, Reginald H. *The New Testament in Current Study.* London: SCM, 1963.

Funk, Robert W., Roy W. Hoover, and the Jesus Seminar. *The Five Gospels: The Search for the Authentic Words of Jesus.* Sonoma, Calif.: Polebridge, 1993.

Garsky, Albrecht, Christoph Heil, Thomas Hieke, and Josef E. Amon. Volume editor Shawn Carruth. *Q 12:49–59. Children against Parents — Judging the Time — Settling out of Court.* In *Documenta Q: Reconstructions of Q through Two Centuries of Gospel Research Excerpted, Sorted and Evaluated.* Leuven: Peeters, 1997.

Gaston, L. *Horae Synopticae Electronicae: Word Statistics of the Synoptic Gospels.* Missoula, Mont.: SBL, 1973.

Goodacre, Mark. *Goulder and the Gospels: An Examination of a New Paradigm.* JSNTSup, 133. Sheffield: Sheffield Academic Press, 1996.

———. *The Synoptic Problem: A Way Through the Maze.* The Biblical Seminar, 80. Sheffield: Sheffield Academic Press, 2001.

———. " 'Drawing from the Treasure Both New and Old': Current Trends in New Testament Studies." *Scripture Bulletin* 27/2 (July 1997): 66–77.

———. "Fatigue in the Synoptics." *NTS* 44 (1998): 45–58. Reproduced on *The Case Against Q* web site, *http://ntgateway.com/Q.*

———. "Beyond the Q Impasse or Down a Blind Alley?" *JSNT* 76 (1999): 33–52.

———. "The Synoptic Jesus and the Celluloid Christ: Solving the Synoptic Problem Through Film." *JSNT* 80 (2000): 31–44.

———. "A Monopoly on Marcan Priority? Fallacies at the Heart of Q." *Society of Biblical Literature Seminar Papers 2000.* Atlanta: Society of Biblical Literature, 2000, 538–622. Reproduced on *The Case Against Q* web site, *http://ntgateway.com/Q.*

———. Review of Kim Paffenroth. *The Story of Jesus According to L. JBL* 118 (1999): 363–64.

———. Review of Alan Kirk, *The Composition of the Sayings Source. NovT* 42 (2000): 185–87.

———. Review of David L. Dungan, *A History of the Synoptic Problem. SJT,* forthcoming.

Goulder, Michael. *Midrash and Lection in Matthew.* London: SPCK, 1974.

———. *Luke: A New Paradigm.* JSNTSup, 20. Sheffield: Sheffield Academic Press, 1989.

———. "The Composition of the Lord's Prayer," *JTS* 14 (1964): 32–45.

———. "On Putting Q to the Test." *NTS* 24 (1978): 218–34.

———. "Mark 16.1–8 and Parallels." *NTS* 24 (1978): 235–40.

———. "Farrer on Q." *Theology* 83 (1980): 190–95.

———. "Some Observations on Professor Farmer's 'Certain Results. . . .' " In *Synoptic Studies: The Ampleforth Conferences of 1982 and 1983.* Edited by C. M. Tuckett. JSNTSup, 7. Sheffield: JSOT Press (1984): 99–104.

———. "The Order of a Crank." In *Synoptic Studies: The Ampleforth Conferences of 1982 and 1983.* Edited by C. M. Tuckett. JSNTSup, 7. Sheffield: JSOT Press (1984): 111–30.

———. "A House Built on Sand." In *Alternative Approaches to New Testament Study.* Edited by A. E. Harvey. London: SPCK, 1985, 1–24.

———. "Luke's Knowledge of Matthew." In *Minor Agreements: Symposium Göttingen, 1991.* Edited by G. Strecker. Göttingen: Vandenhoeck & Ruprecht, 1993): 143–60.

———. "Luke's Compositional Conventions." *NTS* 39 (1993): 150–52.

———. "Is Q a Juggernaut?" *JBL* 115 (1996): 667–81. Reproduced on *The Case Against Q* web site, *http://ntgateway.com/Q.*

———. "Self-Contradiction in the IQP." *JBL* 118 (1999): 506–17.

Gowler, David B. "Heteroglossic Trends in Biblical Studies: Polyphoic Dialogues or Clanging Cymbals?" *Review and Exposition* 27/4 (2000): 443–66.

Grayston, K. "Sermon on the Mount." In *IDB,* ad loc.

Green, H. Benedict. *The Gospel According to Matthew.* Oxford: Clarendon, 1975.

———. *Matthew: Poet of the Beatitudes.* JSNTSup 203. Sheffield: Sheffield Academic Press, 2001.

———. "The Credibility of Luke's Transformation of Matthew." In *Synoptic Studies: The Ampleforth Conferences of 1982 and 1983.* Edited by C. M. Tuckett. JSNTSup, 7. Sheffield: JSOT Press (1984): 131–56.

———. "Matthew 12.22–50 and Parallels: An Alternative to Matthaean Conflation." In *Synoptic Studies: The Ampleforth Conferences of 1982 and 1983.* Edited by C. M. Tuckett. JSNTSup, 7. Sheffield: JSOT Press (1984): 157–76.

Green, Joel B. *The Gospel of Luke.* The New International Commentary on the New Testament. Grand Rapids: Eerdmans, 1997.

Green, Joel B., ed. *Hearing the New Testament: Strategies for Interpretation.* Grand Rapids: Eerdmans; Carlisle: Paternoster, 1995.

Guillaumont, A., H.-Ch. Puech, G. Quispel, W. Till, and Yassah 'Abd al Masih, eds. *The Gospel According to Thomas: Coptic Text Established and Translated.* Leiden: Brill, 1959.

Gundry, R. H. *Matthew: A Commentary on His Literary and Theological Art.* Grand Rapids: Eerdmans, 1982. 2d ed. published as *Matthew: A Commentary on His Handbook for a Mixed Church Under Persecution.* Grand Rapids: Eerdmans, 1994.

————. "Matthean Foreign Bodies in Agreements of Luke with Matthew against Mark. Evidence That Luke used Matthew." In *The Four Gospels 1992. Festschrift Frans Neirynck. Volume II.* Edited by F. Van Segbroeck et al. BETL, 100. Leuven: Leuven University Press, 1992. 1467–95.

Harnack, Adolph von. *New Testament Studies II: The Sayings of Jesus. The Second Source of St. Matthew and St. Luke.* Trans. J. R. Wilkinson. New York: G. P. Putnam's Sons; London: Williams & Norgate, 1908.

Harvey, A. E., ed. *Alternative Approaches to New Testament Study.* London: SPCK, 1985.

Hawkins, J. C. *Horae Synopticae: Contributions to the Study of the Synoptic Problem.* 2d ed. Oxford: Clarendon, 1909.

Head, Peter M. *Christology and the Synoptic Problem: An Argument for Markan Priority.* SNTSMS, 94. Cambridge: Cambridge University Press, 1997.

Hengel, Martin, and Anna Maria Schwemer. *Paul Between Damascus and Antioch: The Unknown Years.* London: SCM, 1997.

Highet, Gilbert. *The Classical Tradition: Greek and Roman Influences on Western Literature.* New York and London: Oxford University Press, 1949.

Hobbs, Edward. "A Quarter Century Without Q." *Perkins School of Theology Journal* 33/4 (1980): 10–19. Reproduced on *The Case Against Q* web site, *http://ntgateway.com/Q.*

Hoffmann, Paul. *Studien zur Theologie der Logienquelle.* NTAbh NF, 8. Münster: Verlag Aschendorff, 1972.

————. "The Redaction of Q and the Son of Man: A Preliminary Sketch." In *The Gospels behind the Gospels. Current Studies on Q.* Edited by Ronald A. Piper. NovTSup, 75. Leiden: Brill, 1994, 159–98.

Hoffmann, Paul, Josef E. Amon, Ulrike Brauner, Thomas Hieke, M. Eugene Boring, and Jon Ma. Asgeirsson. Volume editor Christoph Heil. *Q 12:8–12. Confessing or Denying — Speaking against the Holy Spirit — Hearings before Synagogues* in *Documenta Q: Reconstructions of Q through Two Centuries of Gospel Research Excerpted, Sorted and Evaluated* Leuven: Peeters, 1997.

Hoffmann, Paul, Stefan H. Brandenburger, Ulrike Brauner and Thomas Hieke. Volume editor Christoph Heil. *Q 22:28–30. You Will Judge the Twelve Tribes of Israel.* In *Documenta Q: Reconstructions of Q through Two Centuries of Gospel Research Excerpted, Sorted and Evaluated.* Leuven: Peeters, 1998.

Holtzmann, H. J. *Die synoptischen Evangelien, Ihr Ursprung und geschichtlicher Charakter.* Leipzig: Engelmann, 1863.

Hooker, Morna. *A Commentary on the Gospel According to St. Mark.* London: A & C Black, 1991.

Huck, A., and H. Greeven, *Synopse der drei ersten Evangelien — Synopsis of the First Three Gospels.* 13th rev. ed. Tübingen: Mohr (Paul Siebeck), 1981.

Hünzinger, C.-H. "Aussersynoptisches Traditionsgut im Thomas-Evangelium." *Theologische Literaturzeitung* 85 (1960): col. 843–44.

Jacobson, Arland. *The First Gospel: An Introduction to Q.* Foundations & Facets. Sonoma, Calif.: Polebridge, 1992.

———. "The Literary Unity of Q." *JBL* 101 (1982): 365–89. Partially reproduced in *The Shape of Q: Signal Essays on the Sayings Gospel.* Edited by John Kloppenborg. Minneapolis: Fortress, 1994, 98–115.

Jameson, H. G. *The Origin of the Synoptic Gospels: A Revision of the Synoptic Problem.* Oxford: Basil Blackwell, 1922.

Jeremias, J. *The Eucharistic Words of Jesus.* English Trans. London: SCM, 1966.

———. *Die Sprache des Lukasevangeliums.* Kritisch-exegetischer Kommentar über das Neue Testament; Sonderband; Göttingen: Vandenhoeck & Ruprecht, 1980.

Johnson, Luke T. *The Writings of the New Testament.* London: SCM, 1986.

———. "Luke-Acts, Book of." *ABD* IV, ad loc.

Johnson, Sherman E. *The Griesbach Hypothesis and Redaction Criticism.* SBLDS, 41. Atlanta: Scholars, 1990.

Juel, Donald H. *The Gospel of Mark.* Interpreting Biblical Texts. Nashville: Abingdon, 1999.

Keck, Leander E. "Oral Traditional Literature and the Gospels." In *The Relationships Among the Gospels: An Interdisciplinary Dialogue.* Edited by William O. Walker. Trinity University Monographs in Religion 5. San Antonio: Trinity University Press, 1978, 103–22.

Keck, L. E., and J. L. Martyn, eds. *Studies in Luke-Acts.* London: SPCK, 1968.

Kee, Howard Clark. "Synoptic Studies." Chapter 9 in *The New Testament and Its Modern Interpreters.* Edited by Eldon Jay Epp and George W. MacRae. Atlanta: Scholars Press, 1989, 245–69.

Kermode, Frank, and Robert Alter, eds. *The Literary Guide to the Bible.* Cambridge, Mass.: Harvard University Press, 1987.

Kirk, Alan. *The Composition of the Sayings Source: Genre, Synchrony, and Wisdom Redaction in Q.* NovTSup, 91. Leiden: Brill, 1998.

Klerk, Johannes C. de. "The Literariness of the New Testament Gospels." *Religion and Theology* 4/3 (1997): 204–15.

Kloppenborg, John S. *The Formation of Q: Trajectories in Ancient Wisdom Collections.* Studies in Antiquity and Christianity. Philadelphia: Fortress, 1987.

———. *Q Parallels: Synopsis, Critical Notes and Concordance.* Foundations and Facets: New Testament. Sonoma, Calif.: Polebridge, 1988.

———. "The Theological Stakes in the Synoptic Problem" In *The Four Gospels 1992: Festschrift Frans Neirynck.* Vol. 1. Edited by F. Van Segbroeck et al. BETL 100. Leuven: Leuven University Press, 1992, 93–120.

————. "The Sayings Gospel Q and the Quest of the Historical Jesus." *HTR* 89:4 (1996): 307–44 (with responses by Helmut Koester, 345–49; and Ron Cameron, 351–54).

————. Review of Allan J. McNicol et al., eds. *Beyond the Q Impasse, CBQ* 61 (1999): 370–72.

Kloppenborg, John S., ed. *The Shape of Q: Signal Essays on the Sayings Gospel.* Minneapolis: Fortress, 1994.

————. *Conflict and Invention: Literary, Rhetorical, and Social Studies on the Sayings Gospel Q.* Philadelphia: Trinity Press International, 1995.

Kloppenborg, John S., Marvin W. Meyer, Stephen J. Patterson, and Michael G. Steinhauser. *Q Thomas Reader.* Sonoma, Calif.: Polebridge, 1990.

Kloppenborg Verbin, John S. *Excavating Q: The History and Setting of the Sayings Gospel.* Minneapolis: Fortress; Edinburgh: T & T Clark, 2000.

Knight, Jonathan. *Luke's Gospel.* New Testament Readings; London and New York: Routledge, 1998.

Koester, Helmut. *Synoptische Überlieferung bei den apostolischen Vätern.* Berlin: Akademie-Verlag, 1957.

————. *Ancient Christian Gospels: Their History and Development.* London: SCM; Philadelphia: Trinity Press International, 1990.

————. "One Jesus and Four Primitive Gospels." In *Trajectories Through Early Christianity.* By J. M. Robinson and H. Koester. Philadelphia: Fortress, 1971, 158–204.

————. "ΓΝΩΜΑΙ ΔΙΑΦΟΡΟΙ: The Origin and Nature of Diversification in the History of Early Christianity." *HTR* 58 (1965): 279–318. Reprinted in James M. Robinson and Helmut Koester, *Trajectories Through Early Christianity* (Philadelphia: Fortress, 1971): 114–57.

Kreitzer, L. J. *The New Testament in Fiction and Film: On Reversing the Hermeneutical Flow.* The Biblical Seminar, 17. Sheffield: JSOT Press, 1993.

Kümmel, W. G. *Introduction to the New Testament.* English Trans. London: SCM, 1966; rev. ed., 1975.

Kvalbein, Hans. "Die Wunder der Endzeit. Beobachtungen zu 4Q521 und Matth 11,5p." *ZNW* 88 (1997): 111–25.

Lambdin, Thomas O. "The Coptic Gospel According to Thomas." In *Nag Hammadi Codex II, 2–7,* vol. 1 of 2 vols. NHS 20–21. Edited by Bentley Layton. The Coptic Gnostic Library. Leiden: Brill (1989): 52–93.

Levine, Amy-Jill. "Who's Catering the Q Affair? Feminist Observations on Q Paraenesis." In *Paraenesis: Act and Form.* Edited by Leo G. Perdue and John G. Gammie. *Semeia* 50 (1990): 145–61.

Loisy, A. *Les Évangiles synoptiques.* 2 vols. Paris: Ceffonds, 1907, 1908.

————. *L'Évangile selon Luc.* Paris; n.p., 1924; reprint: Frankfurt: Minerva GmbH, 1971.

Longstaff, Thomas R. W. *Evidence of Conflation in Mark? A Study in the Synoptic Problem.* SBLDS, 28. Missoula, Mont.: Scholars Press, 1977.

———. "Crisis and Christology: The Theology of Mark." In *New Synoptic Studies: The Cambridge Gospel Conference and Beyond.* Edited by William R. Farmer. Macon, Ga.: Mercer University Press, 1983, 373–92.

Lührmann, Dieter. *Die Redaktion der Logienquelle.* WMANT, 33. Neukirchen-Vluyn: Neukirchener Verlag, 1969.

———. "Q: Sayings of Jesus or Logia?" In *The Gospels behind the Gospels. Current Studies on Q.* Edited by Ronald A. Piper. NovTSup, 75. Leiden: Brill, 1994, 97–116.

Lummis, E. W. *How Luke Was Written.* Cambridge: Cambridge University Press, 1915.

Luz, Ulrich. *Matthew 1–7.* English Trans. Edinburgh: T & T Clark, 1990.

Mack, Burton L. *The Lost Gospel: The Book of Q and Christian Origins.* San Francisco: HarperSanFrancisco, 1993.

———. *Who Wrote the New Testament: The Making of the Christian Myth.* San Francisco: HarperSanFrancisco, 1995.

Marshall, I. H. *The Gospel of Luke: A Commentary on the Greek Text.* Exeter: Paternoster, 1978.

Marxsen, W. *Introduction to the New Testament.* English Trans. Philadelphia: Fortress, 1968.

Matson, Mark. "Luke's Rewriting of the Sermon on the Mount." *Society of Biblical Literature Seminar Papers 2000.* Society of Biblical Literature Seminar Paper Series, 39. Atlanta: Society of Biblical Literature, 2000, 623–50.

McNicol, Allan. *Jesus' Directions for the Future: A Source and Redaction-History Study of the Use of the Eschatological Traditions in Paul and in the Synoptic Accounts of Jesus' Last Eschatological Discourse.* New Gospel Studies, 9. Macon, Ga.: Mercer University Press, 1996.

McNicol, Allan J., with David L. Dungan and David B. Peabody, eds. *Beyond the Q Impasse — Luke's Use of Matthew: A Demonstration by the Research Team of the International Institute for Gospel Studies.* Valley Forge, Pa.: Trinity Press International, 1996.

Meadors, Edward P. *Jesus the Messianic Herald of Salvation.* WUNT, 2/72. Tübingen: J. C. B. Mohr (Paul Siebeck), 1995.

———. "The 'Messianic' Implications of the Q Material." *JBL* 118 (1999): 253–77.

Moore, Stephen D. *Literary Criticism and the Gospels: The Theoretical Challenge.* New Haven: Yale University Press, 1989.

Morgenthaler, R. *Statistische Synopse.* Zürich: Gotthelf Verlag, 1971.

———. *Statistik des neutestamentlichen Wortschatzes.* Zürich: Gotthelf Verlag, 1973.

Muddiman, John. Review of Michael Goulder, *Luke. JTS* 43 (1992): 176–80.

Muller, Dieter. "Kingdom of Heaven or Kingdom of God?" *Vigiliae Christianae* 27 (1973): 266–76.

Myllykoski, Matti. "The Social History of Q and the Jewish War." In *Symbols and Strata: Essays on the Sayings Gospel Q.* Edited by Risto Uro. Suomen

Eksegeettisen Seuran Julkaisuja. Publications of the Finnish Exegetical Society 65. Helsinki: Finnish Exegetical Society; Göttingen: Vandenhoeck & Ruprecht (1996): 143–99.

Neirynck, Frans. *The Minor Agreements of Matthew and Luke against Mark with a Cumulative List.* BETL, 37. Leuven: Leuven University Press, 1974.

———. *Evangelica: Gospel Studies — Etudes d'évangile: Collected Essays.* Edited by F. Van Segbroeck. BETL 60. Leuven: Leuven University Press, 1982.

———. *Q-Synopsis. The Double Tradition Passages in Greek.* Leuven: Leuven University Press, 1988.

———. *L'Evangile de Luc — The Gospel of Luke.* BETL, 32. Leuven: Leuven University Press, 1989.

———. *Evangelica II. 1982–91: Collected Essays.* Edited by F. Van Segbroeck. BETL 99. Leuven: Leuven University Press, 1991.

———. "The Synoptic Problem." In *The New Jerome Biblical Commentary.* Edited by Raymond E. Brown, Joseph A. Fitzmyer, and Roland E. Murphy. Englewood Cliffs, N.J.: Prentice Hall, 1990, 587–95.

———. "Recent Developments in the Study of Q." In *Logia. Les paroles de Jésus — The Sayings of Jesus.* Edited by J. Delobel. Mémorial J. Coppens. BETL 59. Leuven: Leuven University Press — Peeters, 1982, 29–75=F. Neirynck, *Evangelica II. 1982–1991.* Edited by F. Van Segbroeck. BETL 99. Leuven: Leuven University Press, 1991, 409–64.

———. "ΤΙΣ ΕΣΤΙΝ Ο ΠΑΙΣΑΣ ΣΕ, Matt. 26.68 / Luke 22.64 (diff. Mark 14.65)." *ETL* 63 (1987): 5–47; reprinted in F. Neirynck, *Evangelica II* 1982–1991. Edited by F. Van Segbroeck. BETL 99. Leuven: Leuven University Press, 1991, 95–138.

———. "From Source to Gospel." *ETL* 71 (1995): 421–30.

———. "Goulder and the Minor Agreements." *ETL* 73 (1997): 84–93.

———. "NAZARA in Q: Pro and Con." In *From Quest to Q. Festschrift James M. Robinson.* Edited by Jon Ma. Asgeirsson, Kristin de Troyer and Marvin W. Meyer. BETL, 146. Leuven: Leuven University Press, 2000, 159–69.

———. "Q." In *IDBSupp.,* ad loc.

Neirynck, F., and T. A. Friedrichsen. "Note on Luke 9.22, A Response to M. D. Goulder." *ETL* 65 (1989): 390–94; also in F. Neirynck, *L'Evangile de Luc — The Gospel of Luke.* BETL, 32. Leuven: Leuven University Press, 1991, 393–98 and *Evangelica II. 1982–91: Collected Essays.* Edited by F. Van Segbroeck. BETL, 99. Leuven: Leuven University Press, 1991, 43–48.

Neville, David. *Arguments from Order in Synoptic Source Criticism: A History and Critique.* New Gospel Studies 7. Leuven: Peeters; Macon, Ga.: Mercer University Press, 1994.

Newport, Kenneth G. C. *The Sources and Sitz-im-Leben of Matthew 23.* JSNTSup, 117. Sheffield: Sheffield Academic Press, 1995.

Painter, John. *Just James: The Brother of Jesus in History and Tradition.* Studies on Personalities of the New Testament. Columbia: University of South Carolina Press, 1998.

Parker, David. *The Living Text of the Gospels.* Cambridge: Cambridge University Press, 1997.

Parker, David, David Taylor, and Mark Goodacre, "The Dura-Europos Gospel Harmony." *Studies in the Early Text of the Gospels and Acts.* Texts and Studies: Contributions to Biblical and Patristic Literature (Third Series). Vol. 1. Edited by David Taylor. Birmingham: University of Birmingham Press, 1999, 192–228.

Patterson, Stephen J. *The Gospel of Thomas and Jesus.* Sonoma, Calif.: Polebridge, 1993.

————. Review of C. M. Tuckett, *Q and the History of Early Christianity. JBL* 117 (1998): 744–46. Also available online at *SBL Review of Biblical Literature, http://www.bookreviews.org.*

Peabody, David B. "Luke's Sequential Use of the Sayings of Jesus from Matthew's Great Discourses. A Chapter in the Source-Critical Analysis of Luke on the Two Gospel (Neo-Griesbach) Hypothesis." In *Literary Studies in Luke-Acts. Essays in Honor of Joseph B. Tyson.* Edited by Richard P. Thompson and Thomas E. Phillips. Macon, Ga.: Mercer University Press, 1998, 37–58.

Peabody David B., ed., with Lamar Cope and Allan J. McNicol. *One Gospel from Two: Mark's Use of Matthew and Luke.* Harrisburg, Pa.: Trinity Press International, 2002.

Perdue, Leo G., and John G. Gammie, eds. *Paraenesis: Act and Form. Semeia* 50 (1990).

Peterson, Jeffrey. "A Pioneer Narrative Critic and His Synoptic Hypothesis." *Society of Biblical Literature Seminar Papers 2000.* Society of Biblical Literature Seminar Paper Series, 39; Atlanta: Society of Biblical Literature, 2000, 651–72.

Piper Ronald A., ed. *The Gospels behind the Gospels. Current Studies on Q.* NovTSup, 75. Leiden: Brill, 1994.

Polag, Athanasius. *Fragmenta Q: Textheft zur Logienquelle.* Neukirchen-Vluyn: Neukircher Verlag, 1979.

Porter S. E., et al., eds. *Crossing the Boundaries: Essays in Biblical Interpretation in Honour of Michael D. Goulder.* Leiden: Brill, 1994.

Powell, Mark Allan. *What Is Narrative Criticism?* Guides to Biblical Scholarship Series. Minneapolis: Fortress, 1990.

————. *The Jesus Debate.* Oxford: Lion Publishing, 1999.

————. "Narrative Criticism." In *Hearing the New Testament: Strategies for Interpretation.* Edited by Joel B. Green. Grand Rapids: Eerdmans; Carlisle: Paternoster, 1995, 239–55.

Przybylski, Benno. *Righteousness in Matthew and his World of Thought.* SNTSMS, 41. Cambridge: Cambridge University Press, 1980.

Riches, John. *Matthew.* New Testament Guides. Sheffield: Sheffield Academic Press, 1996.

Robinson, James M. "Jesus from Easter to Valentinus (or to the Apostles' Creed)." *JBL* 101 (1982): 5–37.

———. "The Sermon on the Mount/Plain: Work Sheets for the Reconstruction of Q." In *Society of Biblical Literature. 1983. Seminar Papers.* Edited by Kent Harold Richards. Society of Biblical Literature Seminar Paper Series, 22. Chico, Calif.: Scholars Press, 1983, 451–54.

———. "The Sayings Gospel Q." In *The Four Gospels 1992.* Edited by F. Van Segbroeck et al. Festschrift Frans Neirynck. BETL 100.1. Leuven: Leuven University Press, 1992, 361–88.

———. "The Jesus of Q as Liberation Theologian" In *The Gospels behind the Gospels. Current studies on Q.* Edited by Ronald A. Piper. NovTSup, 75. Leiden: Brill, 1994, 259–74.

Robinson, James M., and Helmut Koester. *Trajectories in Early Christianity.* Philadelphia: Fortress, 1971.

Robinson, James M., Paul Hoffmann, and John S. Kloppenborg Verbin. *Critical Edition of Q in a Synopsis, Including the Gospels of Matthew and Luke, Mark and Thomas, with English, German and French Translations of Q and Thomas.* Hermeneia. Philadelphia: Fortress, 2000.

Ropes, James Hardy. *The Synoptic Gospels.* Cambridge, Mass.: Harvard University Press, 1934; Second Impression with New Preface, London: Oxford University Press, 1960.

Sanday, W., ed. *Studies in the Synoptic Problem by Members of the University of Oxford.* Oxford: Clarendon Press, 1911.

Sanders, E. P. *The Tendencies of the Synoptic Tradition.* SNTSMS, 9. Cambridge: Cambridge University Press, 1969.

———. *Jesus and Judaism.* London: SCM, 1985.

———. *The Historical Figure of Jesus.* London: Allen Lane, 1993.

———. "The Argument from Order and the Relationship between Matthew and Luke." *NTS* 15 (1968–69): 249–61.

———. "The Overlaps of Mark and Q and the Synoptic Problem." *NTS* 19 (1972–73): 453–65.

Sanders, E. P., and M. Davies: *Studying the Synoptic Gospels.* Philadelphia: Trinity Press International; London: SCM, 1989.

Sato, Migaku. *Q und Prophetie: Studien zur Gattungs- und Traditionsgeschichte der Quelle Q.* WUNT 2/29. Tübingen: J. C. B. Mohr (Paul Siebeck), 1988.

Schaberg, Jane. *The Illegitimacy of Jesus: A Feminist Theological Interpretation of the Infancy Narratives.* Sheffield: Sheffield Academic Press, 1995.

Schenck, W. *Synopse zur Redenquelle der Evangelien.* Düsseldorf: Patmos, 1978.

Schmid, J. *Matthäus und Lukas: Eine Untersuchung des Verhältnisses ihrer Evangelien.* Freiburg: Herder, 1930.

Schmithals, W. *Einleitung in die drei ersten Evangelien.* Berlin: Walter de Gruyter, 1985.

Schottroff, Luise. "Itinerant Prophetesses: A Feminist Analysis of the Sayings Source Q." In *The Gospels behind the Gospels. Current studies on Q.* Edited by Ronald A. Piper. NovTSup, 75. Leiden: Brill (1994): 348–60.

————. "The Sayings Source Q." In *Searching the Scriptures*, vol. 2, *A Feminist Commentary*. Edited by Elisabeth Schüssler Fiorenza. New York: Crossroad, 1994; London: SCM, 1995, 510–34.

Schottroff, L., and W. Stegemann. *Jesus von Nazareth — Hoffnung der Armen*. 3d ed. Stuttgart: Kohlhammer, 1990.

Schrage, W. *Das Verhältnis des Thomas-Evangeliums zur synoptischen Tradition und zu den koptischen Evangelienübersetzungen. Zugleich ein Beitrag zur gnostischen Synoptikerdeutung*. BZNW, 29. Berlin: Töpelmann, 1964.

Schulz, S. *Q. Die Spruchquelle der Evangelisten*. Zürich: Theologischer Verlag, 1972.

Schürmann, Heinz. *Das Lukasevangelium. 1: Kommentar zu Kap. 1, 1–9,50. 2/1: Kommentar zu Kapitel 9,51–11,54*. HTKNT 3/1–2/1. Freiburg: Herder, 1969–84.

Schüssler Fiorenza, Elisabeth. *Jesus: Miriam's Child, Sophia's Prophet: Critical Issues in Feminist Christology*. London: SCM, 1995.

Schüssler Fiorenza, Elisabeth, ed. *Searching the Scriptures: Volume 2, A Feminist Commentary*. New York: Crossroad, 1994; London: SCM, 1995.

Shellard, Barbara. *New Light on Luke: Its Purpose, Sources and Literary Context*. JSNTSup, 215. Sheffield: Sheffield Academic Press, 2002.

Simons, E. *Hat der dritte Evangelist den kanonischen Matthäus benutzt?* Bonn: Universitäts-Buchdruckerei von Carl Georgi, 1880.

Simpson, R. T. "The Major Agreements of Matthew and Luke Against Mark." *NTS* 12 (1965–66): 273–84. Reprinted in *The Two Source Hypothesis: A Critical Appraisal*. Edited by A. J. Bellinzoni, J. B. Tyson and W. O. Walker. Macon, Ga.: Mercer University Press, 1985, 381–95.

Soards, Marion L. *The Passion According to Luke: The Special Material of Luke 22*. JSNTSup, 14. Sheffield: JSOT Press, 1987.

Stanton, Graham N. *The Gospels and Jesus*. Oxford: Oxford University Press, 1989.

————. *A Gospel for a New People: Studies in Matthew*. Edinburgh: T & T Clark, 1992.

————. *Gospel Truth? New Light on Jesus and the Gospels*. London: HarperCollins, 1995.

————. "Matthew, Gospel of." *DBI*, ad loc.

Stein, Robert. *The Synoptic Problem: An Introduction*. Grand Rapids: Baker Book House, 1987.

Stoldt, H.-H. *Geschichte und Kritik der Markus-hypothese*. Göttingen: Vandenhoeck & Ruprecht, 1977; 2d ed. 1986.

Strecker, G., ed. *Minor Agreements: Symposium Göttingen, 1991*. Göttingen: Vandenhoeck & Ruprecht, 1993.

Streeter, B. H. *The Four Gospels: A Study of Origins, Treating of the Manuscript Tradition, Sources, Authorship and Dates*. London: Macmillan, 1924.

————. Review of H. G. Jameson, *The Origin of the Synoptic Gospels*. *Theology* 7/37 (July 1923): 60.

Styler, G. M. Excursus 4 in C. F. D. Moule, *The Birth of the New Testament*. 3d ed. London: Black, 1981, 285–316.

———. "Synoptic Problem." In *The Oxford Companion to the Bible*. Edited by Bruce M. Metzger and Michael D. Coogan. Oxford: Oxford University Press, 1993, 724–27.

Tabor, James D., and Michael O. Wise. "4Q521 'On Resurrection' and the Synoptic Gospel Tradition: a Preliminary Study." In *Qumran Questions*. Edited by James H. Charlesworth. The Biblical Seminar, 36. Sheffield: Sheffield Academic Press, 1995, 151–63.

Tannehill, Robert C. *The Narrative Unity of Luke-Acts. A Literary Interpretation: 1. The Gospel according to Luke*. Philadelphia: Fortress, 1991.

———. *Luke*. Abingdon New Testament Commentaries. Nashville: Abingdon, 1996.

Tatum, W. Barnes. *Jesus at the Movies: A Guide to the First Hundred Years*. Sonoma, Calif.: Polebridge, 1997.

Taylor, Vincent. *Behind the Third Gospel: A Study of the Proto-Luke Hypothesis*. Oxford: Clarendon, 1926.

———. *The First Draft of St Luke's Gospel*. London: SPCK, 1927.

Telford, W. R. "The New Testament in Fiction and Film: A Biblical Scholar's Perspective." In *Words Remembered, Texts Renewed: Essays in Honour of John F. A. Sawyer*. Edited by Jon Davies, Graham Harvey, and Wilfred Watson. JSOTSup, 195. Sheffield: Sheffield Academic Press (1995): 360–94.

———. "Jesus Christ Movie Star: The Depiction of Jesus in the Cinema." In *Explorations in Theology and Film: Movies and Meaning*. Edited by Clive Marsh and Gaye Ortiz. Oxford: Blackwell, 1997, 115–39.

Theissen, Gerd, and Annette Merz. *The Historical Jesus: A Comprehensive Guide*. English Trans. London: SCM, 1998.

Thiselton, Anthony. "New Testament Interpretation in Historical Perspective." In *Hearing the New Testament: Strategies for Interpretation*. Edited by Joel B. Green. Grand Rapids: Eerdmans; Carlisle: Paternoster, 1995, 10–36.

Thompson, D., and I. Christie, eds. *Scorsese on Scorsese*. Updated ed. London: Faber & Faber, 1996.

Tuckett, Christopher M. *The Revival of the Griesbach Hypothesis: An Analysis and Appraisal*. SNTSMS 44. Cambridge: Cambridge University Press, 1983.

———. *Q and the History of Early Christianity: Studies on Q*. Edinburgh: T & T Clark, 1996.

———. "On the Relationship Between Matthew and Luke." *NTS* 30 (1984): 130–42.

———. "Arguments from Order: Definition and Evaluation." In *Synoptic Studies: The Ampleforth Conferences of 1982 and 1983*. Edited by Christopher M. Tuckett. JSNTSup, 7. Sheffield: JSOT Press (1984): 197–220.

———. "Thomas and the Synoptics." *NovT* 30 (1988): 132–57.

————. "The Minor Agreements and Textual Criticism." In *Minor Agreements: Symposium Göttingen 1991*. Edited by G. Strecker. Göttingen: Vandenhoeck & Ruprecht, 1993, 119–41.

————. "The Existence of Q." In *The Gospel Behind the Gospels: Current Studies on Q*. Edited by R. A. Piper. NovTSup, 75. Leiden: Brill (1994): 19–47.

————. "Synoptic Problem." In *ABD*, VI, 263–70.

————. Review of Allan J. McNicol et al., eds., *Beyond the Q Impasse*, *JBL* 117 (1998): 363–65.

Tuckett, Christopher M., ed. *Synoptic Studies: The Ampleforth Conferences of 1982 and 1983*. JSNTSup, 7. Sheffield: JSOT Press, 1984.

————. *Luke's Literary Achievement. Collected Essays*. JSNTSup, 116. Sheffield: Sheffield Academic Press, 1995.

Tuckett, Christopher M., and Michael D. Goulder. "The Beatitudes: A Source-Critical Study." *NovT* 25 (1983): 193–216.

Tyson, J. "The Synoptic Problem." In *The New Testament and Early Christianity*. New York: Macmillan; London: Collier Macmillan, 1984, 148–58.

Uro, Risto, ed. *Symbols and Strata: Essays on the Sayings Gospel Q*. Suomen Eksegeettisen Seuran Julkaisuja. Publications of the Finnish Exegetical Society 65; Helsinki: Finnish Exegetical Society. Göttingen: Vandenhoeck & Ruprecht, 1996.

————. *Thomas at the Crossroads: Essays on the Gospel of Thomas*. Edinburgh: T & T Clark, 1998.

Valantasis, Richard. *The Gospel of Thomas*. New Testament Readings. London and New York: Routledge, 1997.

Van Segbroeck, F., et al., eds. *The Four Gospels*. Fs. F. Neirynck. 3 vols. BETL, 100. Leuven: Leuven University Press, 1992.

Vassiliadis, Petros. "The Nature and Extent of the Q Document." *NovT* 20 (1978): 49–73.

Vinson, Richard B. *The Significance of the Minor Agreements as An Argument Against the Two-Document Hypothesis*. Duke University Ph.D. thesis, 1984.

Walker William O., ed. *The Relationships Among the Gospels: An Interdisciplinary Dialogue*. Trinity University Monographs in Religion 5. San Antonio, Tex.: Trinity University Press, 1978.

Wansbrough, H., ed. *Jesus and the Oral Gospel Tradition*. JSNTSup, 64. Sheffield: Sheffield Academic Press, 1991.

Wenham, J. W. *Redating Matthew, Mark and Luke: A Fresh Assault on the Synoptic Problem*. London: Hodder & Stoughton, 1991.

Wheeler, F. *Text Criticism and the Synoptic Problem: A Textual Commentary on the Minor Agreements of Matthew and Luke Against Mark*. Doctoral Dissertation, Baylor University, Waco, Tex., 1985.

Wills, Lawrence M. *The Quest of the Historical Gospel: Mark, John and the Origins of the Gospel Genre*. London and New York: Routledge, 1997.

Wright, N. T. *Jesus and the Victory of God: Christian Origins and the Question of God.* Vol. 2. London: SPCK, 1996.

Wright, N. T., and Marcus Borg. *The Meaning of Jesus: Two Visions.* London: SPCK, 1999.

York, John O. *The Last Shall Be First: The Rhetoric of Reversal in Luke.* JSNTSup, 46. Sheffield: JSOT Press, 1991.

Films

Hayes, Derek W., and Stanislav Sokolov. *The Miracle Maker.* 1999.

Jones, Terry. *Monty Python's Life of Brian.* 1979.

Krish, John, and Peter Sykes. *Jesus.* 1979.

Pasolini, Pier Paolo. *The Gospel According to St Matthew.* 1964.

Ray, Nicholas. *King of Kings.* 1961.

Scorsese, Martin. *The Last Temptation of Christ.* 1988.

Stevens, George. *The Greatest Story Ever Told.* 1965.

Zeffirelli, Franco. *Jesus of Nazareth.* 1977.

Web Sites

Goodacre, Mark. *The New Testament Gateway* (*http://ntgateway.com*, 1997–present).

———. *The Case Against Q Web Site* (*http://ntgateway.com/Q*, 1997–present).

Index of Ancient Texts

INDEX OF AUTHORS

INDEX OF SUBJECTS